DIVINE EROS

Hymns of St Symeon the New Theologian

T0338802

ST VLADIMIR'S SEMINARY PRESS
Popular Patristics Series
Number 40

The Popular Patristics Series published by St Vladimir's Seminary Press provides readable and accurate translations of a wide range of early Christian literature to a wide audience—students of Christian history to lay Christians reading for spiritual benefit. Recognized scholars in their fields provide short but comprehensive and clear introductions to the material. The texts include classics of Christian literature, thematic volumes, collections of homilies, letters on spiritual counsel, and poetical works from a variety of geographical contexts and historical backgrounds. The mission of the series is to mine the riches of the early Church and to make these treasures available to all.

Series Editor
BOGDAN BUCUR

Associate Editor
IGNATIUS GREEN

* * *

Series Editor
1999–2020
JOHN BEHR

Divine Eros

HYMNS OF ST SYMEON
THE NEW THEOLOGIAN

Translation and Introduction by
DANIEL K. GRIGGS

ST VLADIMIR'S SEMINARY PRESS
CRESTWOOD, NEW YORK

Library of Congress Cataloging-in-Publication Data

Symeon, the New Theologian, Saint, 949–1022.
  [Hymns of the divine loves. English]
  Divine eros : hymns of St. Symeon, the New Theologian / translation and
introduction by Daniel K. Griggs.
      p. cm. — (Popular patristics series ; ser. no. 1, no. 40)
      Includes bibliographical references.
      ISBN 978-0-88141-349-6
      1. Hymns, Greek—Translations into English. I. Griggs, Daniel K. II. Title.

BV467.S9 2010
242—dc22

2010029865

COPYRIGHT © 2010 BY

ST VLADIMIR'S SEMINARY PRESS
575 Scarsdale Road, Crestwood, NY 10707
1-800-204-2665
www.svspress.com

ISBN 978–088141–349–6
ISSN 1555–5755

PRINTED IN THE UNITED STATES OF AMERICA

For
Father Thomas
and
Brother Gerard

Contents

Introduction

Symeon the New Theologian was an abbot and ascetic writer in tenth-century Constantinople.[1] He was born in Galatia, Asia Minor, in AD 949. Symeon was just nine years older than the great Emperor Basil II, so his life corresponds with the zenith of the empire. While still a boy, Symeon sought a political career in Constantinople under the patronage of his uncle. His career in politics survived the vicissitudes of Basil II's minority, but ended when the young Emperor came of age and began to consolidate his power. Thus in AD 977, at the age of twenty-seven, Symeon became a monk, and about three years later, he became abbot of Saint Mamas Monastery. As a result of his conflicts with the Church's hierarchy and the imperial court, Symeon was exiled in AD 1009. He spent his last years across the Bosporus where he rebuilt the monastery of Saint Marina. Symeon died in AD 1022, still in exile.

The edition of Symeon's works fills nine volumes in the Sources chrétiennes series.[2] These writings include theological and ascetic chapters, tracts, prayers, and fifty-eight poems styled "hymns."[3]

[1] This introduction is based on Daniel K. Griggs, "Religious Experience in Symeon the New Theologian's Hymns" (Ph.D. diss., University of Leeds, U.K., 1999). I shall refer to Nicetas Stethatos's hagiography of Symeon as the *Vie*: the edition is found in *Un grand mystique byzantin: Vie de Syméon le Nouveau Théologien*, ed. Irénée Hausherr, trans. Gabriel Horn, OCA 12 (Rome: Pontifical Institute of Oriental Studies, 1928); I follow the chronology established by Hausherr in the introduction, pp. lxxx–xci.

[2] For a brief review of Symeon's works, see Basil Krivochéine, "The Writings of St Symeon the New Theologian," *OCP* 20 (1954): 298–328. Krivochéine's article was written before the SC editions of Symeon's works, so he concentrates on issues of authenticity and redaction.

[3] Τῶν θείων ὕμνων οἱ ἔρωτες. Translating this title is difficult; a literal rendering would be "Loves of the Divine Hymns." A freer translation would be "Love Expressed in Holy Hymns." "Hymns of Divine Love" captures the gist in colloquial English.

Symeon wrote the *Hymns* throughout his monastic career, though most of them probably date from his maturity, especially during his exile.[4] The short biography that follows provides a context for Symeon's *Hymns*. Though it is tempting to provide the reader with a synopsis of Symeon's favorite doctrines, such as tears, dispassion, yearning, deification, luminous vision, and spiritual fatherhood, an extensive analysis is beyond the scope of this introduction. Therefore, I shall discuss at length only Symeon's most characteristic doctrine—that is, that the vision of God in this life is necessary for salvation in the hereafter. What is more, Symeon's *Hymns* best speak for themselves. Any reader who values prayer and intimacy with God will certainly be inspired by Symeon's zeal and the personal immediacy with which he conveys Christian orthodoxy.

BIOGRAPHICAL CONTEXT OF SYMEON'S *HYMNS*

In AD 960, when Symeon was eleven years of age, his parents took him to Constantinople to prepare for a career in politics. They placed Symeon under the care and patronage of his paternal uncle who was a courtier. Symeon studied Greek, rhetoric, and calligraphy under a grammarian.[5] Symeon's writings demonstrate good language skills, yet little exposure to classical literature; even his knowledge of the Fathers was not extensive.[6] In AD 963, Symeon's uncle was killed, probably during the *coup d'état* of Nicephoros Phocas or during the unrest that followed. Though the palace revolution of 963 probably frightened Symeon and interrupted his education, he was able to find a new patron. Before long he was managing a patrician's household and frequenting the palace on business.[7]

---

[4] *Vie* 111, p. 154; Johannes Koder, introduction, in Syméon le Nouveau Théologien, *Hymnes 1–15*, ed. Johannes Koder, trans. Joseph Paramelle, SC 156 (Paris: Cerf, 1969), 76–77.

[5] *Vie* 2, pp. 2–4.

[6] H. J. M. Turner, *St Symeon the New Theologian and Spiritual Fatherhood* (Leiden/New York: E. J. Brill, 1990), 37–38, 45.

[7] *Catechesis* 22.71–72, in Syméon le Nouveau Théologien, *Catéchèses 6–22*, ed.

Six years later, when he was twenty, Symeon visited Stoudios monastery and sought the counsel of a monk named Symeon Eulabes. Eulabes was a well-informed adviser and a good addition to Symeon's sociopolitical network.[8] Symeon, like most Byzantines, also saw the monastery as a refuge, either temporary or permanent. As a disciple of Eulabes, Symeon would have ready access to Stoudios as a place of retreat in the event that his life or career in the imperial court should be endangered.[9]

Soon after Symeon came under Eulabes' spiritual direction, during a regime of fasting, prayer, and vigils, Symeon experienced his first luminous vision.[10] In this vision, Symeon saw, and was enveloped in, a luminous cloud. Most significant for him was that he saw his spiritual father, Eulabes, glorified, standing next to the light. Symeon had considered his confessor to be an intercessor, his patron before God rather like one's patron before the emperor.[11] This first vision assured Symeon that he had found a living saint and a powerful intercessor. The fact that he found a great saint and intercessor in an unordained monk may also have influenced his notion of authority, which, as we shall see, was notably charismatic. Nevertheless, a drastic conversion was still seven years away when Symeon would find his career failing due to changes in imperial politics.[12] Symeon himself admits that he

Basile Krivochéine, trans. Joseph Paramelle, SC 104 (Paris: Cerf, 1964), 370; English translation may be found in *The Discourses*, trans. C. J. deCatanzaro, intro. George Maloney, CWS (New York: Paulist Press, 1980), 274.

[8]Rosemary Morris, "Spiritual Fathers and Temporal Patrons: Logic and Contradiction in Byzantine Monasticism in the Tenth Century," *RBén* 103 (1993): 288; and Morris, "The Political Saint of the Eleventh Century," in *The Byzantine Saint*, ed. Sergei Hackel (London: Fellowship of St Alban and St Sergius, 1981), 47; Hilarion Alfeyev, "St Symeon the New Theologian, St Symeon the Pious, and the Studite Tradition," *StudMon* 36 (1994): 191, 195.

[9]Cf. Joan M. Hussey, *Church and Learning in the Byzantine Empire: 867–1185* (New York: Russell, 1963), 158, 159, 162.

[10]*Catechesis* 22.71–74, 171–73; SC 104:371, 378; deCatanzaro, *Discourses*, 345, 348.

[11]*Actions de graces* 1.71–80 [hereafter *Graces*] in Syméon le Nouveau Théologien, *Catéchèses 23–34: Actions de graces 1–2*, ed. Basile Krivochéine, trans. Joseph Paramelle, SC 113 (Paris: Cerf, 1965), 310; deCatanzaro, *Discourses*, 361.

[12]John A. McGuckin, "Symeon the New Theologian (d. 1022) and Byzantine Monasticism," in *Mount Athos and Byzantine Monasticism*, ed. Anthony Bryer (London: Variorum, 1996), 20.

had not yet understood the significance of the light, and by slackness and neglect, he fell back into his former sins.[13]

Symeon continued his career during the seven years of the reign of Emperor John Zimiskes, but 9/6–9/8 were the years of another *coup*, this time by General Bardos Scleros, and of young Basil II's struggle for his throne.[14] Both Bardos Scleros and Basil II had anti-aristocratic policies,[15] so perhaps as early as AD 976 Symeon knew that his political career had no future.[16] Symeon had expressed a desire to become a monk, but his spiritual father had put him off. Given a new and hostile regime, the time seemed right for Symeon to give up his political career in the imperial court in favor of monastic life. Eulabes then consented to take in Symeon as a novice monk.

The *hegoumenos* (abbot) Peter of Stoudios monastery agreed to put Eulabes in charge of Symeon as his spiritual father.[17] Symeon's novitiate at Stoudios may have lasted only a matter of weeks.[18] Fortunately, the ambitious young courtier's vocation as a monk was confirmed soon after he entered monastic life. This assurance came in the form of a second luminous vision in which Symeon realized that God himself was revealed in the light, that God had been intimately involved in his life, that his calling to the monastery was not just a retreat from the hazards of Byzantine politics, but a genuine vocation.[19]

Symeon soon transferred to the smaller monastery of Saint Mamas (AD 980), and within three years he was ordained priest and elected abbot. As abbot, he rebuilt the structures of Saint Mamas. The monastery's church had been built by the sister of Emperor Maurice (ruled AD 582–623) and contained the tombs of Maurice,

[13]*Graces* 1.114–16, SC 113:314; deCatanzaro, *Discourses*, 362.
[14]Romilly J. H. Jenkins, *Byzantium: The Imperial Centuries, AD 610–1071* (London: Weidenfeld, 1966), 302ff.
[15]Ibid. 305, 310, 311.
[16]McGuckin, "Symeon the New Theologian," 23.
[17]*Vie* 11, p. 18.
[18]McGuckin, "Symeon the New Theologian," 24.
[19]*Graces* 1.156–95, SC 113:316–20; deCatanzaro, *Discourses*, 364–65.

his wife, and family.[20] Symeon refurbished the church, removed the corpses, and laid a new tile floor.[21] John McGuckin argues that Symeon was actually wiping out signs of the original imperial patronage and thereby refounding the monastery and establishing himself as its patron.[22]

Symeon was no stranger to controversy, even within his own community. Nicetas describes Saint Mamas as a dilapidated ruin and a refuge for a few worldly monks. In the *Vie* 34–38, he reports that Symeon's first fifteen years as its abbot were a time of rebuilding, efforts to reform the monks, an increase in vocations, the beginning of Symeon's literary activity, and continued growth in Symeon's own personal holiness.[23] Nevertheless, some time between 995 and 998, thirty of Symeon's monks rebelled against his leadership. During his usual morning conference, thirty monks raised a vociferous protest in the church and threatened Symeon with physical violence. The monks then ran out of the monastery and brought their protest to the patriarch, Sisinnios II. The thirty monks were not just a disgruntled minority; they constituted nearly the entire community.[24] Nevertheless, the patriarch met with Symeon the day after the rebellion and ruled in his favor.

Why did the monks reject Symeon? What may have been truly radical, and perhaps for his monks intolerable, was Symeon's teaching that luminous vision should be regarded as normative for monks, and even the goal of monastic life.[25] This doctrine will

[20] Alice-Mary Talbot, "Mamas, Monastery of Saint," in *The Oxford Dictionary of Byzantium*, ed. Alexander P. Kazhdan et al., 3 vols. (Oxford: Oxford University Press, 1991), 2:1278.

[21] *Vie* 34, p. 46.

[22] McGuckin, "Symeon the New Theologian," 26.

[23] *Vie* 34–38, pp. 46–50.

[24] The *Vie* says that the thirty rebels left Symeon alone with some pious monks, and later Symeon was saddened to find his sheepfold empty (*Vie* 39, 41, p. 52, 54). Cf. Peter Charanis, "The Monk in Byzantine Society," *DOP* 25 (1971): 72; Dirk Krausmüller, "Monastic Communities of Studios and St Mamas in the Second Half of the Tenth Century," in *The Theotokos Evergetis and Eleventh-Century Monasticism*, ed. Margaret Mullett and Anthony Kirby, Belfast Byzantine Texts and Translations 6.1 (Belfast: Byzantine Enterprises, 1994), 70; McGuckin, "Symeon the New Theologian," 28.

[25] E.g., *Hymn* 1; cf. McGuckin, "Symeon the New Theologian," 33.

be discussed further below. Another policy that would have had a direct, personal, and practical impact on his monks was Symeon's policy that all of his monks confess to him and obey him as a novice would his spiritual father.[26]

Symeon's troubles began anew in AD 1003. The main villain in the *Vie* is Stephen of Alexina who was synkellos (chancellor) to the patriarch and former metropolitan of Nicomedia. Stephen was a great scholar who, according to Nicetas, became insanely jealous of Symeon's renown for wisdom.[27] In AD 1003, Stephen challenged Symeon's status with a theological question: "How do you separate the Son from the Father, by a *notional* or *actual* fact?"[28] This was a loaded question rife with peril for anyone lacking in extensive theological training. Symeon recognized the trap and he agreed to respond in writing. His answer came in the form of *Hymn* 21, which briefly answers Stephen's question but focuses on the real issue—that is, the nature of religious authority.[29] The abbot of Saint Mamas argued that academic training is incidental, even superfluous, to one (such as himself) who has the empirical knowledge that comes with religious experience.[30] The abbot of Saint Mamas was ambitious, but he was inexperienced in monastic life when he became abbot,

[26]McGuckin, "Symeon the New Theologian," 32–33; Turner, *St Symeon*, 191ff., 221ff.

[27]*Vie* 74, p. 100.

[28]*Vie* 75, pp. 102–4.

[29]*Hymn* 21 in Syméon le Nouveau Théologien, *Hymnes 16–40*, ed. Johannes Koder, trans. Louis Neyrand, SC 174 (Paris: Cerf, 1971), 130–68.

[30]*Hymn* 21 could also be viewed as a reaction to the conservative and academic style of theology that emerged out of the "Encyclopedist Movement" in the ninth century. Scholars like Photius (born AD 810) and Michael Psellos (AD 1018–78) promoted encyclopedic curiosity and copying of ancient manuscripts. On the other hand, this interest in classical philosophy coexisted with a conservative Orthodoxy that encouraged only standardization and citing of the Fathers (see Symeon the New Theologian, *On the Mystical Life: The Ethical Discourses*, trans. Alexander Golitzin, 3 vols. (Crestwood, NY: St Vladimir's Seminary Press, 1995–1997), 3:13–18; John Meyendorff, *Byzantine Theology: Historical Trends and Doctrinal Themes* (New York: Fordham University Press, 1983), 55. Byzantine theology did not synthesize humanist philosophy with theology into a new style, and theological competence was measured by one's mastery of the Fathers and the Councils' doctrines.

and he also lacked higher theological training. Therefore, he sought to strengthen his legitimacy on the basis of his relationship with his spiritual father (Eulabes), and on his own luminous visions. This issue of Symeon's authority erupted during the rebellion of the thirty monks and peaked during his conflict with the synkellos Stephen. In *Hymn* 21, Symeon exhorted the theologian to asceticism, virtue, and contemplation.[31] He minimized the value of formal education: "They have the Spirit as their teacher; they do not need education from human beings."[32] *Hymn* 21 argues that Saint Paul's genius was his possession of the Holy Spirit and his contemplative experiences, and so the authentic theologian should be able to claim similar experience and authority.[33] Perhaps Stephen was astonished that Symeon would make himself equal to Saint Paul and expect the same of others. Elsewhere in the *Hymns*, Symeon teaches that all the Fathers of the Church were illuminated saints who shared in the Holy Spirit.[34] The importance of personal experience in authentic theology is well attested among the Fathers, but none stress contemplation and conscious possession of the Holy Spirit so strongly as Symeon.[35]

---

[31]*Hymn* 21.1–24, 54–196, 238–455; SC 174:130–64.

[32]*Hymn* 21.102–3; SC 174:138. Cf. Pseudo-Makarios, *Spiritual Homilies* 15.20; PG 34:589. English translation in *Pseudo-Macarius: The Fifty Spiritual Homilies*, trans. and intro. George A. Maloney, CWS (New York: Paulist Press, 1992), 115–16.

[33]*Hymn* 21.174–76; SC 174:144.

[34]*Hymn* 34.83–98, SC 174:434; *Hymn* 29.94–104, SC 174:320–22; *Hymn* 52.91–153 in Syméon le Nouveau Théologien, *Hymnes 41–58*, ed. Johannes Koder, trans. Joseph Paramelle and Louis Neyrand, SC 196 (Paris: Cerf, 1973), 206–10.

[35]A few examples:

Isaac the Syrian, *Homily* 3, in *The Ascetical Homilies of Saint Isaac the Syrian* (Boston: Holy Transfiguration Monastery, 1984), 391–92; cf. *Homily* 61, pp. 295–96.

Mark the Ascetic, *On the Spiritual Law* 79–80, 85 [81, 87 in PG], PG 65:916; English translation in *Philokalia* 1:115–16. See also Mark the Ascetic's *On those who think that they are justified by works* 7, 11, PG 65:932, *Philokalia* 1:125–26.

Diadochos of Photiki, *Chapters on Spiritual Perfection* 9–11 in *Oeuvres spirituelles*, intro., ed., and trans. Edouard des Places, SC 5 bis (Paris: Cerf, 1955), 88–89; English translation in *Philokalia* 1:255.

Pseudo-Makarios, *Spiritual Homilies* 15, 17, PG 34:585, 589, 629, 632, 637–40; English translation in Maloney, *Pseudo-Macarius*, 114–16, 138–39, 143.

Symeon's Retirement and Exile

In AD 1005, the patriarch dismissed Symeon as *hegoumenos* of Saint Mamas. According to Nicetas, Symeon wanted to retire from the abbot's responsibilities so to enjoy more quietude. Stephen continued to persecute Symeon by attacking the cult of Eulabes whose feast Symeon kept each year with great pomp. Stephen insisted that Eulabes was unworthy of veneration.[36] This put Symeon's reputation at stake once again. Part of Symeon's claim to authority was that he was a disciple of a great saint, Eulabes. In order to strengthen this position and to popularize the cult, Symeon had for sixteen years celebrated Eulabes' feast day at Saint Mamas. The *Vie* describes Symeon as defending icons and the cult of saints against Stephen, who is portrayed as an iconoclast. This seems rather anachronistic. The issue was actually a clash between two models of authority. Emperor Basil II's policies were geared toward centralization of power at the expense of the aristocracy.[37] At the same time, the Church was imposing standardization and conformity in liturgy and the calendar of the saints. Symeon resisted these trends in favor of a more diffused model of authority among the aristocracy's social networks. Symeon could rightfully claim that he was keeping a time-honored custom of venerating holy men and women. On the other hand, Stephen could argue that the cult of Symeon Eulabes as *new*, and therefore unprecedented, untraditional, and suspect.

In AD 1009, the synod condemned Symeon to exile. He was sent to the village of Paloukiton, which is across the Bosporus but not far from the capital. Symeon was not left completely destitute; in the

---

Gregory Nazianzen, who exerted an undeniably great influence on Symeon, stressed both experience and scholarship for theology; see *Orations* 27.3, 28.1, in Grégoire de Nazianze, *Discours 27–31*, ed. and trans. Paul Gallay, SC 250 (Paris: Cerf, 1978), 76, 100; English translation in *St Gregory of Nazianzus: On God and Christ: The Five Theological Orations and Two Letters to Cledonius* (Crestwood, N.Y.: St Vladimir's Seminary Press, 2002), 26–27, 37. Cf. *Hymn* 21.159–60, SC 174:142.

[36] *Vie* 81, p. 110.

[37] Jenkins, *Byzantium*, 305–21.

same location was the derelict monastery of Saint Marina, which belonged to one of Symeon's own influential disciples.[38] Symeon rebuilt Saint Marina and spent the last twelve years of his life in exile with a few of his monks. Apparently Symeon penned most of his *Hymns* at Saint Marina, and he began editing some of his previous works.[39] He died of dysentery, still in exile, on March 12, 1022.

Symeon's conversion to monastic life, his writings, and even his contemplative experiences did not happen in a vacuum. His political, social, and biographical context need not be ignored when reading even the most intimate of Symeon's *Hymns*. His writings often include doctrines that justify his own authority, which he based on his own religious experience and his relationship with his spiritual father. The synkellos Stephen challenged Symeon's authority on both points: he challenged Symeon's charismatic style of authority by questioning his competence as a theologian. Stephen later challenged Symeon's status by questioning the holiness of his spiritual father, Symeon Eulabes. These issues influenced the style and content of Symeon's doctrine. Let us now consider the *Hymns* in the context of Greek poetry and ascetic literature.

HYMNS OF DIVINE LOVE

Symeon uses three types of verse in the *Hymns*: eight of them have a meter of eight syllables per line; eleven have a meter of twelve syllables; most of the *Hymns* have fifteen syllables per line. *Hymns* 20, 21, 39, and 40 have a mixed meter. *Hymn* 5 is unique in that it is arranged alphabetically. *Hymn* 6 is the only one that is arranged in quatrains. The *Hymns* range in length from seven lines to eight hundred and fifty-eight lines. Symeon often employs dialogue, which may be between Symeon and God, or between Symeon and an unnamed antagonist. In *Hymn* 18.133ff, the dialogue is a somewhat

[38] *Vie* 95, 100, p. 130, 138.
[39] *Vie* 111, p. 154.

theatrical allegory based on Exodus. *Hymn* 10, one of the shortest, is actually a funeral poem. Most of the *Hymns* are ascetic exhortations, theological tracts, and prayers. Symeon's *Hymns* are occasional works that do not constitute an organized system of theology. They do not take the form of traditional verse sermons (*kontakia*),[40] nor were they composed for liturgical purposes.[41]

Symeon's Hymns and Byzantine Poetry

Certainly in terms of religious experience, Symeon's *Hymns* are the most intimate of all patristic and Byzantine verse. Nevertheless, personal and heartfelt poetry was not without precedent. Gregory Nazianzen's longest poem, *Concerning His Own Life* (Περὶ τὸν ἑαυτοῦ βίον), is considered a landmark in poetic autobiography because of its pathos and true feeling.[42] This poem is personal in that Gregory relates his feelings and perceptions about his life.[43] Gregory freely expresses his feelings in two other poems: *Concerning His Own Affairs* and *Lament Over the Sufferings of His Soul,* both of which have been compared to Saint Augustine's *Confessions.*[44] Although these poems are not so intimate and theological as Symeon's *Hymns,* at least one passage reminds one of Symeon's rhapsodic style:

Long ago I tore my spirit from the world and mingled it with the shining spirits of heaven. The lofty mind bore me far from the flesh, set me in that place, and hid me in the

[40]*Kontakia* were most popular from the fifth to seventh centuries. A *kontakion* consists of an introduction and verses joined by a refrain. See "Kontakion" in *The Oxford Dictionary of Byzantium*, 2:1148.

[41]C. A. Trypanis, *Greek Poetry: From Homer to Seferis* (London: Faber, 1981), 417, 468.

[42]Ibid., 410.

[43]See Gregory Nazianzen, Περὶ τὸν ἑαυτοῦ βίον, PG 37:1029–1166; translation in *Saint Gregory Nazianzus: Three Poems Concerning His Own Affairs, Concerning Himself and the Bishops, Concerning His Own Life*, trans. Denis Molaise Meehan, FC 75 (Washington, DC: Catholic University of America Press, 1987), 75–130.

[44]Trypanis, *Greek Poetry*, 410.

recesses of the heavenly abode. There the light of the Trinity shone upon my eyes, a light than which I have known nothing brighter. It is throned on high and gives off an ineffable and harmonious radiance, which is the principle of all those things that time shuts off from heaven.[45]

This experiential and contemplative passage may have been an inspiration for Symeon's *Hymns*.[46]

Symeon must also have been familiar with Romanos the Melodist's hymns through the liturgy, yet there is scarcely any evidence that Symeon's *Hymns* had a direct literary dependence on Romanos. Granted, both Symeon and Romanos employed dialogue, but Romanos's dialogues are extensions of scriptural narratives. Symeon's dialogues are almost never scriptural midrash.[47] What is more, the structure of Symeon's *Hymns* in no way resembles that of *kontakia*. Still, Romanos's *kontakion* "On the Sinful Woman" bears some affinity with Symeon's doctrine and imagery. The penitential subject matter lends itself to some natural similarity, and the sinful woman of Lk 7.37 is one of Symeon's favorite penitent saints.[48] Most striking is the fact that Romanos describes Christ as shining in the woman's heart, and a little further, he describes Christ as both light and a sun, as Symeon often does. Finally, the woman's desire for Christ, tears, and remorse are cherished themes in Symeon's *Hymns*.[49] Both Romanos and Gregory Nazianzen may have inspired Symeon to write his own poetry, but the literary influence of Romanos on Symeon seems to be

---

[45]Gregory Nazianzen, Περὶ τῶν καθ' ἑαυτόν [*Concerning His Own Affairs*], 195–201, PG 37:985, FC 75:31.

[46]Cf. *Hymn* 2.75–94; SC 156:182. *Hymn* 24.237–51, SC 174:244.

[47]Cf. Koder, introduction to Syméon le Nouveau Théologien, *Hymnes 1–15*, SC 156:78–79.

[48]E.g., *Hymn* 17.76, SC 174:20; *Hymn* 42.52, SC 196:40.

[49]Romanos the Melodist, *Cantica* 10.4–6, in *Sancti Romani Melodi Cantica*: *Cantica genuina*, ed. Paul Maas and C. A. Trypanis (Oxford: Clarendon, 1963), 75; English translation in R.J. Schork, *Sacred Song from the Byzantine Pulpit: Romanus the Melodist* (Gainesville: University of Florida Press, 1995), 79–80. Cf. *Hymn* 7.4, SC 156:208; *Hymn* 8.69, SC 156:220.

minimal. The poetic influence of Gregory Nazianzen may be minor, but his doctrinal influence on Symeon must not be understated. Symeon even cites Gregory by name twice in the *Hymns*.[50]

According to the modern scholar C. A. Trypanis, Symeon's poetry is strikingly original, second in importance only to Romanos.[51] Symeon was the first to employ extensively the fifteen-syllable meter in long religious hymns. This "political verse" eventually came to dominate Greek poetry.[52] Trypanis argues that, though the *Hymns* for the most part do not reach the level of truly great poetry, nevertheless:

> Symeon's unusual personality marks him out as one of the few Byzantine religious poets who is original . . . . In the fossilized monotony of his contemporary verse he chose the living fifteen-syllable line as a suitable vehicle for expressing his tortured heart and established it in the field of personal poetry, turning it into a narrative rhythm capable of expressing deep and moving mystical experiences.[53]

Why did Symeon write poetry? Some of the *Hymns*, especially number 21, are polemic. Alice Gardner suggests that the connection between controversy and verse was very close in early times. She gives the examples of Arius' theological sea shanties and, later, Theodore the Stoudite's verses against iconoclasts.[54] Poetic tracts may appeal to a wider audience, and thus gain a broader publication. For example, Michael Psellus (AD 1018–1098) published a parody of liturgical canon in a dispute with a monk named Jacob. So it seems

---

[50]*Hymn* 19.81, SC 174:100; *Hymn* 23.415, SC 174:216.

[51]Trypanis, *Greek Poetry*, 543.

[52]Ibid., 543. See also C. A. Trypanis, *Medieval and Modern Greek Poetry: An Anthology* (Oxford: Clarendon, 1951), xviii. This political verse predates Symeon by about two generations; nevertheless, Symeon's copious use of it probably helped to popularize it; see Trypanis, *Greek Poetry*, 455, 467.

[53]Trypanis, *Greek Poetry*, 469.

[54]Alice Gardner, *Theodore of Studium: His Life and Times* (London: Arnold, 1905), 243–44.

that, in the generation following Symeon, publishing polemics in verse was a clever, often base and bombastic, way to rebuke one's critics.[55] Nevertheless, most of Symeon's poems are inspirational exhortations. The advantage of writing homilies in verse is that they are more easily memorized, and the aesthetic makes them more emotive. Did Symeon intend his *Hymns* for the private meditation of his monks? Did he hope to bring the thoughtful reader into the cathartic and contemplative experiences he describes?

Symeon's Hymns for Spiritual Reading

There are few studies of *lectio divina* in Byzantine monasticism. The obvious reason for this is that *lectio divina* is a technical term for a Benedictine (Western) practice. An equivalent term is lacking in the East, so I shall refer to meditation on biblical and patristic texts as "spiritual reading." Though a technical term for it is lacking, there is no doubt that eastern monks meditated upon the Scriptures. Robert Meyer has published a study on spiritual reading among the desert Fathers, as recounted by Palladius. Although the desert Fathers were not Byzantines, their influence on Greek monasticism is beyond question. In his article, Meyer shows that spiritual reading consisted of both meditating upon and memorizing Scriptures.[56] The monks would attentively read the Bible and apply it to their own life; this included what we would call meditation. The highest type of manual labor for the monks was copying Scripture because doing so nourishes both body and soul.[57] Nicetas reports that reading Scripture and lives of the saints, and copying divine books were part of Symeon's own monastic routine.[58] Symeon himself confirms

[55]See Trypanis, *Greek Poetry*, 467.

[56]Robert Meyer, "Lectio Divina in Palladius," in *Kyriakon: Festschrift Johannes Quasten*, ed. Patrick Granfield and Josef A. Jungmann, 2 vols. (Münster: Aschendorff, 1970), 2:580–84.

[57]Ibid., 584.

[58]*Vie* 26, 27, pp. 36–38. Both Theodore the Studite and his uncle Plato were eulogized as fine calligraphers, cf. Gardner, *Theodore of Studium*, 77.

that he practiced spiritual reading. In *Catéchèse* 26, which describes the horarium at Saint Mamas, Symeon exhorts the monk to give attention to the readings during liturgy and offices, and during the common meal.[59] Symeon recommends that the monk study during morning and afternoon intervals.[60] Finally, Symeon advises the monk to read "about six pages with attention," alone after the evening office.[61] This last example is most clearly spiritual reading in the fullest sense. Symeon's own evening reading may have been the occasion of one of his contemplative experiences. He describes himself as "examining the sayings and considering the passages . . . meditating on these things" just before a luminous vision.[62]

It is safe to conclude that Symeon intended the *Hymns* to become part of the tradition of spiritual reading. He chose verse and an emotive, prayerful, inspirational style that make them unique in Byzantine religious poetry. Symeon unabashedly spoke about his own religious experiences and exhorted the reader to follow him to intimacy with God. This provides the reader with a rare glimpse into a Byzantine monk's contemplative experience that seems spontaneous but is also in the language, imagery, and theology of Scripture and the Fathers. In other words, the *Hymns* stem from both experience and scholarship; they are theological reflections on Symeon's religious experiences.

One of the most distinctive and characteristic of Symeon's teachings is his emphasis on religious experience. What follows is an overview of Symeon's doctrine on the importance of religious experience—even contemplative visions—for salvation.

---

[59]*Catechesis* 26.26–40, 137–140, SC 113:70–72, 80–82; deCatanzaro, *Discourses*, 275, 278.
[60]*Catechesis* 26.74, 249, SC 113:76, 90; deCatanzaro, *Discourses*, 276, 281.
[61]*Catechesis* 26.273, SC 113:92; deCatanzaro, *Discourses*, 282.
[62]*Hymn* 25.7–10, SC 174:254.

The Necessity of Contemplation

In the *Hymns*, Symeon argues that putting on Christ, possessing the Holy Spirit, union with God, and grace in general must be perceived as conscious data in the individual's senses, knowledge, and contemplation. The vision of God in this life is even necessary for salvation in the next. This is one of the most distinctive and characteristic aspects of Symeon's doctrine and is well attested in the *Hymns*. When Symeon argues that mystical experience is necessary for salvation, he makes three main points. First, God is all good things; he is not only the *agent* of salvation, he is beatitude itself. Second, for the dead, there is no place of repose outside of God; one either abides with God or suffers in hell. Third, if one has not seen God in this life, then there is no hope to see him in the afterlife.

Symeon argues that God is life, glory, and happiness for all beings. The vision of God is ultimately the only beatitude and salvation.[63] The contemplation of God's face is the very definition of joy both now and in the age to come:

> But you are all good things, you always give
> them to your servants who see your light,
> as you are life, and you provide life with all other
> good things, which, I say, are You yourself.
> And one who has you truly has all things in you.[64]

As such, separation from God is the worst thing that can happen: it is hell itself.[65]

Hymn 1 insists on the necessity of seeing God in this life for salvation in the next. The basic assumption is that if one is spiritually blind and out of touch with God in this life, then so also in the afterlife. There is no way to develop one's spiritual vision after death.

---

[63]*Hymn* 2.75ff., SC 156:182.
[64]*Hymn* 45.96–100, SC 196:110. Cf. *Hymn* 55.14–24, SC 196:254.
[65]*Hymn* 1.88–98, SC 156:164.

Thus spiritual blindness, though subjective, is hell itself because it cuts one off from God. Similar teachings may also be found in *Hymns* 34, 42, 44, and 50. Symeon's antagonists say that it is enough to avoid the fires of hell and to abide in a "place of repose" that is outside of God, but is not hell:

> And they say there is no need for your eternal glory
> or the kingdom of heaven, but it is enough to be in repose.[66]
> you who say: "I do not want to be
> within his pure kingdom
> nor to enjoy those good things,
> but I wish only to be outside punishment
> and not to receive the experience of fire at all."[67]

According to Symeon, there can be no such place of repose because any existence outside of God, who is all beatitude, is hell itself.[68] Isaac the Syrian makes a similar argument against those who would say: "It is sufficient for me to escape Gehenna, but I do not seek to enter into the kingdom!"[69] The language and arguments in Isaac's homily and in Symeon's *Hymn* 1 are similar enough to suggest literary dependence. Nevertheless, unlike Isaac, Symeon offers a biblical argument in the form of an exegesis of Lk 16.23–26. In the parable of Lazarus and the poor man, Jesus mentions no rest outside the kingdom: between heaven and hell lies only a chasm that cannot be crossed. The alienation and torment of the chasm is even worse than hell itself.[70] Isaac bases his argument more on the division of the sheep from the goats in Mt 25.32.[71] What is more, Isaac's argu-

[66]*Hymn* 1.111–12, SC 156:166.
[67]*Hymn* 50.267–71, SC 196:176. Cf. *Hymn* 42.162–63,170–76, SC 196:50; *Hymn* 17.445–50, SC 174:44.
[68]*Hymn* 1.88–98, 132–46,160–79, SC 156:164–72.
[69]Isaac, *Homily* 6, *The Ascetical Homilies*, pp. 56–57.
[70]*Hymn* 1.104–31, SC 156:164–66.
[71]Isaac, *Homily* 6, pp. 56–57. Symeon also cites Mt 25; compare *Hymn* 1.74, SC 156:162.

ment is more in terms of the necessity of asceticism rather than contemplation.

Symeon's teaching that luminous vision is necessary for one's very salvation puts him on the fringe of traditional orthodoxy, and it is one of the teachings that his monks probably found most difficult to accept. Most Christian ascetic writers, and even many in East Asian traditions, had grave reservations about visions, ecstasies, and the like because they can be delusions; lead to pride, heresy; or be considered ends in themselves.[72] It is worth considering Diadochos of Photiki's doctrine on visions because his emphasis on affectivity probably had a direct influence on Symeon's works. Diadochos was suspicious of visions.[73] He concedes that the soul can perceive God's grace, but somatic, fiery apparitions must be dismissed:

> Let no one who hears us speak of the perceptive faculty of the intellect imagine that by this we mean that the glory of God appears to man visibly. We do indeed affirm that the soul, when pure, perceives God's grace, tasting it in some ineffable manner; but no invisible reality appears to it in a visible form, since now "we walk by faith, not by sight," as Saint Paul says (2 Cor 5.7). If light or some fiery form should be seen by one pursuing the spiritual way, he should not on any account accept such a vision.[74]

This starkly contrasts the importance that Symeon gives to luminous visions. What is more, Symeon would have rejected Diadochos' use of the expression "by faith, not by sight."[75] Still, both Diadochos and Symeon would agree that the divine light is more noetic than somatic. Diadochos goes a step further by distinguishing between

---

[72]Tomás Spidlík, *Spirituality of the Christian East: A Systematic Handbook*, CSS 79 (Kalamazoo, MI: Cistercian Publications, 1986), 74–75; Caroline Franks Davis, *The Evidential Force of Religious Experience* (Oxford: Clarendon Press, 1989), 39.

[73]See Edouard des Places, introduction, SC 5 bis:44–46.

[74]Diadochos *Chap.* 36, SC 5 bis:105, *Philokalia* 1:263.

[75]*Hymn* 17.558ff., SC 174:52; *Hymn* 50.172ff., SC 196:168.

the natural light of the mind (which the purified mind can see) from the light of demonic deceptions:

> You should not doubt that the intellect, when it begins to be strongly energized by the divine light, becomes so completely translucent that it sees its own light vividly. This takes place when the power of the soul gains control over the passions. But when Saint Paul says that "Satan himself is transformed into an angel of light" (2 Cor 11.14), he definitely teaches us that everything which appears to the intellect, whether as light or as fire, if it has a shape, is the product of the evil artifice of the enemy. So we should not embark on the ascetic life in the hope of seeing visions clothed with form or shape; for if we do, Satan will find it easy to lead our soul astray. Our one purpose must be to reach the point when we perceive the love of God fully and consciously in our heart.[76]

It would seem that Symeon did not heed Diadochos' *caveat* concerning luminous visions. Symeon appropriated Diadochos's notion of a divine light that energizes the *nous*: this light is a perception of divine love "fully and consciously" perceived in one's heart. With respect to contemplating divine love, the difference between Diadochos and Symeon is that Symeon freely spoke of divine love as a luminous vision and God himself. The New Theologian was less worried about whether visions were from God or a deception, at least in the *Hymns*. In the *Traités éthiques,* Symeon gives an example of a monk (himself) reporting a visionary experience to his spiritual father.[77] This is an example of discerning the authenticity of a vision, but he includes no warnings about demonic deceptions.

Symeon's polemics often seem too demanding. He seems to impose his subjective experience on others and to make luminous

---

[76]Diadochos *Chap.* 40, SC 5 bis:108, *Philokalia* 1:265.

[77]*Traités éthiques* 5, in Syméon le Nouveau Théologien, *Traités théologiques et éthiques, II: Éthiques 4–15,* ed. Jean Darrouzès, SC 129 (Paris: Cerf, 1967); English translation in *The Ethical Discourses*, 2:52–54. See also Turner, *St Symeon*, 189.

vision not only the goal of monastic life, but the test of one's salvation. This was probably one of the reasons for the conflict between Symeon and his monks. Is this doctrine too demanding? Did Symeon really expect everyone to have luminous visions akin to his own, or did he concede the sincere quest for God is enough?

Contemplation as Love and a Foretaste

In *Hymn* 17, Symeon describes love as the source of transcendence and contemplation; he identifies love with the luminous vision and the Holy Spirit himself. It follows that Symeon would proclaim the necessity of love in language akin to that of *Hymn* 1, which argues for the necessity of contemplation:

> But if it is possible to be saved
> without love, O my Christ,
> how shall this be?
> Impossible! If we were separated from the light,
> how shall we flee the darkness?
> If we were deprived of joy,
> how would we be free from sorrow?
> Having been found outside the bridal chamber, (Mt 25.10–11)
> how would we be completely happy?
> Having fallen out of the kingdom
> —I am speaking of your vision, Savior—
> what other salvation,
> and what sort of consolation,
> or in what other kind of place
> would we be able to find salvation?
> Certainly, absolutely nowhere.[78]

[78]*Hymn* 17.426–41, SC 174:42–44. Cf. *Hymn* 1.66–131, SC 156:162–66.

One must seek and possess the kingdom—which is divine love—here below "if you wish to enter the kingdom after death also."[79]

Of course, the connection between divine love and contemplation is well attested among the Fathers. For example, Isaac the Syrian sometimes speaks of contemplation as divine love: "For love is the place of spiritual things and it dwells in purity of soul. When the intellect is established in the realm of love, grace is active, and the mind receives spiritual divine vision and becomes a beholder of hidden things."[80] Maximos the Confessor also spoke of divine love, knowledge, and light interchangeably, and he taught that one who is alienated from love is also alienated from God who *is* love.[81] Nevertheless, Symeon went a step further by arguing that contemplation is necessary for salvation. He claimed that failure to behold the light of the Spirit after Baptism is only for lack of love, so let no one say that contemplation is impossible.[82] The New Theologian identified the divine light with love and the Holy Spirit.

Symeon's doctrine on the necessity of contemplation for salvation is most distinctive and one must not trivialize its significance. Nevertheless, Symeon had more sober and tolerant passages in which he admitted that the fullness of divine vision is reserved for the final resurrection, and not all of the elect can expect their experiences to be like his own. For all his insistence on contemplation and possessing the kingdom here below, Symeon recognized that the contemplative sees only a part, as a foretaste and pledge.[83] Symeon used the term "pledge" five times in the *Hymns*. Twice he described the luminous vision as a pledge of things to come. Elsewhere, the pledge is variously described as the Holy Spirit, deification, pos-

---

[79] *Hymn* 17.750–54, SC 174:64.

[80] Isaac the Syrian, *An Epistle to Abba Symeon of Caesarea*, in *The Ascetical Homilies*, 443. See also Isaac, *Homily* 46, *The Ascetical Homilies*, 223–25, where he speaks of love as the goal of ascetic life: "When we attain to love, we attain to God."

[81] Maximos, *Chapters on Love* 1.9, 1.31–34, 1.38, in PG 90:964, 968; English translation in *Philokalia* 2:54, 56.

[82] See also *Traités éthiques* 13.222–77, SC 129:416–20, *The Ethical Discourses*, 2:171–72.

[83] E.g., *Traités éthiques* 5.317–46, SC 129:102–4, *The Ethical Discourses*, 2:54–55.

session of God, and the experience of the kingdom in this life.[84] The notions of the pledge and foretaste strengthen the biblical basis of Symeon's argument. They also convey the "already, but not yet" aspect of the kingdom, which is both at hand and still to come.

In his more sober moments, Symeon recognized that his luminous visions were special to himself. He acknowledged that other people's experience may be less rich, despite their best efforts. On the other hand, these more tolerant teachings are found in his *Traités éthiques* and *Catéchèses*; there are no parallel teachings in the *Hymns*.[85] Because the *Hymns* are among Symeon's later works, one may assume that his doctrine on the necessity of contemplation was not just from the zeal of his youth but was the conviction of his maturity. Still, this doctrine seems less extreme when one considers that he understood contemplation as love and as a sensitivity to spiritual values.

Symeon's degree of emphasis on affectivity and visionary experience was without precedent but always expressed in biblical and Orthodox terms. I see Symeon's doctrine as incarnational. That is, he deeply believed in Providence and that, by the power of the Holy Spirit, one may encounter Christ in one's daily life: in the events of the day, in reading Scripture, by participating in a Christian community, and—where they all come together—in the liturgy. Religious experience may be regarded as normal for practicing Christians, but one's experience must be discerned and understood through the lens of Orthodoxy. Therein lies a strength of Symeon's *Hymns*: with heartfelt zeal and biblical imagery, Symeon makes the doctrines of the Fathers intimately relevant for the individual.

---

[84]*Hymn* 1.73, SC 156:162; *Hymn* 28.219, SC 174:312; H*ymn* 17.817, 854, SC 174:68, 70; *Hymn* 52.63, SC 196:204.

[85]*Catechesis* 22.264–66, SC 104:386; deCatanzaro, *Discourses*, 250. See also *Traités éthiques* 7.446–508, SC 129:188–90, *The Ethical Discourses*, 2:96–97; *Traités éthiques* 10.817–21, SC 129:318, *The Ethical Discourses*, 1:167.

Translator's Note

The translation is based on the edition in the *Sources Chrétiennes* series (SC), volumes 156, 174, 196. Some of the Greek words that are more technical or difficult to render into English are provided in footnotes; a Glossary is also found at the end of the translation. I have made no attempt to convey the meter in these poems; rather, I have tried to translate as literally as English grammar and idiom allow, without sacrificing the meaning. I have included the line numbers, according to the SC edition, for those who wish to compare the translation with the Greek. Still, the reader must be aware that differences between English and Greek sentence structure did not allow for a literal, line by line translation. I have corrected some of the Scripture citations found in the edition.

Mystical Prayer

Mystical prayer of our father among the saints Symeon, through which he invokes the Holy Spirit whom he saw before him.

Come, true light (Jn 1.9). Come, eternal life (1 Jn 5.20). Come, hidden mystery (Eph 3.9). Come, nameless treasure. Come, [5] ineffable reality. Come, incomprehensible face. Come, everlasting exultation. Come, unfading light. Come, trusty expectation of all who are going to be saved. Come, awakening of those who sleep. Come, resurrection of the dead (Jn 11.25). Come, Mighty One who always creates, who re-creates and who transforms all things by his will alone. Come, invisible, and [10] untouchable, and in every way intangible. Come, you who always remain immutable, and who at every hour are wholly altered, and are coming to us who lie in hell, you who are above all the heavens (Eph 4.10). Come, most beloved name repeated again and again, ‹a name› entirely forbidden for us to speak or to know the very person you are, the kind or quality. Come, eternal joy.[15] Come, imperishable crown (1 Pet 5.4). Come, purple of our great God and King. Come, crystalline cincture set with gems. Come, unapproachable sandal. Come, royal, purple robe and truly autocratic right hand! Come, you whom my miserable soul has desired and desires. Come, the Alone to the alone, because I am alone, as you see![20] Come, you who separated me from everyone and made me alone on the Earth. Come, you who have become desire itself in me and who made me desire you, the utterly unapproachable one. Come, my breath and my life (Acts 17.25). Come consolation of my dejected soul. Come, my joy, and glory, and endless luxury.

I thank you because you have become one spirit with me (1 Cor 6.17), unmixing,[25] unmoved, immutable God over all things,

33

and because you yourself have become the all in all for me,[1]
utterly inexpressible food, and utterly without expense, ‹food
that› is endlessly overflowing the lips of my soul, and gushing out
in the fountain of my heart (Prov 5,16), garment flashing forth
and burning up the demons, purification through incorruptible
and holy tears [30] that wash me out, tears that you give freely to
those whom you visit. I thank you because you have become an
unfading light and an unsetting sun to me, you who have nowhere
to hide, who fill the universe with your glory.[2] For you have never
been hidden from anyone, but we always hide ourselves from
you, not wishing to come to you. For where would you hide, you
who nowhere [35] have a place of rest? Why ‹would you hide›?
you who never turn away anyone at all, and you do not turn from
anyone of them. And so now Master, dwell in me and inhabit
me,[3] and remain continually and inseparably in me your slave,
until my death, Good One, so that I also may be found both in
my departure and after my departure in you (Phil 3.9), Good
One, and I shall reign [40] with you (2 Tim 2.12), God over all
things (Rom 9.5)! Remain, Master, and let me not be alone, so
that when my enemies come, always seeking to devour my soul
(1 Pet 5.8), when they find you remaining in me, they shall flee
entirely and shall have no strength against me, when they see you
who are more powerful than everything, seated within the home
of my humbled soul (Mk 3.27). Verily Master, [45] When you
remembered me, when I was in the world of my ignorance, and
you yourself picked me out, and separated me from the world,
and set me before the face of your glory (Jude 24). So now also
keep me within, always standing upright and immovable in your
dwelling within me. So that watching you continually, I the corpse,
may live; and holding you, I, a poor hired man,[50] will always
be rich, even richer than all kings;[4] and eating and drinking you

[1]Rom 3.5; 1 Cor 15.28.
[2]Acts 7.49; Is 66.1.
[3]Jn 1.14; Eph 3.17.
[4]Lk 15.25; Rom 13.14.

(Jn 6.54), and every hour being vested with you, I will be reveling in unspeakable holy things. For you are every good, and every glory, and every enjoyment, and to you glory is fitting, you the Holy, Consubstantial, and life-giving Trinity. The Trinity in Father, and Son, and Holy Spirit venerated, and [55] proclaimed, and worshipped, and served by all the faithful now, and always forever and ever. Amen.

Hymn 1

Concerning divine illumination and the light of the Holy Spirit: that God is the one place in which all the saints have rest after death, that one who falls away from God into the other place will have no rest in the life to come.

What is this spine-chilling mystery that is being accomplished
    in me?
In no way can a word recount, nor can
my miserable hand write to the praise and glory
of him who is above praise, of him who is beyond telling.
    (Phil 1.11)
5 For, tell me, if the things now being accomplished in me the
    profligate
are inexpressible and unutterable, how would
he who is the author and maker of such wonders
need praise from us, or need to receive glory?
No, for he who has been glorified cannot be glorified,
    (2 Cor 3.10)
10 in the same way that the sun that is seen by us in the cosmos
could not be illumined nor partake of light;
the sun gives light, it is not enlightened; it enlightens, it does
    not receive light.
For the sun has the light that it received from the beginning,
    from the Creator.

And so if God, the Creator of everything, has made the sun,
15 and has created without need, only to bring to light a
       bounteous flame,
   and in no way from any other greater need,
   how would he receive glory from lowly me?
   For he is the utterly gracious Creator of the sun;
   he fills everything with all good things,
20 with just a nod and an intention he possesses the power.
   In this also my tongue is at a loss for words;
   my mind sees the things being accomplished; it does not
       explain them.
   It sees, and desires to speak, and does not find the words.
   For the mind looks upon invisible things that are utterly
       without form:
25 whole, simple, uncompounded, infinite in magnitude.
       (Rom 1.20)
   For my mind perceives no beginning, it sees no end at all,
   it knows no center. And how would it tell what it sees?
   It seems to me that the totality is seen
   not all at once in its essence, but by participation.
30 For when you ignite something from a fire you take the whole
       fire.
   And there it remains undivided, it remains as before.
   Moreover, what is given is separated from the first fire
   and is made into many lamps, for it is material fire.
   This is a spiritual, undivided fire,
35 and utterly indivisible and inseparable,
   for in communicating to many it is not divided into parts.
   But it remains both undivided and in myself;
   it springs up in me from within my wretched
   heart like the sun or like the solar disc, (Ps 111.4)
40 spherical, and showing itself radiant like a flame,
   I do not know, as was said, what to say about this,
   and I wish to keep silent—if only I could!

but the awesome marvel stirs my heart,
and opens my filthied mouth,
45 and makes me speak and write unwillingly.
you who now dawn in my darkened heart, (2 Pet 1.19)
you who have shown to me marvels that my eyes did not see,
you who come down into me as to the last of all, (1 Cor 15.8)
you who designated as a son and a disciple of an apostle me
50 whom the terrible, murderous dragon held previously
as an accomplice who commits every transgression.
you who are the sun shining in hell before all ages,
and who enlighten my darkened soul ever more,
and give to me an endless day
55 —a difficult thing for timid and lazy types like me to believe!
you who fill my beggary full of all good things,
may you also give to me speech and supply for me the words
to describe your wonder-working to everyone,
and to describe all that you do today with us your servants,
60 so that the worthless ones sleeping in darkness,
and those who say: "It is impossible for sinners to save
            themselves
the way that Peter and the other holy, religious,
and just apostles found mercy,"
so that they may know and may learn that, by
65 your goodness, this is, was, and shall be easy!
And those who suppose that they have you, the light of all the
            cosmos, (Jn 8.12)
yet say that they do not see you, that they do not live in the
            light,
they are not enlightened, they do not continually contemplate
            you, O Savior.
May they learn that you have neither enlightened their mind,
70 nor have you dwelt in their dirty hearts, (Eph 3.17)
and in vain do they exult in their empty hopes,
expecting that they will see your light after death.

For here is the pledge money, the seal thus given by you,[1]
Savior, to the sheep on your right. (Mt 25.32)
75   For if the death of each obtains a final closure,
and likewise for all, after death, one can effect nothing,
and one cannot do either good or worthless things,
my Savior, without question each will remain as they were
       found at death. (2 Cor 5.3)
This frightens me, Master, this makes me tremble,
80   this makes all my senses melt away,
that one who dies blind and departs from here
shall nevermore see this sun with the senses
even if they were resurrected and were again to receive the
       light of their eyes,
so also one whose mind is blind, if they should die, (2 Cor 4.4)
85   they shall not gaze upon you the rational sun, my God,
but having come from darkness they shall dwell in darkness,
and for eternity they shall be separated from you.
No person, Master, among those who put faith in you,
no one among those who have been baptized in your name,
       (Acts 8.16)
90   shall withstand this huge and horrible burden
of separation from you, O Compassionate One; for this is a
       terrible calamity,
terrible, unbearable, eternal suffering.
For what would be worse than separation from you, O Savior?
And what is more grievous than to be cut off from life,
95   and from thence to live as a corpse deprived of life,
at once to have all goods taken away?
For one who is separated from you is deprived of every good.
For then it will not be as it is now on earth.
For now, those who are ignorant of you live in bodily self-
       indulgence,

[1] 2 Cor 1.22; Rev 9.4.

100 and here they exult like leaping, irrational beasts.[2]
    They have all things that you have given for the enjoyments of
        life,
    and seeing only these things, they suppose it will be
    the same after the departure of their soul and of their life.
    But they speculate badly, and badly do they believe
105 when they say that they are not with you, but still they
    prepare a certain place of repose—oh the folly!—(Jn 14.2)
    They do not receive light, yet they have no share in darkness,
    they are outside the kingdom, but also outside of hell,
    both outside the bridal chamber, and away from the fire of
        punishment, (Jude 7)
110 the wretched pray to arrive in such a place.
    And they say there is no need for your eternal glory
    or the kingdom of heaven, but it is enough to be in repose.
        (Mt 3.2)
    Alas for their darkness! Alas for their ignorance!
    Alas their wretchedness and vain hopes!
115 Nowhere has this been written nor shall this be,
    but only those who do holy things are in the light of good
        things,
    and the workers of worthless things shall be in the darkness of
        vengeance. (1 Jn 3.18–21)
    In between a terrifying chasm divides the two,
    as you yourself have taught, you who have prepared these
        things. (Lk 16.26)
120 And for the person falling into the middle ‹of the chasm›
    it will be a punishment beyond all the most frightful tortures,
    into the abyss of punishment, into the chaos of destruction.
    Unfortunate for the person who tumbles and who is brought
        down,
    for those who are in torments *there* it is difficult to climb up,
        (Lk 16.23–26)

[2] 2 Pet 2.12; Jude 10.

125 difficult to cross over into the land of the just;
     they would prefer to be reduced to cinders in a terrible fire,
     or to throw themselves into the horrible chaos.
     And so those who wish to be in the chasm after death
     are worthy of weeping and mourning,
130 because like irrational beasts they are entirely senseless;
     they call down curses upon themselves and lead themselves
           astray.
     You the kingdom of heaven, you Christ, the land of the meek,
           (Mt 5.5)
     you the young grass, the paradise, you the divine bridal
           chamber.
     You the secret nuptial bed, you the table for everyone,
135 you the bread of life, you the freshest drink, (Jn 6.35)
     and you are both the bowl of water and the water of life,
           (Rev 21.6)
     and you are an unquenchable lamp to each one of the saints
           individually,
     and you are the garment, and the crown, and the one who
           distributes the crowns.
     And you are the joy and repose; you are the pleasure and glory.
140 And you are the exultation, and you are the merriment,
     my God; your grace, the grace of the All-Holy Spirit,
     shall shine like the sun in all the saints. (Mt 17.2)
     And you, the unapproachable sun, shall shine in the middle of
           them, (1 Tim 6.16)
     and all shall gain glory in proportion
145 to their faith, practice, hope, and their love,
     their purification, and their enlightenment from your Spirit.
     O God, Alone, Long-suffering, and Judge of all, (Heb 12.23)
     those who shall receive mansions and different places,
           (Jn 14.2–3)
     the measure of their illumination, the measure of their love,
150 and the measure of their contemplation shall be the measure of

their grandeur and glory, their luxury and fame
that distinguishes their homes and their wonderful mansions.
These are the different tents, the many houses,
the brilliant robes of the many dignities,
155   and the variegated crowns, stones, and pearls,
and unfading flowers that have a strange appearance,
both the sofas and the bedding, both the tables and the
        thrones,
and all that is the sweetest luxury,
was, is, and shall be to see you and you alone.
160   And like I said, those who neither see your light,
nor are seen by you, but have been separated
from the vision of you, the All-Good, are deprived of all goods.
Where would they find repose or a place free from pain?
In what place shall they dwell, those who have not been made
        upright?
165   For the upright dwell with your face; (Ps 139.14)
and you have formed ‹your likeness› in their upright heart,
and in you they dwell with your form, my Christ. (Gal 4.19)
O marvel, O paradoxical gift of goodness!
All humans have been made in the form of God, (Phil 2.6)
170   and in all of them is formed he who cannot be contained,
the immutable God, unmoved by nature,
the one who desires to dwell in all who are worthy,
as each one has within them the whole King,
the kingdom itself, and the goods of the kingdom,
175   and each one shines like my resurrected God has shone,
exceeding the rays of this visible sun, (Mt 17.2)
and thus are those who have stood by God who glorified
        them,
they persevere, astounded by the excess of glory (2 Cor 4.17)
and by the endless addition of divinity's splendor.
180   For the end will be eternal progress,
the condition of additional, endless fulfillment,

and shall make an attainment of the Unattainable, and God
of whom no one can get enough, shall become the source of
    satisfaction for all.[3]
But the full measure of him and the glory of his light
185 will be an abyss of progress, and an endless beginning;
and just as those who have Christ transformed within them
stand by him who shines unapproachably,
so also the end in them becomes a beginning of glory.
And—in order to make the idea more clear to you—
190 in the end they shall have a beginning, and in the beginning an
    end. (Rev 21.6)
Understand me, one who is overflowing needs no addition,
and runners do not overtake the end of the infinite.
For if this sky that we see passes away, (Mt 5.18)
as well as the earth and all things in the earth, then seek what
    I say;
195 it will be the attainment of the place where you shall find
    fulfillment.
I do not mean bodily fulfillment, but you shall be able, by your
    mind,
to attain the full measure of the incorporeal world;
but it is not the world, but the air as it was before,
but not the air, but an inexpressible receptacle, which they call
    the All,
200 and it is an utterly endless abyss,
equally whole from every direction, from one part and from
    others;
this All is filled with the divine divinity.
And so those who have a share in him, those who dwell in
    him,
how may they embrace all of him, and so be satisfied?
205 How, tell me, would they grasp the end of the endless?

---

[3]καὶ προσκορὴς γενήσεται ὁ ἀκόρεστος πᾶσιν. This is difficult to render into concise English.

It is impossible and by all means impracticable.
For thus neither for the saints still in the body,
nor for those departed to God
can such a thought at all penetrate them.
210 For they also are covered by the light of divine glory;
they are enlightened, and they shine, and they revel in all these
    things.
And they truly know as though by every certainty
that their perfection shall be endless,
and the progress of their glory shall be everlasting.
215 I wonder where those who fall away from God stand,
those who stand afar off from him who is everywhere?
And truly, brothers, this is a great wonder that is full of fear;
one needs the consideration of an enlightened mind,
in order to perceive this properly and not fall
220 into heresy, like one who does not have faith in the words of
    the divine Spirit.
These also shall certainly be within the All,
but they shall be outside the divine light and certainly outside
    of God;
for just like those who do not see when the sun shines,
even if they are illuminated all around, they finish their lives
    outside the light,
225 they are separated from the sun by perception and
    contemplation;[4]
so also is the light of the Triune Divinity in the All,
and in the middle of the light the sinners are enclosed in
    darkness,
not seeing, not having any divine perception at all,
but burning in their conscience,
230 and being condemned, they shall have unspeakable calamity,
and an unutterable suffering unto eternity.

[4]αἰσθήσει θεωρίᾳ.

Hymn 2

What change came upon this father, and how by the highest purity
he was united to God, and what sort of person he was, and what he
became; here his words of love addressed to God reveal these things,
and at the end he who theologizes speaks about angels.

What is your immeasurable compassion, Savior?
How have you deigned that I be made your member,
I the impure one, the profligate, the prostitute?[1]
How have you vested me with a brilliant robe, (Lk 15.22)
5   flashing forth with the radiance of immortality,
and turning all my members into light?
For your body is immaculate and divine,
flashing forth entirely with the fire of your divinity,
unspeakably mixed and commingled.
10 And so you have given this to me, my God.
For this dirty and perishable tent
was united to your all-immaculate body,
and my blood mixed with your blood.
I was united, I know, to your divinity also,
15 and I have become your most pure body,
a resplendent member, a truly holy member,
far-shining, and transparent, and gleaming.
I see the beauty; I look at the luster;
I reflect the light of your grace,
20 and I am astonished at the mystery of the radiance,
and I am beside myself when I consider myself,
from what a lowly condition I have come, what a marvel!
And I wait quietly and stand in awe at myself,
and I fear and reverence as though before you yourself.
25 I am in great difficulty, wholly given to reverent fear,
where shall I sit, and whom will I approach,

[1]Eph 5.5; Lk 7.36–50.

and where do I lay down these members of yours?
For what works and what actions
may I use these awesome and divine members?
30 Grant that I may both speak and practice what I preach.
O my craftsman, and sculptor, and my God!
For if there is anything I say that I do not fulfill in deeds,
then I have become a brass gong making a big noise in vain,
        (1 Cor 13.1)
and I do not even perceive the sound of the loud noise.
35 But do not cast me aside nor abandon me,
nor allow me to be led astray, my Savior,
I am wretched, poor, a stranger,
the one who owes to you countless talents, (Mt 18.24)
but as you have done before, do also now, O Logos!
40 For once upon a time, from my inheritance, and all the
        paternal land
of my father, brothers, mother, relatives, guests, (Mt 19.29)
and from all other relations and friends,
you separated me, when I was sinful and
more worthless than all of these, O Savior,
45 and you took me into your immaculate arms,
though I was revealed to be hard-hearted toward your
        blessings.
Thus may you now also have mercy on me, O Compassionate
        One,
and so more greatly, my God, may you
be moved with compassion, and protect me,
50 and calm the movements of my anger,[2]
and give me strength to bear with patience
all the trials and suffering of life,
as many trials as I myself imprudently procure,
and as many as the jealous nature of the demons tempts me
        with.

[2]Anger = θυμοῦ can also be translated as: life, breath, heart, rage.

55   And the weak ones among my brothers,
     by deed and by word they manipulate me; woe is me,
     because my members consume me,
     and again I suffer through these things.
     I am led by my feet ‹though› it is my fate to be the head,[3]
60   and barefoot I am stabbed by thorns,
     and I am violently distressed as I bear the pain.
     One of my feet goes forward
     and again the other turns back;
     hither and thither they drag me, they draw me,
65   and I trip and fall down.
     And so I am not able to follow everyone:
     to lie down is bad, and so to go away
     is worse than lying down,
     as though surpassing all other misfortunes.
70   Lord, give to me compunction and remorse,
     and deign that in the darkness of life,
     in this world, in the place of suffering,
     I may serve you, and worship you well,
     and keep your holy commandments!
75   I thank you because you gave life to me,
     so that I may know you, and fall down and worship, my God.
     For this is life, to know you alone, (Jn 17.3)
     God, creator and maker of all things,
     unbegotten, uncreated, without beginning, unique,
80   and to know your Son begotten from you,
     and the Holy Spirit proceeding from you,
     the all-praised, triune unity
     whom to worship and to give religious service
     is above all other glory
85   that one might speak of on earth or in heaven. (Phil 2.10)
     For what is the glory of the angels, of the archangels,
     of dominions, of cherubim, of seraphim,

[3]That is, abbot of Saint Mamas.

and of all other heavenly hosts,
what is their glory, or the light of their immortality,
90   or their joy, or the radiance of their immaterial life
if not the one light of the Holy Trinity,
indivisibly divided into three,
which is one in three persons,[4]
unknowably known, insofar as he wishes.
95   For it is not possible for a creature
to know at all the Creator as he knows
himself by nature.
Every angel and every created nature
sees and perceives[5] according to grace,
100   not comprehending, but perceiving,
insofar as he shall wish to be known or revealed
to the blind or even to those who see plainly.
For even an eye does not see without light,
but takes its vision from light.
105   Because by the light vision was made,
and whether you speak of the incorporeal or the corporeal,
you shall find that God has made all things.
And if you should also hear of anything in heaven,
the things on earth, and things in the depths,
110   of all these there is one life and glory,
one desire, and one kingdom,
one wealth, one happiness, crown, victory, peace,
and every other dignity,
is the full knowledge of the beginning and the cause,
115   whence all things were brought forth and came to be.
This is the upholding of things above and things below;
this is the ordering of all things perceived;
this is the subjection of all things seen,
the angels held this as a firm status,

[4]χαρακτῆρσι.
[5]νοοῦσιν.

120 receiving greater knowledge and fear
     when they saw Satan falling, (Lk 10.18)
     and all those with him were brought under by self-conceit;
     for however many angels merely forgot this
     and fell enslaved by pride,
125 but all those who held to this knowledge
     were raised up by fear, and by love
     they stuck to their Master.
     Thence the full knowledge of God's lordship
     also made an increase in love,
130 because the more they saw the flashing lightning
     of the Trinity, the more clearly they saw the Trinity's radiance,
     and again this beat off all other thought,
     and made immutable those who
     at the beginning received a mutable nature,
135 and who now remain in the heights of heaven.

Hymn 3

What is a monk and what is his practice, and to what heights of contemplation he has been raised.

     The monk is one who is not mixed with the world
     and always converses with God alone,
     seeing he is seen, loving he is loved,
     and he becomes a light mysteriously shining.
5   Being glorified he seems all the more a beggar,
     and belonging he is like a stranger.
     Oh marvel that is in every way strange and inexpressible!
     On account of boundless riches I am a poor man,
     and possessing much I seem to have nothing.
10   And I say that I thirst through an abundance of waters,
     and I ask who shall give to me what I have in abundance,
     and where shall I find what I see each day?

And how shall I grasp what is both within me
and outside the world, for it is entirely unseen?

15 If anyone has ears to hear, let them hear (Mt 11.15)
and truly understand the words of an illiterate!

Hymn 4

A teaching to monks who have just renounced the world and those who are in the world; and concerning what sort of faith one ought to have toward one's own father.

Get rid of the whole world and those in the world!
Embrace only the blessed remorse! (Mt 5.4)
Mourn only because of wicked deeds,
because these deeds separated you from the Maker of all
    things,

5 from Christ, and from all things holy!
Be anxious about nothing other than that.
But regard even your body as a stranger,
and look down as one who has been condemned,
as one who is slowly walking the road to death;

10 always sigh from the depths of your heart,
and wash your face only with tears!
And your feet, which have been running to wicked things,
    (Prov 1.16)
by no means may you wish to wash them with water.
Yes indeed, also keep your hands together;

15 may you not shamelessly hold them out to God,
these hands, which you have often stretched toward sin!
Conquer the reckless tongue by however much power,[1]—
for the tongue also is easily given to sin—
seeing that through their tongue alone

---

[1] ὅση δύναμις, "power," is in the vocative, the subject of the imperative κράτει, "conquer."

20   many of the great ones strayed from the straight path
     and lost the kingdom of heaven.
     Firstly, stop up your ears (Prov 21.13)
     so to hear nothing shameful or profane,
     and then perhaps you shall master even your tongue.
25   Listen only to the admonitions of your father,
     give to him humble answers,
     and tell him your thoughts as to God,
     even mere temptations, and may you hide nothing from him,
     nor do anything without his opinion,
30   neither go to sleep, nor eat, nor drink!
     And when you have kept these things over time,
     do not suppose that you have accomplished anything great,
     for though you have sown in sweat and toil,
     you have not yet picked the fruit of your labors. (Ps 127.2)
35   Therefore do not be led astray, nor suppose that you have
           found,
     before you have acquired spiritual eyes,
     and before the ears of your heart have been cleansed
     by your tears that wash out the filth,
     before all your senses begin to be changed,
40   and you begin to see and to hear spiritually.
     For you shall gaze upon many things beyond telling,
     and you shall hear extraordinarily more things,
     which you cannot express with your tongue. (1 Cor 14.2)
     And so to hear spiritually is a spine-chilling wonder,
45   and so also to see the wonder of wonders!
     This sort of person never understands bodily,
     but treads the earth as though walking in air;
     the spiritual person sees everything, even into the abysses,
     and understands all creatures,
50   gains knowledge of God, and is astonished by fear.
     The spiritual person worships and glorifies God as creator.
     It is a great thing to discover God's lordship,

although everyone may believe that they know it,
do not doubt that most are deceived!
55   Those who are enlightened know this,
but all the others, oh terrible ignorance,
are more in the dark than even the devils.
But, O Lord and Creator of all things,
you who have made me from earth, both living and mortal,
60   and you Who have honored me with immortal grace,
and you have given to me life, and speech, and motion,
     (Acts 17.28)
and to glorify you, the Master of all things,
you yourself, Master, grant that I the miserable one
may prostrate myself before you and ask for what is fitting!
65   For I do not know how I was brought into the world
and I do not know what are the things which people suppose
     exist here.
What is my vision, O my God,
and what are the visible things, I cannot say
how all we humans have been given to vanity,[2]
70   and we have no correct judgment of beings.
I came just yesterday, and tomorrow I depart,
and I suppose that I am immortal here below.
I confess to everyone that I have you as my God,
but I deny you by my actions each day.
75   I am taught that you are the maker of all things,
without you I force myself to have everything.
You rule things above and things below,
and I alone resist you without trembling.
Give to the helpless one, grant to me the all-wretched one,
80   that I may renounce all the wickedness of my soul,
which both my swell-headedness and empty pride
crush and break to pieces, alas!
Give humility, give a helping hand,

[2]Rom 1.21; Ps 61.9.

and cleanse the filth of my soul,
85   and grant to me tears of repentance,
tears of yearning, tears of salvation,
tears that cleanse the gloom from my mind,
and in the end make me radiant from on high,
desiring to see you the light of the world, (Jn 8.12)
90   the light of my eyes, of me the miserable one, (Tob 10.5)
of the one who has a heart full of this life's evil,
full of many afflictions and jealousy,
full of the actors of my exile,
or, to say more, of my benefactors,
95   of my masters, of my true friends.
Give to them good things instead of bad, my Christ,
      (Rom 12.17)
eternal things, divine things, and riches,
which you have prepared unto ages of ages
for those who ardently desire and love you! (1 Cor 2.9)

Hymn 5

(without the glosses of Nicetas)

Alphabetical doublets by the same author urging and guiding those who have just withdrawn from the world to the perfection of life.

At the beginning make Christ and fervent faith your own.
Proceed by fleeing relatives and friends!
Go forward to the immaterial, stripped of material things.
Renounce all cowardice from yourself.
5   All the more embrace hope without doubt!
Take up the easy yoke, the Lord, (Mt 11.30)
the Gift who saves all of us mortals,
the Lord who renders us gods by the power of him who calls
      us,

so that by a work, you may know the outcome of the works.
10 To cut out your desires is a good advantage for you.
Accomplish the words and commands of your father,
even unto death, for this is the great summit.
Consider yourself to be the most worthless of all,
a stranger poorer and more humble than others!
15 May you be entirely an imitator of your master. (Eph 5.1)
May daily mourning achieve everything,
teaching you the knowledge of things that perish and things
    that remain.
Practice the habit of silence, which guards all these virtues.
Keep at all times the memory of death.
20 By these means one is purified and enlightened at heart.
May you merit to see clearly the divine,
but Christ is perfect love;
he enlightens souls who seek him.
O deifying love that is God!

Hymn 5

(including the glosses of Nicetas)

At the beginning make Christ and fervent faith your own.
    [Thus withdraw from the world.]
Proceed by fleeing relatives and friends!
    [For this benefits beginners.]
Go forward stripped of material things for the immaterial.
    [You shall find nothing better for the struggle.]
Renounce all cowardice from yourself.
    [For you flee to a powerful master.]
5 All the more, without doubt, embrace hope!
    [For he is concerned even for the little sparrows.]
    (Mt 10.29)

Take up the easy yoke, the Lord, (Mt 11.30)
>   [For there is much return in the future.]
the Gift who saves all of us mortals,
>   [Since we have been saved by divine blood.] (Rev 5.9)
the Lord who renders us gods by the power of him who calls
>   us,
>   [For this was the reason for the Incarnation of the Master.]
so that by a work, you may know the outcome of the works.
>   [More astonishing than all visible things.]
10   To cut out your desires is a good advantage for you.
>   [It reveals you as a martyr in conscience.] (2 Cor 1.12)
Accomplish the words and commands of your father,
>   [For they will lead the way without stumbling.]
even unto death, for this is the great summit.
>   [God is revealed as he who achieves this for your sake.]
Consider yourself to be the most worthless of all,
>   [This makes you first in the kingdom.] (Mt 20.21, 27)
a stranger poorer and more humble than others!
>   [These are the great virtues if you would accomplish
>   them.]
15   May you be entirely an imitator of your master. (Eph 5.1)
>   [And what is better than this?]
May daily mourning achieve everything,
>   [For this is sweeter beyond food and drink.]
teaching you the knowledge of things that perish and things
>   that remain.
>   [Because first one keeps away from all the world.]
Practice the habit of silence, which guards all these virtues.
>   [For it cuts off all sorts of hurtful roots.]
Keep at all times the memory of death.
>   [For this is the source of humility.]
20   By these means one is purified and enlightened at heart.
>   [Oh marvel sought by all.]

May you merit to see clearly the divine light.
>   [For the light is an immaterial missile from the
>   Immaterial.]
But Christ is perfect love;
>   [One who has this love is God by adoption.]
He enlightens souls who seek him.
>   [These alone shall live, let no one be deceived!] (Ps 68.33)
O deifying love that is God!
>   [Astonishment and an impenetrable reality.]

Hymn 6

Quatrains by the same author that show his passionate love for God here on earth.

How are you both a fire gushing forth,
and also a sprinkling water,
how do you both inflame and sweeten,
how do you make mortality disappear?

5 How do you turn humans into gods,
how do you make darkness light,
how do you raise up from hell,
how do you prevent mortals from perishing?

How do you drag darkness to the light,
10 how do you seize the night,
how do you illuminate my heart,
how do you entirely transform me?

How do you become one with human beings,
how do you make them children of God,[1]
15 how do you make them burn with desire for you,
how do you wound without a sword?

[1]Mt 5.9; Jn 1.12.

How do you endure, how do you tolerate,
how do you not immediately render what is due,
how is it that you who dwell beyond everyone
20 see the duties of all?

How, though you are far from us,
do you look down on the practice of each?
Give patient endurance to your servants,
so that afflictions do not bury them! (Rom 5.3)

Hymn 7

A petition to God, and how when he was united to God and saw the glory of God operating in himself he was astonished.

How do I worship you within me, and how do I see you far
　　away?
How do I observe you in myself, and see you in heaven?
You alone know this, you who do these things and shine like
the sun in my material heart immaterially.
5 You who made the light of your glory to shine through me, my
　　God,
by means of your apostle, disciple, and servant,
the all-holy Symeon, shine upon me even now
and teach me to sing hymns to him in the Spirit,
hymns new and at the same time ancient, both divine and
　　secret.
10 So that through me, my God, your knowledge may be revered,
　　(Ps 138.6)
and your great wisdom may be displayed all the more,
and all who hear shall praise you, my Christ,
because by your grace I speak in new tongues. (Mk 16.17)
Amen, so be it, Lord, according to your will! (Mt 26.42)
15 I toil hard, I suffer in my humbled soul,

when your light appears within it shining brightly.
Within me yearning is called suffering, and it truly is.
Distress because I am not able to embrace you entirely,
and to be satisfied, as I yearn to be, so it is for me and I groan.
20   Nevertheless I also see you, and that is sufficient for me,
and that shall be glory, and joy, and a royal crown,
and above all pleasures and desires of the world.
And this shall render me like the angels,
perhaps you shall make me even greater than them, my Master.
25   Even though by your essence you are invisible to them,
and by your nature you are unapproachable, but still you are
          perceived by me,
and you are altogether mixed with me by the essence of your
          nature,[1]
for your attributes are not separated nor cut off at all,
but your nature is your essence and your essence your nature.
30   And so when I participate in your flesh I participate in your
          nature,
and I truly partake of your essence,
having a share in divinity, but I am also
made an heir in body, I suppose that I am greater than
incorporeal beings. I am made a son of God,[2] as you have said,
35   not to the angels, but to us, calling us gods:
"I have said: You are gods and all children of the Most High."[3]
Glory to your compassion and your divine plan,
because, being God by nature, you were made human
without changing, without mixing, you remain both human
          and God.
40   And you made me God, though I am mortal by nature.
God by adoption and by your grace, through your Spirit,
as God, incredibly you have united these two extremes.

---

[1]πάντως καὶ τῇ τῆς φύσεώς σου μίγνουσαί μοι οὐσίᾳ.
[2]Jn 1.12; Mt 5.9.
[3]Jn 10.34; Ps 81.6.

Hymn 8

To whom God reveals himself and who comes into possession of virtue through practice of the commandments.

Being hidden, how do you see, how do you watch over all
    things,
how are you not seen by us, yet you see all of us?
But not all whom you see do you also know, my God,
but you know and love only those who love you,[1]
5   and you manifest yourself specially to them; (Jn 14.21)
being a hidden sun to every mortal nature,
you spring up within those who belong to you are seen by
    them,
and those who were formerly in darkness rise in you:
fornicators, adulterers, and those despairing of salvation,
    sinners, publicans. (Mt 9.10)
10   Repenting, they become children of your divine light, (Jn 12.36)
and light certainly produces light, and so these also are light,
little children of God, as was written, gods by grace. (Jn 1.12)
However many shall keep well your divine commands,
however many shall renounce the vain and deceiving world,
15   however many shall hate parents and brothers without hate,
    (Lk 14.26)
regarding them as strangers and passersby in this life,
however many shall become naked of wealth and property,
and shall utterly deny their attachment to them,
however many, by means of heaven's glory, shall loathe
20   from their soul the empty glory and praises of human beings,
however many have completely cut out self-will
and have become as guileless sheep to their shepherds,
however many have become dead in body toward every evil
    practice,

[1]Prov 8.17; 1 Cor 8.3.

sweating over the hard work of virtue,
25 and living only by the will of their pilot,
mortified by obedience, but living anew,
however many by the fear of God and the memory of death
weep each day and every night,
and mentally[2] they fall at the feet of the Master,[3]
30 begging mercy and forgiveness of faults,
these are the ones who come into possession of moral beauty by every
practice of the virtues, wailing each day,
and knocking without ceasing, they gain mercy.
These, by many prayers, unutterable sayings, (Rom 8.26)
35 and rivers of tears, purify their soul.
Such as these, seeing their soul purified,
receive the fire of desire and the fire of yearning,
of a longing to look upon the soul thoroughly purified.
But since they are unable to find the perfection of the light,
40 purification is endless for such as these.
For the more I shall be purified and illumincd, I the wretched one,
the more also shall be seen the Spirit who purifies me,
it always seems to me a beginning of both cleansing and seeing.
For in an infinite depth, in an immeasurable height,
45 who shall be able to find a middle or an end?
I know that it is great, but I do not know how great.
I long for more and I continually groan,
because even though I suppose it to be much, what is given is small
compared to what I suspect exists far away from me
50 when I see the very thing that I desire, and I seem to have nothing,
not entirely sensing the wealth ‹already› given to me.

[2]νοερῶς.
[3]Mk 5.22; Lk 7.36ff.

Because I see the sun, I do not consider this.
And how? Listen, believe the very thing I experience.
The sun is unspeakably sweet in sensation,
55 dragging the soul to a desire that is divine and beyond telling.
This soul who sees burns ‹with passion› and is inflamed by
    desire.
She wishes to possess within her the whole of that which is
    revealed,
but she is not able, and she is distressed by this,
and she does not consider it good ‹merely› to see or to
    experience.
60 And so then he who is seen, being uncontainable to all things,
truly unapproachable, shall wish to have mercy
upon my afflicted and humbled soul.
Of a sudden, he appears shining before my face,
such a one as he makes himself appear flashing in me,
65 and he fills all of me with total joy, every desire,
and sweetness of vision, me the humbled one.
The sudden change, the strange transformation
being accomplished in me is beyond telling.
For if this sun which we all see,
70 someone saw going down within ‹their heart›
and in like manner all of it shining and swelling ‹within›,
would they not be speechless as a corpse at this marvel,
and would not all who saw this be out of their senses?
And one seeing the Maker of the sun like a torch
75 shining out, operating, speaking within them,
seeing this how shall they not be out of their senses? How shall
    they not tremble?
How shall they not love the One who gives life?
Human beings love other humans who are like themselves
whenever they seem to have something more than others.
80 On seeing the Maker of all things—the One who alone is
    immortal—

the One who is all-powerful to everyone, who shall not desire
   him?
Most people, believing from hearing, love ‹him›, (Rom 10.17)
and for his sake the saints died and lived. (2 Cor 6.9)
But those participating in his vision and light,
85   being known and knowing him, how shall they not yearn ‹for
       him›? (Gal 4.9)
Tell me, how shall they not grieve continually on his account?
How shall they not despise the world and things in the world?
       (1 Jn 2.15)
And how shall they not utterly reject all honor and glory?
       Those who
have come above the glory on earth, and above every honor,
90   those who yearn for the Master who is beyond the earth,
       beyond all things seen,
or rather he who created all things seen
and certainly even things unseen, (Col 1.16)
and those who find and receive immortal glory,
and from thence fully possess every good,
95   but also every desire, every yearning
for eternal goods and for divine realities.
They have been filled from the ever-living source,
from which, Master, give to us also to be abundantly satiated,
and to those who seek you, and ardently desire you,
100   as we ourselves may also enjoy with your saints
the eternal goods forever and ever. Amen.

Hymn 9

That when one has been made a participant of the Holy Spirit, one is snatched away by the Spirit's light and carried above all the passions, and one is not injured by their approach.

Oh. Oh, God. Lord, Almighty!
Who may have their fill of your invisible beauty?
Who may be filled with your incomprehensibility?
Who may walk worthily by your commands, (Lk 1.6)
5   and who shall see the light of your face, (Ps 4.6)
the great light, wonderful, not at all contained
in this burdensome and darkened world;
the light takes the one who sees it from the world
with their body. Oh strange mystery!
10   Who is the one who, having passed over the fortification of
       their flesh,
and having crossed over the gloom of mortality,
and having left the whole world behind, was hidden from
       view?
Oh the deficiency of knowledge and words!
For where has been hidden the one who passed through the
       world
15   and taken outside of everything that they see?
Tell me, refuted wisdom of the wise,
so that I do not say that it is wisdom that God made foolish,
       (1 Cor 1.19–20)
as Paul and any of God's servants would say.
This is a man[1] of desires, desires of the spirit, (Dan 9.23)
20   he who associates with bodies, by means of his body,
can still be holy by means of the spirit.
For beyond the world and outside these bodies
there is no yearning for fleshly experience,

[1] ἀνήρ.

but a certain dispassion. One who kisses this dispassion
25   also gains life from their kiss.[2]
Even if you truly see such a one behaving disgracefully,
as if deserting to his own practice,
know that it is a dead body doing this! (Rom 8.10)
I do not mean a body apart from its soul, by which it is moved,
30   but apart from external evil desire,
for the pleasure of beautiful dispassion,
from which the light mysteriously kisses me,
it snatches away and transports my whole mind,
and seizes my naked mind with an immaterial hand,
35   it does not allow me to fall away from his love,
nor to consider a thought of passion,
but it embraces me incessantly,
and yearning inflames my soul,
and there is no other sensation in me.
40   For as much as the purest bread is
sweeter and more prized than dung,
so much the more are the things above incomparably
superior to the things below for those who have experienced
     them well.
Shame on you, wisdom of the wise,
45   deprived of the real knowledge! (1 Cor 1.27)
For the simplicity of our words
has gained, in practice, the true wisdom
by approaching God and prostrating in worship,
God from whom all wisdom of life is given,
50   by which I am formed anew or even deified
as I contemplate God forever and ever. Amen.

---

[2]"kisses … kiss" = φιλήσας … φιλήματος. The sense may be that of love, affection.

Hymn 10

That, through grief, death strikes even the stronger among us.

I have learned a strange thing of astonishment,
an immaterial nature, more solid than rock,
a nature as enduring as a diamond[1]
which is softened by neither fire nor iron,
5   has been turned to wax interwoven with lead.
Only just now do I believe that a little flow of water
over a long time hollows a hard rock,
and truly nothing is immutable among the things in life.
From now on let no one think that I am deceived![2]
10   Alas for the one who considers the fleeting things in life,
seeing them as things to be held and by which one is satisfied!
They shall suffer[3] these things which I—the wretched one—
   have suffered.
Night has separated me from my very sweet brother,
dividing the indivisible light of love.

Hymn 11

*Here our astonished father describes how God was seen by him as by
the Apostles Paul and Stephen.*

What is this unforeseen wonder that is happening even now?
Does God now wish to be seen by sinners also,
he who long ago ascended on high, and has taken his seat on a
   throne
in his Father's heaven, and remains hidden?

[1] ἴσον ἀδάμαντος καλουμένου παθοῦσαν. Rendered more literally: "Suffering
like that which is called the unconquerable."

[2] Μηδείς μ᾽ ἐκ τοῦ νῦν ἀπατᾶν νομιζέτω! Apparently this is an intransitive use
of ἀπατᾶν. An alternate rendering would be: "From now on let no one think that I
deceive!"

[3] πείσεται may also be translated as "Shall be persuaded."

5 For he was hidden from the eyes of the divine apostles,
   (Acts 1.9)
 and afterward, as we have heard, only Stephen
 saw the heavens opened and then said:
 "I see the Son standing at the right hand of the glory
 of the Father." And as if he were speaking blasphemy,
10 he was stoned by the teachers of the law.[1]
 He died by the law of nature and lives forever.
 Although he was an apostle, he was also sanctified
 and completely full of the All-Holy Spirit. (Acts 7.55)
 But it was the beginning of the proclamation[2] and there was a
   crowd of unbelievers
15 who by trusting in Christ through the apostles
 received the grace which is a gift of faith.[3]
 Now then, what does this strange thing mean,
 this thing happening in me? What would this frightening
   terror
 that is now accomplished signify?
20 What sort of benevolence has just now been manifested,
 a strange wealth of kindness, another fountain of mercy
   (Titus 3.4)
 having much more mercy than the marvels of old?
 For many have found mercy by divine benevolence,
 but they were each offering their own thing: their faith,
25 or even other virtues, and acceptable works.
 But perceiving myself as deprived of all these virtues,
 I am driven out of my senses and unable to bear
 the things happening to me—profligate from the womb—
 at the hand of the God who created all creation with a word.
30 I shudder to consider these very things, and how shall I write
   them in words?

[1]Acts 7.56; 6.1.
[2]That is, of the Gospel.
[3]Acts 5.12, 14; Eph 2.8.

What sort of hand shall conduct the service, what sort of pen
    shall write?
What sort of word shall recount, what nature of tongue shall
    speak out?
What sort of lips shall say the things seen happening in me,
things being accomplished throughout the day?
35 Furthermore, in both night itself and in darkness itself,
I see Christ frightfully opening the heavens for me, (Acts 7.56)
himself stooping to look and to be seen by me
at the same time with the Father and the Spirit, the thrice holy
    light,
a light that is one in three and three in one.
40 By all means they are the light, and the one light is the three
which also enlightens my soul more than the sun,
and illuminates my darkened mind.
For what my mind saw, it did not see from the beginning.
But it was blind, you may trust, and did not see,
45 and because of this the wonder struck me down with
    amazement all the more
when somehow Christ opened the eye of my mind, (Lk 24.31,
    45)
and somehow he both gives the vision and is the one seen.
For he is revealed both *as* light and *in* light to those who look,
    (Ps 35.9)
and those looking see him again in the light.
50 For those who look see in the light of the Spirit,
and those who see in this light look upon the Son.
But one who is worthy to see the Son, sees the Father, (Jn 14.9)
and one who looks on the Father certainly sees him with the
    Son.
Like we said, what now is being accomplished in me,
55 and the things which cannot be known I have somewhat
    understood,
and now from afar I look upon the beautiful invisible things,

I am violently struck down with astonishment by the
    unapproachableness
of the light, the unbearableness of the glory, oppressed by
    trembling,
even though I see but one drop from an abyss.
60 As the whole of water is displayed in a drop,
the quality of its nature and its form,
and as from the top edge the whole robe,
and, as they say, by the claws the beast, the lion,
so also I see the whole in a fragment when I am embraced.
65 I fall down and worship him, the Christ and my God.
I had in my mind the small consolation that he
neither consumed me nor burned me completely,
like wax near a fire, as the prophet says.[4]
The fact that I am far from the unapproachable fire,
70 and standing in the middle of darkness, and hidden in it,
as a result I become dizzy, as though seeing through a tiny hole.
I have passed time with my mind engaged in these things,
and as though, it seemed, I gazed into heaven,
and I tremble lest I receive more and He should absorb me.
75 I have found him whom I saw from afar,
Whom Stephen saw when the heavens opened, (Acts 7.56)
and whom again Paul saw afterward when he was blinded,
    (Acts 9.9)
truly and entire like a fire in the middle of my heart.
And so I was troubled by the wonder, and trembling greatly;
80 I was beyond myself, the whole of me fainted, entirely at a loss,
not bearing the unendurable I turned away from the glory,
and during the night I ran away from my perceptions here,
and I was sheltered by my thoughts and concealed among
    them.
As though stepping into a tomb, and instead of a stone,
85 I put on this burdensome body, and so I was covered,

[4]Ps 67.3; Mic 1.4.

and by thinking that I was hidden from him who is
    omnipresent,
the one who of old raised me up when I was a buried corpse.
Trembling and unable to look at his glory,
I preferred to enter secretly, and to cleave to the tomb,
90   and to dwell with the dead, myself living in the tomb, (Ps 67.6)
rather than to be burned up and to perish utterly.
Having settled there, it is by all means necessary that I mourn
    without ceasing,
and it is necessary for me, the profligate, to lament because I
    lost the one
I yearned for, and I have become one lying in the tomb.
95   But I the living corpse, under the earth, covered by a stone,
    (Rev 1.18)
I have found life, the one who gives life,
to whom is fitting glory and honor now and unto the ages.
    Amen.

Hymn 12

Theology concerning all aspects of the unity of the divine, triune essence. And throughout Symeon speaks about himself using humiliation ‹and thereby› turns around the self-conceit of those who suppose themselves to be something.

How, my God, do the things that you once made disappear live
    in me again?
And how do they fill me with darkness and affliction?
Passions of both anger and fury from which
a rising smoke comes upon me, a mist upon my head,
5   and they impair the eyes of my mind,[1]
since ‹these eyes› are covered, alas, and compelled

---

[1]καὶ πήρωσιν τοῖς νοεροῖς ὄμμασί μου ποιοῦσι. Literally: and they make an impairment for my noetic eyes.

to close by the gloom, I am deprived of you,
you the light whom everyone longs for, but few seek out.
But those deemed worthy to participate in your mysteries,

10 and to partake materially in an immaterial sensation
of fearful mysteries that are inexpressible to all,
and to know the invisible glory in visible things,
and the strange mystery that was accomplished in the world,
those so worthy, I well know, are certainly very few,

15 and those who have come into clear contemplation
from him who was in the beginning before all ages,
from the Father, with the Spirit of the Son, from God and
     Logos,
from the triple light in the one, and from the one in the three.
And each in one light: Father, Son, and Spirit,

20 being undivided in three persons without confusion,
who are according to the divine nature,
of one dominion, glory, power, and one will.
For the Three appeared to me, as in one face,[2]
two beautiful eyes filled with light.

25 Tell me, how do the eyes see apart from the face?
It is entirely unfitting to call it the face without the eyes,
for it is deprived of the larger part, or rather the whole.
For the sun, if deprived of the light of its beauty,
would itself first be destroyed and then also the whole creation

30 that has obtained from it enlightenment and vision.
So also for the noetic beings;[3] if God were deprived of one,
either Son or Spirit, he would no longer be Father,
but he would not be living, having lost the Spirit,
from Whom is given to all to live and to be. (Acts 17.28)

35 Let every truly rational nature therefore be in awe,
however many under the sun or beyond it,

---

[2]προσώπῳ = face. Often in theology of the Trinity προσώπων must be translated
as "person" (as in line 20), but in this case that would be heresy. Cf. *Hymn* 24.253.
     [3]τοῖς νοητοῖς or "rational beings."

⟨be in awe before⟩ the utterly inexplicable nature in three
    persons![4]
For anyone among human beings does not know the name,
    nature, appearance,
form, nor hypostasis of God

40   in order to speak, and to write and to give a share to another.
But as the shining sun penetrates the clouds,
and yet itself is not seen, nor is it wholly revealed by its light,
but dimly provides its light to those on earth,
so also understand that my God is hidden from us,

45   and a great and profound darkness overpowers all of us.
But understand an entirely more marvelous wonder:
for the light of God does not set like the sun,
but it even shines everywhere and illuminates all things,
and in the middle of all this ⟨light⟩ I am surrounded by
    darkness,

50   and I am deprived of the Light who made me.
And so who would not lament, and who would not mourn for
    me,
and who would not groan and weep over me?
Because God is in everything and everywhere,
and he himself is entirely light, in whom is not

55   the least shadow of change, nor presence of night, (Jas 1.17)
there is absolutely no hindrance of darkness,
but he is unfolded above every thing, and he shines
    unapproachably,
and to those who are worthy he is approachable, and
    apprehendable, and seen
to a small degree as we said, compared to the whole ray,

60   and compared to the sun itself, when it will wholly reveal itself,
but so much the more for those sitting in darkness (Is 42.7)
because they have been deemed worthy to see a little sunbeam.
But I, the miserable one, prefer the darkness,

[4] φύσιν τὴν τρισυπόστατον.

and I am anxious about the things in it, and I add to my gloom,
65 and it becomes thicker in my humbled soul
from which the passions increase and are vivified in me,
and they become to me dragons, and reptiles, and snakes
always throwing into confusion the members of my soul.
Furthermore the vain and impious glory bites me,
70 and has planted its teeth in my heart
when I was entirely faint and helpless, from my heart
came savage dogs, came a multitude of beasts,
and finding me lying down they chewed me to pieces.
For wantonness and praise have thrown into disorder
75 my marrow and sinews, the strength and zeal of my soul.
Alas, how shall I write all this? ‹The passions› have taken away
        from me ‹my strength›.
Like bandits, having put upon me self-conceit and hesitation,
pleasure, and anxiety as to how I shall please human beings,
dragging me to and fro, they divide me among themselves.
80 The one showing my discretion and my sobriety,
the other showing my good works and my inspired actions,
they rendered me a corpse,
and ‹what is› great, extraordinary, and awesome
is that they have left self-conceit in me, the defiled one.
85 For tell me how is it not wonderful, how is it not pitiful,
that such passions fall upon me unawares,
rendering me dead and naked of every virtue,
again without noticing myself, having learned nothing of what
        happened,
but supposing myself to be greater than everyone,
90 a wise theologian both dispassionate and holy,
rightly honored by all persons,
but also praised as though worthy of praises,
summoning everyone, I supposed that I am gathering honor.
For when the people are gathering I puff myself up the more,
95 and I constantly look around me, lest somewhere someone

has been left out who was not present and did not see me,
and if somewhere someone was found looking suspiciously at
         me
then I bear it with malice, and revile, and tear them to pieces,
so that after they hear and cannot bear my censures,
100   they will come, greet me, and show themselves under my
             obligation,
and as if in need of my prayer and love,
and I say to all the others: "such a one comes
and seeks my prayers, and to listen to my words,
and to my teaching." Woe is me, such simplicity!
105   So how do I not see the nakedness of my suffering,
nor sense the blows, nor be distressed, nor cry,
nor seek healing lying in a hospital,
how do I not call doctors, showing to them my bruises,
stripping bare even my secret passions[5] for them,
110   so that they may apply dressings, bandages, and cautery,
and I may steadfastly endure through my healing?
But how is it instead that every day I add to my wounds?
But, O my God, have pity on me as I am led astray,
and implant fear of you in my heart,
115   so that I may flee the world according to your commands,
and I shall have hatred toward it, and prudently lower the
             world ‹in my esteem›,
and may you not allow me, Christ, to be led astray in the midst
             of the world,
because it is you alone I love, though I have not yet loved you,
and I intend to keep only your commandments,
120   though I am entirely in the passions, and I have not yet
             understood you.
For who among those who know you needs the glory of the
             world?
Or who among those loving you seeks more of the world,

---

[5]Πάθη here could also be rendered "sufferings."

either to call everyone to themselves, or to flatter some,
or who shall make haste to be a friend of humans?
125 No one among your legitimate servants has done these things,
and on account of this I am afflicted, and I suffer, my God,
because in these things I see myself enslaved,
and I cannot obey nor be humbled,
nor do I wish to see your glory and yours alone,
130 by which I am shown to be faithful and your servant,
and by which I can be raised higher than everyone,
especially in thrift, and poverty, and works,
not only exceeding powerful men, but even kings.
Incline toward my humbled soul and have mercy on it.
135 God, the Creator of all, who has given what is good to me,
give to me also true knowledge, so that to all your eternal
        goods
I may wisely attach myself and to them alone!
And I shall love and seek your glory from my soul,
and have no care at all for human or worldly glory,
140 so I shall become one with you now and after death,
and I shall be deemed worthy, Christ, to reign with you,
        (2 Tim 2.12)
you who submitted to a dishonorable
death for me, and fulfilled the whole divine plan.
And then I shall be honored above all mortals.
145 Amen, so be it, Lord, now and unto the ages!

Hymn 13

Exhortation to repentance, and how the will of the flesh united to the will of the Spirit renders a person divine in form.

I lament and I am stung with contrition when the light shines
        on me,
and I see my poverty, and I know where I am,

and the sort of mortal world I dwell in, and I am mortal.
And I am delighted, and I rejoice when I will understand
5   the glory and status given to me from God,
and I suppose that I am an angel of the Lord,
having been wholly dressed in an immaterial garment.
And so the joy lights up my desire for the giver,
and for the God who transforms me, and desire
10   brings up rivers of tears, and makes me more brilliant.
Listen, you who, like me, sin against God,
hasten and run vigorously by your actions[1]
to catch and to seize the material of the immaterial fire
—by saying material, I indicate to you the divine essence—
15   and to rekindle the rational lamp of your soul,
so that you may become suns shining in the world,[2]
though totally unseen by those in the world,
so that you may become as gods possessing
within you the whole glory of God in two essences,
20   by all means in double natures, double energies,
and double wills, as Paul cries out.[3]
For the will of the mercurial flesh is one thing, (Jn 1.13)
and that of the Spirit another, and that of my soul yet another.
Except I am not triple, but double like a human being,
25   my soul is inexpressibly united to my flesh,
but each does not seek its own things respectively,
such as to eat, and to drink, such as to sleep,
which I call the earthly will of the flesh.
But when separated from the soul, the flesh seeks no such
    thing,
30   but dead, senseless, it is as clay.
It seems to me that the one will of a human being is wholly that
    of the soul.

[1]Cf. Heb 12.1; 1 Cor 7.29, 9.24.
[2]Mt 13.43; Phil 2.15.
[3]Eph 2.3; cf. Rom 7–8.

And so one who has united their own spirit to the divine Spirit
becomes divine in form, having received Christ in the breast,
a Christian from Christ, having Christ formed
35 entirely within, who alone is inapprehensible (Gal 4.19)
and truly unapproachable for all creatures.
But, O Immaculate Nature, hidden essence,
benevolence unknown to most human beings,
mercy not seen by those who live foolishly,
40 essence immutable, indivisible, thrice holy,
simple and formless light, completely without composition,
incorporeal, inseparable, incomprehensible to every nature,
how have you been seen like me, you have been known to
    those in darkness,
and you have been held in the hands of your holy mother,
45 and how were you put in chains like a murderer, you suffered
    bodily like an evil-doer,
O King, desiring by all means to save me,
and to bring me back again to a paradise of glory?
This is your divine plan, your advent,
your compassion, and your benevolence
50 which has come into being for all us human beings, O Logos,
for the faithful, the unfaithful, the heathens, the sinners, and
    for the saints.
For your manifestation has become common to all,
salvation and redemption of the living and the dead.
That which has secretly occurred in me, the profligate,
55 is also accomplished in known ignorance
—entirely known by me, but unknown to others—
what sort of tongue would speak, what kind of mind might
    explain,
what sort of word would recount, so that my hand may also
    write?
For it is truly fearful, Master, fearful and beyond telling,

60   that the light seen by me, the light which the world does not
        have,
    and he who is not within this world loves me,
    and I love him who is in no way among things seen.
    I am sitting on my couch, I am outside the world,
    and in the middle of my cell I see him Who is outside
65   being manifested, and I converse with him
    —and to speak boldness—I also love and he loves me,
    I eat, I am nourished well by contemplation alone,
    and being united with him I surpass the heavens,
    and I know this to be true and certain,
70   where my body is, I do not know, (2 Cor 12.2)
    I know that he comes down, he who is immovable,
    I know that he appears to me, he who is invisible,
    I know that he who is separated from every creature
    receives me within himself and I am hidden in his arms,
75   and then I am found outside the whole world.
    Again, small and mortal in the world
    I look upon the whole Creator of the world within me,
    and I know since I shall not die while in life,
    and I have the whole of life gushing forth within me,
80   he is in my heart, and he is in heaven,
    just the same, I see him flashing forth.
    How do these things come about, or how shall I fully know,
    how shall I be able to express what I know and see?
    For they are truly unspeakable and utterly unutterable,
85   things which eye has not seen and ear has not heard,
        (1 Cor 2.9)
    and has never come upon a heart of flesh.
    I thank you, Master, because you had mercy on me,
    and you gave these things for me to see and thus to write,
    to proclaim your benevolence to those with me.
90   So that even now peoples, tribes, and tongues may be initiated
        into the mystery, (Rev 14.6)

so that you may have mercy on everyone who fervently
    repents,
just as to your apostles and to all the saints,
you show them kindness, and honor them, and glorify them,
    my God,
seeing that they seek you with much desire and fear,
95 and looking to you alone, the maker of the world,
to whom is fitting glory, and honor, power, majesty
as to a king, and God, and master of all,
now and always, through all ages forever. Amen.

Hymn 14

A thanksgiving to God for the gifts of which God deigned Symeon
worthy; and that the dignity of the priesthood and abbacy is awesome
even to the angels.

I am not able to speak, Master, even though I wish to.
For what would I utter, I who am unclean in
thoughts, and deeds, and all my intentions?
Moreover, I wound my soul, and I burn within,
5   desiring to speak to you, just a bit, my God.
I see, for you also know my concerns, O my God,
you know that ever since my birth I have defiled
all the members of my body and my soul, being utter
    sinfulness. (Jn 9.1, 34)
I consider your mercy and benevolence,
10 and your many blessings that you have accomplished for me,
and I become speechless, almost despairing,
and afflicted, distressed endlessly, the wretched one,
because I am unworthy of all your goods.
Whenever I go into myself and I want
15 to recount in my mind the multitude of my evils, Christ,
and that I have not done one good thing in life

—and instead of punishments, instead of your just wrath,
which I expected to endure since I often grieved you,
now you have deigned me worthy of more such blessings—
20 I go into despair, I fear your condemnation
because I add even more failures each day,
and I tremble lest you turn your great mercy
and benevolence to the rage of even greater retributions.
Although I have been shown kindness, I am still more
      ungrateful to you.
25 I am your worthless servant, Good Master. (Mt 25.26)
And so all the other things, Lord, provided patience,
they procured hope of eternal life,
on account of which I rejoiced much, as you alone know,
taking courage in your kindness and your mercy.
30 For a good reason you have taken me from everyone, out of the
      world,
and separated me from all relatives and friends,
so that you may have mercy upon me, and save me, my Christ.
Being fully assured by your gifts,
I have insatiable joy, and certain hope.
35 And these last two things I do not know how to express,
you have been well pleased to manifest them to me, my King.
They deprive my soul and my mind of words,
and stop my energies and all intentions,
but also by the greatness of your glory they weigh me down,
40 and convince me to stop a little, my Savior, and neither
to speak, nor to work, nor to touch these things,
and I am at a loss in myself, and suffering dumbfounded.
How have I, the wretched one, given myself to serve
and to minister to such unutterable realities?
45 The angels tremble to gaze upon these realities without
      restraint,
the prophets were at once afraid when they heard
of the unattainability of glory and of the divine plan.

The apostles, and martyrs, and crowd of teachers
shout and scream that they themselves are unworthy,
50 preaching explicitly to all who are in the world.
And how can I, the profligate, and how can I, the fornicator,
and how can I, the humiliated one, have been deemed to
      become
abbot of the brothers, priest, and minister
of the divine mysteries of the immaculate Trinity?
55 For where bread is placed and wine poured
unto the name of your body and blood, O Logos,
you yourself are there, my God and Logos,
and this truly becomes your body and blood
by the arrival of the Spirit, and the power of the Most High,
      (Lk 1.35)
60 and having the boldness we touch the unapproachable God,
but what is more we touch him who dwells in unapproachable
      light, (1 Tim 6.16)
not only unapproachable to this perishable nature and
      humanity,
but even to all the spiritual[1] armies of angels.
And so this is the unspeakable, this is the supernatural,
65 a work and an undertaking which I have been appointed to do,
it persuades me to see death before my eyes.
Hence dismissing enjoyment, I am seized with trembling,
knowing that it is impossible for me—and I would think for
      all—
to serve worthily, and thus to have
70 angelic life in the body, or rather life above angels,
so that, as this discourse has shown and as the truth maintains,
one becomes more intimate with him in dignity than the
      angels,
since one even touches with hands and eats with the mouth

---

[1]νοεραῖς.

the One whom angels can merely stand near and shudder with
    hair standing on end.

75   And the judgment of the brothers whom I have been ordered
    to shepherd,

what sort of soul would endure it, what sort of mind would be
    capable,

of seeking blamelessly the intention of each one,

and of supplying amply everything by oneself,

and of escaping their judgment?

80   To me, this does not seem possible for human beings.

And thus I am convinced, and I prefer to be a disciple, it is
    better

to serve the will of one, listening to the words of one,

and to render finally an account to this one only

than to serve the characters and wishes of the many,

85   and to examine the intentions of these, and to seek out their
    designs,

even more to search out their practice and thoughts

because the judgment awaits me also, and I will have to give an
    account

in return for those who have sinned, those whom I shepherd.

By the mysterious words of God I alone certainly have been
    chosen.

90   For each shall be judged and by all means shall give an account
    (Mt 12.36)

of the things they have done, either worthwhile or worthless,
    (2 Cor 5.10)

but only I shall give an account on behalf of each one.

And how do I wish to be saved or to be shown mercy,

I who have not even one deed to show for the salvation

95   of my lone struggling soul? (Rom 2.15)

What is more, be assured, I do not have anything to declare,

since I have never done a work small or great,

    by which I expect to be saved from the eternal fire. (Jude 23)

But, O benevolent Savior, compassionate, merciful,
100 give to me, the humiliated one, divine power, so by a word
I may guide to the pasture of your divine law
the brothers whom you have given to me to shepherd with
    sagacity,
and to rescue them for the mansions of the kingdom on high,
    (Jn 14.2)
safe and sound, bright with the beauty of their virtues,
105 worthy worshippers of your fearful throne.
But as for me, the unworthy one, take me from the world,
even though I am spotted by many attacks of sin,
but at the same time wholly your servant and useless slave!
    (Mt 25.30)
And count me, together with my disciples,
110 among the choirs of the elect, whom you know by ‹your›
    judgments,
so that we may all at once see your divine glory (Jn 17.24)
and, Christ, we may revel in your inexpressible goods!
For you are the enjoyment, the pleasure, and the glory
of those who fervently love you forever and ever. Amen.

Hymn 15

How when he saw the glory of God Symeon was moved by the All-Holy Spirit, and that divinity is both interior and exterior to everyone, but both apprehensible and inapprehensible to the worthy. And that we are the house of David. And though he becomes many members, our Christ and God is one, and he remains undivided.

When you reveal yourself, Master of all things,
and you show the glory of your face more clearly,
I am entirely oppressed by trembling from above when I look
    upon you,
since it is accessible to me, who am lowly by nature,

5   and being oppressed by fear I am astounded and I say:
         (Lk 8.37)
     All your attributes, my God, are beyond my grasp,
     moreover, I am unclean, utterly unworthy (Is 6.5)
     of seeing you, the pure and holy master,
     whom angels reverence and serve with trembling,
10   and from your face every creature is driven away in confusion.
     But when I would say these things and close my eyes;
     that is to say, when I turn my mind to things below,
     unable to see or to look upon your unbearable vision,
     then I am deprived of your beauty so I wail, my God,
15   unable to bear separation from you who alone are benevolent.
     When I weep and wail you shine all around me.
     Bless me. And I am struck down with astonishment, and I
         weep even more,
     amazed at your compassion toward me, the profligate.
     Then I see so much ungracefulness in my body,
20   and the unworthiness of my wretched soul,
     and when I realize these things I am beside myself crying
         aloud:
     Who am I, God and Maker of the universe,
     and what good at all have I done in life,
     or which of your commandments have I ever practiced,
25   that you should glorify me, the dejected one, with such glory?
         (2 Sam 7.18)
     And from where or through what have you deigned thus to
         shine
     around me, the wretch, both night and day?
     For I have never thirsted while seeking you, my King,
     for I have not suffered distress from the labor of your
         commandments,
30   nor have I endured trials and scourges like all
     the saints who declare these things from the ages,[1]

     [1]Heb 11.36; Acts 3.21.

in such manner you save me, Christ, numbering me among
    those saints!
For you shall not save lazy me while I am devoid of works
even though, as the sculptor of human beings, you are most
    benevolent.

35 I hear Paul saying that faith is dead
without works[2] and I shudder at the retributions
which certainly await me there, for I am negligent.
And so how dare I count myself as faithful,
as with the saints, Master, who do works,

40 I who have never observed even one of your commandments?
    (Jn 14.15)
But I know that you are capable of all things, you make all
    things as you wish,
and, Master, you give to the last as even to the first,
and, oh wonder, to the last *before* the first! (Mt 20.1–16)
Having said these things to you, the Maker of the world,

45 you at first revealed yourself above and then one day concealed
    yourself from me,
and then later you completely surrounded me with splendor.
All of a sudden I see you completely manifested in me,
revealing yourself on high first, but then again hiding
in a cloud, just like the sun completely without rays.

50 And just as that sun is approachable to those who look
and then, what is more, as if the whole is seen by all,
so also you are approachable when hidden within me,
unapproachable to the eyes of my mind,
as you know, appearing, gradually increasing,

55 being shown brighter, flashing brighter. Yet
another time you are revealed to me again as utterly
    unapproachable.
And on this account I extol your incomprehensibility,

[2]Jas 2.26. Symeon has confused a saying of James for one of Paul's, see SC
156:280n1.

I proclaim your goodness, I cry out to you:
Glory to God who has so glorified our essence,
60 glory to your immeasurable condescension, O Savior,
glory to your compassion, glory to your domination,
glory to you for remaining immutable and unchanged.
You are unmoved, yet ever-moving,
and you are wholly outside of creation, wholly in every
     creature.
65 The whole of you fills all things, yet you are completely outside
     of everything,
above all things, Master, above all beginning,[3]
above all essence, above the nature of nature,
beyond all aeons, above every light, Savior,
above rational essences, for these are also your work,
70 rather, they are the work of your design.
For you are not a thing among all beings, but you are superior
     to everything;
for you are the cause of all beings as the Creator of all things,
and on this account you are apart from everything,
so high beyond the perception of any being,
75 invisible, unapproachable, inapprehensible, and intangible,
you are beyond understanding and remain without change,
you are simple, whole, and you are many-faceted,
and a mind is totally unable to understand the
diversity of your glory and the splendor of your beauty.
     (Ps 44.4)
80 And so you are not anything since you are above everything,
you who are outside all things since you are God of all things,
invisible, unapproachable, inapprehensible, and intangible,
and you yourself have become mortal, you have entered into
     the world,
and you were seen by all as approachable in the flesh that you
     assumed.

[3]ἀρχὴν could also be translated as "sovereignty."

85 And to the faithful you were known by the glory of your
divinity,
and you have become attainable to them, you who are
inapprehensible
and completely visible, you who are invisible to all.
And they knew the glory of your divine nature,
and only the faithful see, but even when all the faithless
90 see you they continue on blind, the light of the world. (Jn 8.12)
And so the faithful, both then and now, always see you
and they possess you, the Creator of the universe with them,
you participate and dwell with them in the darkness of this life.
You are like a non-setting sun, like an eternal lamp,
95 wholly ungrasped by the darkness, (Jn 1.5)
but always illuminating those who see you.
But like we said, since you are outside all things,
those whom you illuminate you transport beyond all visible
things,
and like yourself they are with your Father on high,
100 and you yourself are entirely and inseparably with us,
and you are in the world, yet again you cannot be contained by
the world.
For you are in the all, you are above the all.
Thus we your servants are in the midst of perceptible reality,
we are within visible things and you lead us out,
105 and we are with you on high, made completely brilliant by your
light.
You raise us up to yourself and make immortals out of the
mortals,
and remaining what we are, your children by grace,
we are made like you, gods seeing God. (1 Jn 3.2)
And so who would not run to you who alone are benevolent?
110 Who would not follow you, who would not declare out of their
yearning:

Look, we have thrown away everything, we follow you,
    (Mt 19.27)
the sympathetic, the gentle, the compassionate master
Who always await our return,
you who do not wish the death of those who offend you,
115 you who now fully accomplish fearful things in us.
When we hear that these things happened long ago in the
    house of David (Lk 1.69)
we are astonished! These things would be as follows:
we are the house of David since we are the same race as him,
and you yourself, O Creator of all things,
120 became his son, and we your children according to grace;
you are our kin by flesh, we are yours by divinity.
For by receiving the flesh you gave to us your divine Spirit,
and we have become one house of David, all at the same time,
by what is peculiar to you, and by ties of kindred to you.
125 And so you are the Lord of David in the spirit, (Mt 22.43)
and we are children of David, all your divine seed,
and when we gather together we become one house;
that is to say, all one family, all your siblings.
Is this not a fearful wonder? Or how shall anyone not tremble,
130 when they understand this entirely, considering
that you are with us now, and unto all ages, (Mt 28.20)
and that you make each person a home and you dwell within
    everyone,
and you become a home to all, and in you we dwell,
each one of us entirely, Savior, with you entirely,
135 you alone are with each one alone,
and you are entirely alone above us?
And so now you are securing all awesome things in us.
What awesome things? Listen to just a few of the many,
for even if what we have said surpasses all astonishment,
140 then all the same, listen now to things more awesome!

We are made members of Christ, and Christ becomes our
    members, (1 Cor 6.15)
and Christ becomes my hand and the foot of all-wretched me,
and wretched I become the hand of Christ and the foot of
    Christ.
I move my hand and my hand is Christ entire.
145 For, understand me, the divine divinity is indivisible!
I put my foot in motion and behold, it flashes as himself.
Do not say that I blaspheme, but accept these things
and fall down and worship Christ who makes you like this!
For if you also wish, you shall become his member,
150 and thus every member of each one of us
shall become a member of Christ, and Christ our members,
and he shall make all shameful things decent (1 Cor 12.23–24)
by the beauty of his divinity and by his glory he shall adorn
    them,
and when we are united to God we shall at the same time
    become gods,
155 not looking upon the indignity of the body at all,
but completely made like Christ in the whole body,
and each of our members shall be the whole Christ.
For while we become many members he remains one and
    indivisible,
and each part is the whole Christ himself.
160 And so thus you well know that both my finger and my penis
    are Christ.
Do you tremble or feel ashamed?
But God was not ashamed to become like you,
yet you are ashamed to become like him?
"I am not ashamed to become like him.
165 But in saying he is like a shameful member
I suspect that you speak blasphemy."
So then, you suspected badly, for there are no shameful
    members!

They are hidden members of Christ, for they are covered,
and on account of this they are more revered than the rest,
    (1 Cor 12.23)
170 as hidden members of him who is hidden, they are unseen by
        all,
from whom seed is given in divine communion, (1 Jn 3.9)
awesomely deified in the divine form,
from the whole divinity itself, for he is God entire,
he who is united with us, oh spine-chilling mystery!
175 And thus it truly becomes a marriage, unutterable and divine:
He unites with each one, and again I shall say these things
for pleasure, and each is made one with the Master.
And so if you will put the whole Christ on your entire flesh,
    (Rom 13.14)
then you shall understand everything that I say and have no
        cause for shame.
180 But if not entirely, but if you put upon your soul only a small
        patch
—I am speaking of the immaculate inner garment which is
        Christ—
then your old cloak is patched in just one place, (Mt 9.16)
and you are ashamed of all the remaining members,
retaining the whole body as more dirty,
185 then how shall you not blush seeing how you have put on filthy
        garments?
I said frightful things about holy members,
and about seeing much glory and illuminating the mind,
about rejoicing and taking to heart nothing carnal,
but still you see your flesh as defiled,
190 and in your mind you go through your disgusting practices,
and your mind always crawls in such things like a worm.
Wherefore you attribute to Christ and to me your sense of
        shame,
and you say: "Are you not ashamed of the shameful members?

and what is more, you bring Christ down to shameful
    members."
195 But again I say to you: look at Christ in the womb
and notice the things in the womb, and escaping the womb,
and from whence my God went out and passed through!
And there is something more you shall find concerning what I
    have said,
and the things he accepted for our glory,
200 so that no one imitating him need be ashamed
whether one says or suffers the things that he has suffered.
Being truly and entirely God he became fully human,
though not divided, he by all means became a perfect man,
    (1 Cor 1.13)
but he is God himself, whole in all of his members.
205 Thus it happened even now in the final age.
Symeon the holy, the pious Studite,
he was not ashamed about the members of any person,
neither to see any naked people nor to be seen naked;
he possessed the whole Christ, he was the whole Christ
    himself,
210 and all his members and the members of every other
he always saw one and all as Christ,
and he remained unmoved, innocent, and dispassionate,
since he was the whole Christ himself, and he saw
all the baptized, who have put on the whole Christ as Christ.
215 But if *you* are naked and your flesh were to touch flesh,
then you become mad for women like an ass or a horse,
    (Jer 5.8)
so how dare you calumniate the saint,
and why do you blaspheme against Christ who is united to us,
and who has given dispassion to his saints?
220 Furthermore he makes himself a bridegroom—do you hear?—
    each day,

and the souls of all become brides, to whom the Creator is
     united,
and again they to him, and spiritually it becomes a marriage,
as befitting a god he unites to these souls.
He does not utterly spoil them, God forbid, but even if
     previously ruined,
225 he would receive them and unite himself to them, immediately
        he makes them incorrupt,
and they see all the things that were previously defiled by
     corruption
as holy, incorrupt, entirely healed over.
They glorify the compassionate one, they yearn for the
     beautiful one,
and they are all united to the whole of his love,
230 what is more, they acquire the holy seed, as we said,
receiving the whole transformed God within themselves.
And so, fathers, are these things not the truth?
Have we not spoken out rightly concerning divine realities?
Have I not said things identical and equal to the Scriptures?
235 Well then, if you have put on the shame of your flesh,
and you have not stripped bare your mind, you have not
     stripped your soul,
you have not been able to see the light, having been covered by
     darkness,
then what can I do for you, how shall I show you the spine-
     chilling mysteries,
how, alas, am I to bring you to the house of David?
240 What is more, the light is unapproachable for lazy types like
     me,
it is invisible for blind people like me,
it is extremely far from the faithless and the hesitant,
very far from all worthless types, from all who love worldly
     things.
And so the light keeps incomparably far from the vainglorious,

245 as far as the highest heaven is above the depths of the abyss.
And who or how shall one climb all the way to heaven,
or go down below the earth and search out the abysses? (Rom
   10.6–7)
And seeking a pearl, that is very small like
a grain of mustard, how shall one find it? (Mt 13.31, 45)
250 But gather together, O children, but come, O women! (Joel 2.16)
But, O fathers, act before death overtakes you,
and everyone mourn and weep with me, (Joel 1.5)
like little ones receive God in Baptism,
or better, like infants become children of God,
255 because we sinners have been promptly cast out
from the house of David, and we have suffered
this unconsciously,[4] and let us run by repentance!
For by this conversion all we who have been cast out shall enter
   in,
there is no other means of going inside, do not be misled,
260 nor another way to see the mysteries accomplished in David's
   house,
and even now being fully accomplished for endless ages
in Christ my God, to whom is fitting all glory,
honor, and worship now and forever! Amen.

Hymn 16

That by nature only the Divine is desired and longed for, one who participates in divinity has come into the participation of all goods.

Oh what is the reality that is hidden from every created
   essence,
and what is the rational light[1] that is not seen by anyone,
and what is this abundant wealth, which no one in the world

---

[4] ἀναισθήτως could also be translated as "without feeling."
[1] τὸ φῶς τὸ νοητὸν.

has the strength to find entirely or to fully possess?
5   For it is inapprehensible[2] to everyone, uncontainable by the
            world,
        and it is most desirable above the whole world,
        and it is yearned for, as much as God prevails above the whole
        of visible reality, which he has prepared.
        This is why I am wounded by his love, (Song 2.5)
10   insofar as he is not seen by me, I melt away in my senses,[3]
        and groaning, I burn in my mind and heart.
        I walk about, and I burn, seeking here and there,
        and nowhere do I find the lover of my soul. (Song 5–6)
        And I often look around to see the one I desire,
15   and he, as though invisible, is wholly unseen by me. (Mk 5.32)
        But when I begin to mourn like one in despair, then
        he is seen by me and he looks at me, he who looks upon all
            things.
        Amazed, I am astonished at the shapeliness of his beauty,
        and how the Creator stooped down when he opened the
            heavens
20   and displayed his unspeakable and strange glory to me.[4]
        Who therefore shall also come closer to him?
        Or how shall one be carried up to the immeasurable heights?
        When I considered this, he himself was found within me,
        flashing forth within my wretched heart,
25   illuminating me from all directions with immortal radiance,
        shining upon all my members with his rays,
        folding his entire self around me he tenderly kisses all of me.
        He gives his whole self to me, the unworthy,
        and I take my fill of his love and beauty,
30   and I am filled full of divine pleasure and sweetness.

[2]ἄληπτος; the basic sense is "cannot be grasped" in either a physical or mental sense.
[3]φρένας.
[4]Acts 7.56; Is 64.1.

I partake of the light, and I participate in the glory,
and he illuminates my face like that of the one I yearned for,
        (Mt 17.2)
and all my members become bearers of light.
Then finally I become more beautiful than the beautiful,
35   I am richer than the rich, and more powerful
than all the powerful, greater than kings,
and much more honorable than all visible creation,
not only more honorable than the earth, and everyone on
        earth, but even more than
heaven and everyone in heaven, for I have the Creator of all
        things
40   to whom is fitting glory and honor now and forever. Amen.
        (1 Tim 1.17)

Hymn 17

*That fear begets love, and love roots out fear from the soul, and love
alone remains in the soul; love is the Divine and Holy Spirit.*

How shall I sing, how shall I glorify,
how shall I worthily honor
the God who gave little notice
to my many sins?
5   How shall I look to the heights at all,
how shall I lift up my eyes,
how shall I open my mouth, Savior,
how shall I move my lips?
How do I stretch out my hands
10   to the summit of heaven,
what manner of words can I find,
what teachings shall I put forth?
How shall I dare to speak,
how shall I ask forgiveness

15   for my immeasurable stumbling,
      for my many trespasses?
      For certainly I have done deeds
      beyond all pardon!
      You know what I speak of, Savior,
20   I have transgressed all nature,
      I have done works contrary to nature.
      I was seen as worse than irrational beasts,
      worse than all animals of the sea,
      worse than all cattle of the dry land,
25   worse than reptiles and wild beasts.
      I have become truly worse,
      having transgressed your commandments, (Mt 15.3)
      beyond the nature of irrational beasts. (Jas 3.7)
      And so having made a beast of my body,
30   and having defiled my soul,
      how can I be seen by you, how shall I look at you,
      how shall I dare to stand openly
      before your face, I the wretch? (Mt 11.10)
      How shall I not flee your glory
35   and the light of your
      Holy Spirit flashing forth?
      And, all alone, how shall I not give way
      to the darkness? I have done
      works of darkness, shall I not be
40   separated from the crowd of saints? (Rom 13.12)
      How shall I bear your voice
      when it sends me into darkness,
      thereafter bearing
      the condemnation of my works?
45   All shuddering, all trembling,
      totally oppressed by fear
      and consternation I shout to you.
      I know, Savior, that no other

has failed you like I have,
50 nor done the deeds
that I have done, the wretch,
and I have also become a cause
of destruction for others.
But again I know this,
55 I am persuaded of this, my God,
seeing as neither the magnitude of failures,
nor the multitude of sins,
nor the shame of deeds
shall then surpass
60 your great benevolence,
rather beyond great,
and beyond telling, your mercy is beyond
the mind, which you abundantly
pour out to those who fall (Titus 3.6)
65 and fervently repent,
you both purify and enlighten them,
and you make them participants of light,
companions of your divinity, (2 Pet 1.4)
you consort with and converse with them
70 as your legitimate friends. (Ex 33.11)
Oh infinite kindness!
Oh inexpressible love!
On this account I both prostrate
and fervently call to you.
75 Just as you received the prodigal (Lk 15.20)
and the prostitute when they approached, (Lk 7.38)
so you received me, O Merciful One,
I who repent from my soul.
And you have considered the drops
80 of my tears as a fountain always
gushing forth, O my Christ.
In them wash my soul,

wash also my body
of the defilement of the passions!
85 And wash out my heart
from every wickedness!
For that is the root
and the fount of sin.
Wickedness is the seed
90 of the wicked sower.
And there where it is, it sprouts,
and goes up high,
and produces a great many young shoots
of wickedness and evil. (Mt 13.24–30)
95 Tear out their roots
from the depths, my Christ,
and purify my soul,
and implant fear
in the furrows of my heart.
100 O Merciful One, deign that your fear
may take root in the furrows,
and to sprout up well,
so it may grow to the summit
as a safeguard of your commandments,
105 adding by the hour,
by the addition of tears,
adding streams gushing forth,
and being watered by them, (Ps 79.6)
increasing even more,
110 and as much as it is strengthened,
so much the more does it climb unto the summit.
Proportionately, humility
increases with fear,
and by humility all the
115 passions withdraw,
and with them also an army

of demons has been expelled.
And all virtues show themselves
as in a circle around a queen,
120   following along with her,
like guards, and friends,
and handmaids of a mistress.
And these virtues, having assembled
and having united with each other,
125   in the midst of them like a tree
at the outlet of waters
your fear has been planted,[1]
and blooms; after a little while
it shows to me a strange flower.
130   O my Christ, a strange flower!
Strange, I said, because every
nature produces according to its type,
and the seed of all trees
in each one according to its type. (Gen 1.11–12)
135   But your fear displays a
flower with a strange nature
And likewise the fruit is strange
and different from fear.
For fear by nature is
140   full of shame,
and causes those who have acquired it
to look sad always
like slaves that are
worthy of many stripes, (Lk 12.48)
145   as if expecting every hour
to be cut off by death,
and as if seeing the scythe (Rev 14.15)
but not knowing the hour,[2]

[1] Ps 1.3; Ezek 19.10.
[2] Mt 25.13; Rev 3.3.

and not having hope,
150   and truly no guarantee
of complete forgiveness,
but trembling at the end,
but shuddering at the final hour
as though carrying around
155   the uncertain sentence
of this judgment, my God.
At any rate, the flower that fear bears,
is inexpressible in form,
most unutterable in character.
160   For it is seen blooming out,
and immediately it is concealed,
which is not natural,
and is not in conformity,
but it is a nature beyond nature,
165   transcending all nature.
For a time the flower shows itself,
beautiful beyond telling,
and it carries off my whole mind
to the vision of itself,
170   allowing the remembrance of nothing
that knows how to produce fear,
but it then produces for me
forgetfulness of all these
and immediately flies away.
175   But the tree, the tree of fear,
is again without flower,
and I am distressed, and I groan,
and I fervently scream to you,
and again I see the flower
180   among the young shoots of the tree,
and keeping my eye, O my Christ,
only on the flower,

then I do not see the tree.
But more often the flower
185   is blooming, and by desire it draws
the whole of me to itself,
and ends in the fruit of love.
But again the fruit itself
does not suffer to be borne
190   by the tree of fear,
but rather when it will be fully
ripened, only then
is it seen apart from the tree.
For fear is by no means
195   found in love, (1 Jn 4.18)
but then again, without fear
the soul does not bear fruit.
Truly a wonder beyond telling,
beyond all thought,
200   that a tree blossoms forth
with toil and bears fruit,
and again its fruit
uproots the whole tree,
and only the fruit remains.
205   How there is fruit without the tree
by no means can I tell.
While the fruit remains,
love is without the fear
that gave birth to it.
210   And so love is
certainly all cheerfulness, (Acts 14.17)
and joy, and delight,
and fulfils one who possesses it,
and consciously[3] throws
215   you out of the world;

[3]ἐν αἰσθήσει perhaps could be rendered "by your senses."

fear by no means
can accomplish this.
For fear is in the visible realm,
and within perceptible realities,
220 how is fear able to throw one who
has it far away from visible realities,
and then in the senses[4] unite
one's whole being to the invisible realities?
Truly it is by no means able!
225 But the flower and the fruit
which fear has begotten,
is outside the world,
these things know how to snatch away the mind,
and to take up the soul along with it,
230 and to throw them out of the world.
"How, tell me, does love
throw them out of the world,
I would like to know clearly?"
These things are inexpressible, as I said.
235 Nevertheless, pay attention and I shall tell.
Love is the divine Spirit, (1 Jn 4.16)
the light that works and illuminates all things,
but it is not from the world,
nor in any way something of the world,
240 nor a creature, for it is uncreated,
and outside of all creatures,
uncreated among all creatures.
Understand what I say to you child!
For it is separated,
245 and the Uncreated never
accepts to become a creature.
Yet if he should wish it, even this
is possible for him to do.

[4]ἐν αἰσθήσει.

For even the Logos became human
250 with the cooperation of the Spirit
and the approval of the Father,
completely human without changing,
being uncreated God by nature,
he mysteriously became created
255 and he deified the human nature that he assumed,
he showed to me a double marvel
by his two energies
and likewise by his two wills,
a visible marvel and an invisible,
260 graspable and ungraspable,
and showing himself as a creature
amidst all creatures.
Since he was not a creature,
as they supposed, he disappeared.
265 Nevertheless he did not utterly disappear,
but in the midst of all
sensible creatures the Logos
was seen as a creature, united
to his human nature.
270 But having assumed the creature,
and hiding it or taking it up
to the heights, to his own
glory beyond telling,
he immediately hid himself.
275 And they said this,
that the Master has vanished, (Lk 24.31)
but only with respect to them,
for the Creator of all things
is incomprehensible to all beings,
280 and as God he fills everything.
How by any means could he hide himself?
Will you remove the Master from

one place to another,
and will you make him
285 to be hidden from the eyes
of the holy apostles? (Jn 12.36)
Off with you! Lest from ignorance
you should fall into blasphemy!
And listen, if you wish,
290 you may learn the energies
of love and how
love is greater than all!
All of what? Do you not hear
the apostle shouting:
295 "To speak with the tongues of angels,
and those of all human beings,
that to have all faith
so to move mountains,
to know all knowledge
300 and the depth of mysteries,
to disperse all of one's wealth
and to make oneself a beggar,
and to give up one's body to burning
for the sake of Christ,
305 love is greater than these"? (1 Cor 13)
And it is so much greater
that without love these virtues
—either one or all—
have absolutely no advantage
310 for one who acquires them.
And so whoever is deprived of love
and of all the things
we spoke of, tell me,
how will such a person show themselves, what shall they do,
315 how will they dare to say to those who
question them that they are faithful?

Because of this, one must pay attention
to the one who speaks about love.
I am seated in my cell,
320   in the night or in the day,
love is invisibly
with me, unbeknown to me.
Love is outside of all creatures,
then again it is also with all things;
325   it is fire, it is dazzling light,
it becomes a cloud of light, (Mt 17.5)
it completes itself as a sun.
And so as a fire it warms my soul,
and inflames my heart, (Lk 24.32)
330   and excites it to desire,
and to love, love of the Creator.
And sufficiently burned
and inflamed in my soul,
just like every radiance, a light bearer,
335   it all flies around me
sending forth its radiant
beams to my soul,
and illuminates my mind,
and it proves me capable
340   of the heights of contemplation;
love makes a vision.[5]
It was this, what I spoke of before,
as the flower of fear.
And I was beholding the radiance,
345   and was filled with unutterable joy,
and I was not delighted that I saw it,
but having itself filled me
with divine joy, removed and
snatched away my mind,

---

[5]This line could perhaps be rendered "love makes the power of sight."

350 and my senses, and all
my worldly yearning. (Titus 2.12)
And my mind ran down
and sought to overtake by yearning
the manifested radiance.

355 But the creature did not find,
and could not come
completely outside creation
in order to grasp the uncreated
and incomprehensible radiance.

360 Still, my mind was going around everywhere
and contriving to see,
it searched out the air,
and was wandering about the heavens,
and searching out the abysses,

365 and so it seemed that my mind searched out
the ends of the cosmos.
But my mind found nothing in all that
because it is all created.
I was wailing and mourning,

370 and I was aflame in my bosom,
and became as though out of my mind in a trance,
thus was I passing my time.
And so love came as it wished,
and in the appearance

375 of a shining cloud it fell. (Mt 17.5)
It was seen fully settled
on my head,
and caused me to scream
while I was petrified.

380 In like manner it again flew away,
it abandoned me alone,
and while I diligently sought it,
suddenly, again unawares, the whole of it

was consciously found inside me,
385 in the middle of my heart,
like a heavenly body, truly
it was contemplated like the solar disc.
Thus was love revealed
and consciously made known.
390 Love put to flight a column of demons,
it chased away cowardice,
it introduced manliness.
It stripped my mind
of sense perception of the world,
395 and dressed me in the garment
of rational perception,[6]
it separated me from visible things,
and united me to invisible things,
and kindly granted that I see
400 the Uncreated and rejoice,
because I had been separated
from all creatures and visible things,
and from things that are soon destroyed,
and I was united with the uncreated,
405 the incorruptible, the one without beginning,
the one who is invisible to all,
for that is what love is.
Let us run, faithful ones, vigorously!
Let us hasten, slothful ones, diligently!
410 Let us wake up, hesitant ones,
so as to be in possession of love,
or better, may we become
participants in love, and thus (Heb 6.4)
may we pass over the things here below,
415 so that with love we may be present
to our Creator and Master,

[6]αἰσθήσεως . . . νοερᾶς.

having transcended
visible things with love!
Otherwise, being like creatures,
420 we may be left behind in
visible and created things,
in fire, and in the darkest abyss,
and in frightful dungeons,
having been found without it,
425 without love, I mean.
But if it is possible to be saved
without love, O my Christ,
how shall this be?
Impossible! If we were separated from the light,
430 how shall we flee the darkness?
If we were deprived of joy,
how would we be free from sorrow?
Having been found outside the bridal chamber, (Mt 25.10–11)
how would we be completely happy?
435 Having fallen out of the kingdom,
—I speak of seeing you, O Savior—
what other salvation,
and what sort of consolation,
or in what other kind of place
440 would we be able to find salvation?
Certainly, absolutely nowhere,
even if it foolishly seems so to some,
for one who would say that is foolish.
Just the same, someone responding would say:
445 "How outside the kingdom,
and how outside the bridal chamber,
and outside the chorus of the just ones?
Shall there not be another place
of salvation or rest?"[7]

[7]Cf. *Hymn* 1.66–131.

450   "Fool," says love.
      Did you not hear that
      Adam, your first father in paradise, (Gen 3.23ff)
      having transgressed one
      commandment, was stripped
455   of divine glory, and Eve
      with him was immediately
      banished from the paradise, and
      they received in return for pleasure,
      alas, the wretched death
460   and life filled with sweat and hard work, alas, and by this
      they were justly banished to live and to die?
      Understand me! So shall it be then,
      when judgment comes,
      whoever would be found
465   like Adam, truly denuded
      of divine glory, shall be
      immediately cast out
      from paradise, yes, truly
      also from the kingdom, and from
470   the heavenly bridal chamber. (Mt 22.13)
      Even if one were to have no sin,
      but was also without virtue,
      one would stand naked.
      But the first of all virtues,
475   the queen and mistress,
      truly is love.
      She is the head of all,
      their garment and glory.
      But a body without a head
480   is both dead and lifeless.
      And a body without a garment,
      how will it not be naked?
      Virtues without love

are stale, and useless,
485 and naked of divine glory,
one who has no love,
even if they had all the virtues,
stands denuded,
and not bearing their nudity,
490 they prefer rather to hide. (Gen 3.8)
For thus bearing one's shame,
one also has the condemnation
and hears "I do not know you"
from the judge of the universe. (Mt 25.12)
495 The Creator came upon the earth,
he took on a soul and a body,
and he gave the divine Spirit (1 Thess 4.8)
who is love.
And so if he wills it and if you desire
500 to receive the divine Spirit,
then have total faith in God,
in like manner deny yourself, (Lk 9.23)
without doubts lift to your shoulder
and accept the cross,
505 dying on purpose, little child,
so that you shall become
a sharer of immortal life!
Let not deceivers mislead you
by their falsehoods, (Jer 23.32)
510 saying that after death
the dead receive life, lest,
having been so persuaded, you should be negligent.
For then you would not possess life!
Listen to the words of God,
515 listen to the apostles,
listen to the teachers,
to those who preside over the Church,

what Christ shouts hourly:
"Rivers from the belly
520 of those who believe in me
shall flow from the divine fountain,
from ever-living water." (Cf. Jn 7.38)
What is this water he speaks of,
if not the grace of the Spirit?
525 And the pure of heart
he deems blessed, saying these
shall see God here below. (Mt 5.8)
And all the apostles
and teachers cry out that
530 henceforth we receive both
the Spirit and Christ himself
if indeed we intend to be saved.
Listen to the voice of the Master,
listen to the words of the Logos,
535 how he reveals that human beings
receive the kingdom of heaven
even here below.
He says: "⟨The kingdom⟩ may be likened
to a very costly pearl." (Mt 13.45)
540 And having heard of the pearl,
what do you suppose it is?
Do you say it is a stone
that is possessed wholly
or is somehow seen?
545 Away with blasphemy!
For it is an intelligible[8] pearl.
But the merchant who found it,
just tell me how he found it
if it is intangible,
550 if it is invisible?

[8]Νοητός.

And so where did he find it?
Instruct me, how did he look upon it?
And having sold everything how
would he buy this pearl
555   that he has not discovered, that he has not seen,
that he has not held in his hand,
that he did not receive in his pocket?
Will you teach me that by faith alone
and by hope he will be so disposed
560   as though he really had it?
But the Master did *not* say,
as you understand it,
that it was in the *hope* of finding,
in the *hope* of receiving,
565   that he sold his possessions.
Why be led astray?
Why lean upon vain hopes?
And why do you wish to become
culpable for the destruction
570   of others and incur severe punishments
for yourselves by your foolish persuasions?
But he exhorts you to first
find the pearl,
and having considered
575   that it is priceless,
and then selling everything,
you purchase it.
But since you say: "in hope,"
you reveal yourself
580   as not wanting to seek,
as not wanting to find,
as not wanting to sell
your possessions, and to take up
the kingdom of heaven

585 which is within you, if you want it, (Lk 17.21)
     as the Master said it is.
     But likewise if you are poor
     and do not possess gold,
     nor property, nor riches,
590 and you hear that by the sale
     of all possessions
     the priceless pearl is
     purchased, then you might say:
     "How, without having
595 possessions, shall I be able
     to acquire this divine
     and beautiful pearl?"
     And so, concerning this matter, I invite
     you to listen intelligently.
600 If you had the whole world,
     and the things in the world,
     and dispersing them you distributed (Ps 111.9)
     these things to orphans, and to widows,
     and to needy beggars,
605 and you yourself should become a beggar,
     and if you considered
     the payment fully worth
     that which you paid for yourself, saying:
     "Give to me the pearl,
610 for I gave all I had!"
     Immediately you would hear
     the Master saying this to you:
     "What is this "all" of yours that you speak of?
     Naked you came out from
615 your mother's womb,
     and again utterly naked
     shall you go into the tomb." (Job 1.21)
     What things do you claim to be yours?

Do you not feel utterly foolish?
620 And you shall not receive the pearl,
nor will you receive the kingdom.
But if you distributed everything,
absolutely all your possessions,
or you were very poor,
625 and you came forward saying thus:
"Behold now, Savior, a heart
and a soul crushed, (Ps 50.19)
and terribly chastised,
and severely consumed!
630 Behold me naked, Master,
behold me in need,
a stranger to every virtue,
and very poor in these things,
and not having anything to give
635 to purchase you, O Lord,
and have mercy on me, you alone,
my long-suffering God!
For what in the world
shall I find worthy, O my God, (Prov 3.15)
640 that I could give to your honor,
you who created everything?
For what did the prostitute give?
And what did the robber provide?
And the prodigal, my Christ,
645 what sort of wealth did he offer?"
Say these things and you shall hear:
"Yes, they offered gifts to me, (Mt 2.11)
yes, they offered wealth to me,
having given what they had,
650 they received the pearl that is
better than the whole world.
And you, if you wish, give to me

these things and by all means you shall receive.
Come to me with that
655 and immediately I will show to you
the pearl that they received,
and you shall rejoice.
Even if you will give your soul,
you shall believe that it is nothing worthy,
660 you shall reckon that it is nothing worthy,
that which you cast off completely.
For if you were to approach me,
just like the prostitute approached me (Lk 7.37)
—I certainly have the power,
665 I certainly have the pearls,
which even if all the world received them,
and along with this world,
a myriad of other worlds,
not even one pearl
670 would be lacking from my treasure—(Jer 10.13; 28.16)
so shall I provide for you also a gift,
like I provided for the prostitute."
—These things God says to you,
and he shall teach you how the robber
675 approached, and how the prostitute,
those who are sung about in the world,
and how when the prodigal
returned he was immediately welcomed.—
"And by faith the robber was saved, (Lk 23.42–43)
680 he had done many evil things,
and it is just that he alone
among all those who denied me,
and among all those who were scandalized
because I was hanging on the wood,
685 he alone confessed
that I was both God,

and King, and immortal,
he cried aloud from his heart.
Because of this, and before all,
690 he received the kingdom.
What words would show
the yearning of the prostitute?
That desire she bore
in her heart as she approached
695 me as God and Master
of things visible and invisible,
and she offered abundantly
as no one had up till then,
I saw and accepted her desire.
700 And I did not take away her yearning,
but I gave to her the pearl,
and I also let loose her longing,
rather, I enkindled it,
and I raised it to a large torch,
705 and I dismissed her
as more esteemed than virgins.
For suddenly she crossed over
the whole Law like a wall, (Ps 17.30)
or like a ladder, she
710 was lifted over all virtue,
she arrived at the fulfillment
of the Law, which is love, (Rom 10.4; 13.10)
and she went even so far as death,
keeping love unwounded.
715 And likewise the prodigal, (Lk 15.11–32)
having turned around from the depths of his heart,
he sincerely repented,
and though he was my son before,
he did not approach me like my son,
720 rather he asked to become

like one of my hired servants.
And not by his mouth alone,
but he spoke also by his soul,
and by his works, he showed
725 what he said with his words.
His humility drew me
to compassion, and
immediately I enriched him,
and in a short time I glorified him,
730 because I saw him approaching me
from his whole soul,
because he did not turn
his heart at all backward
like many do.
735 And so it is, if each one would approach me
and sincerely prostrate
—Let every creature listen!—
I shall immediately receive them.
But whoever wishes to receive
740 my grace with deceit, and
should they approach me with hypocrisy, (1 Pet 2.1)
or having wickedness within,
or having confidence in their works,
possessed by pride
745 or envy, they have no
share with me, Christ."[9]
Through us, God shouts these things
to you and to everyone every hour.
And if you wish, from other ‹Scriptures›
750 I shall clearly show to you here
that it is necessary for you
to receive the whole kingdom of heaven
if you wish to enter the kingdom

[9] 2 Cor 6.15; Jn 13.8.

after death also.

755 Listen again to God speaking
to you in parables:
"To what shall I liken
the kingdom of heaven?
It is like—pay attention!—

760 a grain of mustard,
which a certain person took
and cast into their garden,
and it grew and certainly became
a large tree." (Lk 13.19)

765 Therefore tell me, you listening,
what is this seed?
What do you suppose it is?
Speak frankly!
But if you will not, then I shall tell you,

770 and I will proclaim the truth.
Certainly he told you the grain
is the kingdom of heaven.
And this grain is
the grace of the divine Spirit,

775 and the garden is the heart
of each person where
one who has received the Spirit
casts him within, and hides him
in the flanks of their bosom,

780 thus no one sees the Spirit,
and one guards the seed with all
precision so that it grows,
so that it becomes a tree
and rises up to heaven.

785 And so if you say, "Not here,
but after death, all
who ardently desire it

shall receive the kingdom,"
then you refute the Savior,
790   and the words of our God.
For if you do not take the seed,
the grain of mustard he spoke of,
if you do not cast it into your garden,
then you remain completely without seed.
795   But if you were to take the seed
and choke it with weeds,
or betray it to the birds,
(and they will carry off the grain) (Lk 8.5)
or you allow the garden to go
800   unwatered through negligence,
(and your seed does not grow,
nor shall it grow, nor bear fruit)
tell me, what shall be the benefit
to you from the seed?
805   When, if not now?
At what other time do you receive the seed?
"After death," you tell me.
But you fall from what is reasonable.
In what garden, after death,
810   will you bury it, I ask you,
and by what works
will you cultivate it so that it grows?
Truly you are totally full of error,
deceived brother.
815   For this is the time for works,
and the future is the time for crowns. (2 Tim 4.8)
"Receive here the pledge-money,"
said the Master,
"receive here the seal.[10]
820   From henceforth light the lamp, (Mt 25.1–12)

[10]Eph 1.13–14; Rev 7.2; 9.4.

     the lamp of your soul,
     before it grows dark, before
     the doors of action are closed!
     Even if you are wise,

825 it is here that I become for you the pearl,
     and I am purchased,
     it is here that I am wheat for you,
     and like a grain of mustard,
     here I become leaven for you, (Lk 13.21)

830 and I leaven your dough,
     here I am like water for you, (Jn 7.37)
     and I become a sweetening fire,
     and here I become for you a garment, (Mt 9.16)
     and nourishment, and every drink

835 if you desire. (Jn 6.55)
     The Master says these things.
     And so if you will discover me
     as such, from things here,
     you shall have me, and thence mysteriously

840 I become all things for you.
     But if you depart, ignorant
     of the energies of my grace,
     in the other world you shall only find
     me an unsympathetic judge."

845 O my Christ, and my God,
     may you not condemn me then,
     and may you not subject me to punishment.
     I who have failed you in many things.
     But receive me as one

850 of the least of your hired servants, (Lk 15.19)
     and deign that henceforth
     I may serve you, my Savior,
     and that I may receive your divine Spirit,
     the pledge money of the kingdom, (2 Cor 1.22)

855　and thence to enjoy
　　　the bridal chamber of your glory,
　　　seeing you, my God,
　　　forever and ever. Amen.

Hymn 18

A teaching with theology concerning the activities of love—that is to say, the light of the Holy Spirit.

　　　Who shall be able, Master, to describe you fully?
　　　Those who do not know you fail, knowing nothing at all,
　　　but those who understand your divinity in faith,
　　　they are gripped by much fear, and with trembling they are
　　　　　astonished, (Lk 8.37)
5　　and they do not have anything to say, for you are beyond the
　　　　　mind,
　　　all-incomprehensible, all-unattainable are
　　　your works, and your glory, and the knowledge of you.
　　　We know that you are, and we see your light,
　　　but we are all ignorant of your type and your nature.
10　　But we have hope, and we seize faith, (1 Cor 13.13)
　　　and we know the love that you gave to us,
　　　infinite, unspeakable, by no means contained,
　　　love is light, light unapproachable, light operating all things.
　　　　　(1 Tim 6.16)
　　　And this is said to be your hand, and is called your eye,[1]
15　　and your all-holy mouth, and power, and glory, (Is 1.20)
　　　and your face is made known beautiful beyond everything.
　　　Love is an unsetting sun to those who are elevated in divine
　　　　　things.
　　　Love is the ever-shining star for those who contain nothing
　　　　　more.

　　[1]Ps 108.27; Sir 23.27.

Love is set against grief, it drives away ill will,
20   and it completely removes satanic jealousy.
In the beginning love makes one melt away, and it threshes one
      by purification.
Love chases away thoughts and humbles emotions.
It teaches the hidden one to be humble,
and does not allow one to be scattered nor to act randomly.
25   Again, love separates the visible world,
and causes one to forget all distressing things in life.
And love makes things grow, and heals thirst,
and freely gives strength to those who toil virtuously. (Mt 11.28)
Love puts out rage, and the seething heart,
30   and it does not allow one to get angry or all upset.
When love flees, it is pursued by those who are wounded,
and it is sought with much love from the heart,
but it returns, and appears, and shines benevolently,
and it makes those who chase it turn away and be humbled,
35   and that which was sought out has them sent away in fear,
as if not worthy of the good which is beyond all creation.
Oh gift beyond telling!
For what has love not accomplished, and what is it not?
Love is delightfulness, and joy, gentleness, and peace,
40   immeasurable mercy, an abyss of compassion,
invisible yet seen, infinite yet comprehended,
impalpable, untouchable, yet capable of being grasped in my
      mind.
When I have love, I do not look upon it,
I quickly hasten to grasp it, and it flies clean away.
45   I am completely at a loss, and I burn, and I learn to beg,
and to seek out with weeping and much humility,
not to suppose that things beyond the nature
of my strength and human exertion are possible,
to seek the compassion of God and his infinite mercy.
50   This time is revealed as short and reduced,

one, but one of the passions it casts out from my heart.
For it is not possible for a person to conquer the passions fully,
if the light does not come to the rescue,
and again, if it does not chase away the whole passion with one
     accord.
55   For the natural[2] person does not have the capacity to receive
the whole Spirit all at once and to become dispassionate,
but when one has accomplished all things within their power:
nakedness, detachment, separation from one's private things,
cutting off from one's will, denial of the world,
60   endurance of trials, and prayer, and remorse,
poverty, humility, then one has all their strength,
then slightly, as a faint and tiny ray,
suddenly encircling the mind, love snatches one into ecstasy,
and leaves quickly lest one die,
65   with the result that the one who sees because of the great
     swiftness
does not understand, nor remember the beauty, nor yield
lest the infantile eat the nourishment of perfect men, (Heb 5.3)
and so burst straight away or be damaged and vomit.
And so from there love leads us by the hand, strengthens,
     teaches,
70   showing itself and then fleeing when we need it,
not whenever we wish, for this belongs to the perfect ones,
but whenever we are at a loss, and utterly faint,
it comes to the rescue, it appears from afar,
and makes me perceive it in my heart.
75   I cry out in distress, I am bound tight wishing to grasp it,
and everything is night, and my wretched hands are empty.
I forget everything and I sit and lament,
without hope of thus seeing the love light ever again.
But when I wail much and want to stop,
80   then love comes mysteriously, and grabs my head,

[2]ψυχικὸς, unspiritual.

and mingles with tears, I know not who it is,
and it shines upon my mind with an exceedingly sweet light.
But whenever I know who it is, love quickly flies away,
leaving for me the fire of its divine desire,
85   which does not allow me to laugh or to look at human beings,
nor to accept desire for any of the visible things.
By small degrees love lights up, by patience it is kindled,
and becomes a great flame seizing the heavens;
relaxation quenches it, the distraction of domestic matters
90   and the care of life's anxieties (for it is in the beginning).
        (Lk 21.34)
Love invites silence, and hatred of every glory,
and being rolled on the ground, and tread upon like dung,
for love enjoyed these things, and wants to be with them,
teaching the all-powerful humility.
95   And so when I attain the flame and become humble,
then love is with me without separation,
it converses with me, enlightens me, love sees me and I see it.
Love is in my heart, it is in heaven,
it explains the Scriptures to me and adds to my knowledge,
        (Lk 24.27)
100   it teaches me mysteries, of which I am unable to speak,
        (1 Cor 14.2)
and love shows to me how it snatched me from the world
and ordered me to have mercy on all those who are in the
        world.
And so walls press round me, and I am seized by my body,
and I am truly outside of it, do not doubt it!
105   I perceive no loud noise, and I hear no voice,
and I do not fear death, for I disregard even that.
Anguish, I do not know what it is, even if everyone were to
        afflict me;
pleasures are bitterness to me, all passions flee,
and through all I see the light, in both night and day.

110 Day appears as night to me, and night is as day, (Ps 138.12)
     and I do not wish to sleep, for that is a loss to me.
     But when all bad things surround me, (Ps 17.6)
     and seeming to drag me down and to overpower me,
     then suddenly I find myself with love outside everything,
115 outside joys, and painful things, and pleasures of the world.
     I revel in the unspeakable and divine joy;
     I make merry in love's beauty, I often embrace it,
     I kiss it, and fall down in worship, I have great thankfulness
     to those who have arranged for me to see what I was desiring,
120 to partake in the inexpressible light, and to become light,
     and to share in the light's gifts here on earth,
     and to obtain the provider of all good things,
     and to lack no spiritual gifts.
     Who, by drawing me, has guided me to these beautiful things?
125 Who brought me up from the depth of worldly deceit?
     Who separated me from father, and brothers, and friends,
          (Mk 10.29)
     from relatives, and pleasures, and the joy of the world?
     Who showed to me the way of repentance, and remorse,
     from whence I found the day that has no end?
130 It was an angel, not a human being, but he is fully human,
     by whom the world is mocked, and the dragon tread upon,
          (Ps 90.13)
     and the demons tremble at his presence. (Jas 2.19)
     How do I tell you, brother, what I saw in Egypt,
     the wonders and signs accomplished by him? (Ex 3.2ff)
135 For now I shall tell you this one, for I cannot tell all.
     For he came down and found me a slave and a sojourner,
     and he said: "Come, my child, I shall lead you to God!"
     But I said to him out of much faithlessness:
     "And what sign will you show to me, to guarantee[3]
140 that you are able to deliver me from Egypt,

[3]Jn 2.18; Ex 4.8.

and to rescue me from the hands of treacherous Pharaoh,[4]
lest by somehow following you I risk greater danger?"
"Light a big fire," he said, "and I will walk into the middle,
and if I do not remain unburned, may you not follow me!"
    (Ex 3.2)

145   This word dumbfounded me, I did what was ordered,
and the flame was enkindled, and he was in the middle,
unharmed, and not offended, and he was calling to me.
"I am frightened," I said, "master, I am a sinner!" (Lk 5.8)
He came out, he came to me and embraced me.

150   "Why were you frightened, tell me, why be afraid and tremble?
A great and fearful wonder, greater than this, you shall see."
    (Jn 1.50)
I was astonished. I said: "I do not dare to approach you,
and I do not wish to appear more daring than the fire,
for I see that you are a human who is superhuman,

155   and I dare not to look at you whom the fire feared."
He brought me nearer, he took me in his arms, (Mk 10.16)
and again he kissed me with a holy kiss, (Rom 16.16)
and the whole of him spread the scent of immortality.
I trusted, I was pleased to follow him,

160   and I desired to become a slave to him alone.
Pharaoh seized me, the terrible overseers
forced me to give heed to brick and straw, (Ex 5.6ff)
alone I had not strength to flee, for I had no weapons.
Moses spoke to God, to do something useful.

165   God whipped Egypt with tenfold plagues,
and Pharaoh did not bend, nor set me free.
And indeed my father intercedes, and God kindly heard,
and he orders his squire to take me by the hand,
and he promises to journey together with us.

170   Being released from Pharaoh, and the evils of Egypt,
he put courage into my heart,

[4]"Pharaoh" is used as a name rather than a title.

and he freely gave the daring not to fear Pharaoh.
Thus also did the workman of God,
he took my hand, and marched before me,
175   and thus we made a beginning so to bring the road to an end.
Lord, give to me sagacity by the intercessions of my father,
give the words to describe the wonders of your hand, (Ps 25.7)
things that you brought to perfection on my account, me the
        profligate and lecherous,
leading me out of Egypt by the hand of your slave!
180   The king of Egypt learned of my departure,
since he despised the departure of one, but he himself did not
        go out,
rather he sent slaves, whom he had bound by contract.
        (Ex 14.5)
They ran down and overtook us at the frontier of Egypt,
all the vain ones turned around, all beat to a pulp,
185   they broke their swords, they exhausted their arrows,
their hands failed to act against us,
and we persevered, sustaining no injury.
The pillar of fire was burning, and the cloud was with us,
        (Ex 14.20)
and alone we were passing through an alien country,
190   in the midst of bandits, among tribes and kings.
The king learned of his army's defeat.
He became enraged and considered it a great indignity
to be mocked and vanquished by one person.
He geared up his chariots, and mustered the soldiers, (Ex 14.6)
195   and he himself gave chase, boasting great things.
He came and found me alone, lying down from exhaustion.
(But Moses was keeping watch and conversing with God.)
Pharaoh ordered my hands to be bound with my feet,
and it seemed they had seized me, and set hands to fetter me.
200   But I was laughing, lying down, arming myself with prayer,
and with the sign of the cross I fought all of them off,

and not daring to touch or come close to me,
standing from a distance where they seemed to fear me,
holding fire in their hands, they threatened to burn me.
205 And they were shouting great cries, and making loud noise,
and, lest they should boast as though doing a great thing,
they saw me become light by the intercessions of my father,
and all of a sudden they retreated in shame. (Ps 39.15)
Moses came out from God, and found me resolute,
210 joyful, and trembling at the miracle.
He asked what happened, I reported the whole thing to him.
I told him that there was Pharaoh, King of Egypt,
arrived just now with an immeasurable army,
and he was not able to bind me, but he wanted to burn me,
215 and all those who came with Pharaoh became a flame,
and out of their mouth they spewed fire against me.
And when they saw me become light by your prayers,
they all became darkness, and just now I am alone.
"Look," Moses answered me, "and you may not be so bold;
220 and may you not look at the visible things, but fear the more
      that which he hides!
Come, let us take flight! As God exhorts,
and Christ shall do battle with the Egyptians in our place."
"Let us go," I said, "I shall not be separated from you,
I shall not transgress your commands, but I shall keep them
      all." Amen. (Mt 19.20)

Hymn 19

*Teaching with theology which concerns both the priesthood and at the
same time dispassionate contemplation.*

How do I proclaim, Master, your strange wonders,
how shall I describe in a word the depths of your judgments,

which you accomplish each day in us your servants?
    (Rom 11.33)
How do you ignore the infinite multitude of my faults,
5   yet you do not reckon, Master, the actions of my evils,
rather you have mercy, and cover me, and enlighten, and
    sustain me, my Savior,
as if I have fulfilled all your commandments?
But you do not just have mercy on me, but what is more,
you deem me worthy to stand in the presence
10   of your glory, and power, and majesty, (Jude 24)
you converse with me, and you speak words of immortality
to the one who is without strength, and dejected, not worthy
    to live.
How do you illuminate my soul which is so stained,
and render it immaculate and divine light?
15   How do you make my wretched hands resplendent?
Hands that have sinned, and I have defiled them with the
    defilement of sin.
How, by the radiance of your divinity, do you change my lips,
transforming them from unclean to holy?
And my filthy tongue, O Christ, how have you purified it,
20   and made it partake of your body by chewing?
How do you deign to see me and to be seen by me,
and to be held by my hands, you who hold all things,
you who are not perceived by heavenly legions,
and who are unapproachable even to Moses, the first among
    prophets?[1]
25   For he was not deemed worthy to see your face,
nor was anyone else among humanity, lest they die.
    (Ex 33.20, 23)
And so you the incomprehensible, you alone the inexpressible,

---

[1]Symeon refers to Moses' vision of God as described in Ex 33. This idea is found elsewhere in the *Hymns*, e.g., 31.104. The Fathers of the Church also spilt much ink over this passage from Exodus, see SC 174:97n2.

you who are uncontainable by all and unapproachable for
    everyone,
how am I deemed worthy to grasp, and to kiss,
30   and to see, and to eat, and to have you in my heart, O Christ,
and I remain unburnt, rejoicing, and at the same time I
    tremble,
and I sing the praises, O Christ, of your bountiful benevolence?
And so the blind and carnal, who do not know you,
who are unfeeling, and show even more their own
35   feebleness, and blindness, and deprivation of all good,
O my Savior, how do they dare to say:
"But why does a person need to have the priesthood,
unless he gain one of these three advantages:
either the nourishment of the body, or the procuring of gold,
40   or the throne of some wealthy bishop among the exalted ones?"
Oh darkness, oh hardness, oh ultimate poverty,
oh so much wretchedness, oh great ignorance,
oh earthly, vain, and empty words,
oh audacity, oh arrogance of the betrayer Judas!
45   For just as Judas reckoned as nothing the awesome things
of the Lord's supper and his immaculate body,
but he regarded a little silver as more excellent, (Mt 26.15)
so also they choose spiritual strangling by preferring
perishable things above imperishable and divine things.
    (Mt 27.5)
50   Tell me, O impious ones, if you understand this!
Who, possessing Christ, needs anything more
of the goods of the present age?
Who, having the grace of the Spirit in the heart,
does not acquire the sublime Trinity abiding within,
55   enlightening and making them God?
And who, having become God by the grace of the Trinity,
and having been deemed worthy of the glory on high and the
    foremost glory,

what would they consider to be a higher honor
than to celebrate the liturgy and to see the most high nature
60 that works all things, inexpressible, and inaccessible to all?
Or, consider now, what would one desire more,
what could be considered more brilliant in this short life,
than the other life, understand me, which has no end?
If you knew the hidden depths of the mysteries
65 you would not coerce me to speak or write these things.
       (Col 1.26)
For with reverence I shudder to engrave the divine things,
and to sketch out with letters what is unspeakable to all.
If you saw Christ, if you received the Spirit
and through these two graces you have been brought to the
       Father,
70 you have to know what I say and what I explain to you,
and that to offer the liturgy is great, and fearful, and beyond
all glory and illumination, and beyond sovereignty and
       authority,[2]
beyond wealth, and power, and all dominion,
when one offers the liturgy to the holy and immaculate Trinity
75 with a pure heart and a clean conscience. (1 Tim 3.9)
And may you not speak to me about innocence of the body,
and, do not bring forth witnesses, the depths of which you do
       not know,
but rather listen to what God says through the apostles,
and the wise Basil, the tongue of fire,
80 and through the simple witnesses of Father Chrysostom
and Gregory who theologized well about these things,[3]
listen and believe, what sort of person it must be
to celebrate the liturgy to God, the Creator of all things!

[2]Jude 25; Rev 4.11.
[3]Gregory Nazianzen, *Oration* 2.14–17; SC 247:106–112, John Chrysostom, *On the Priesthood* 2–3; SC 272:100–224. The reference to Basil may be implied from *On the Priesthood*, which is presented as a dialogue between Chrysostom and Basil. Or it could refer to Basil's *Commentary on the Prophet Isaiah* 103–4; PG 30:285–88.

And from your worthiness and from your virtue
85   you can marvel at the magnitude of the honor.
Do not be led astray, brothers, nor have the audacity
to grasp or approach the unapproachable nature!
For he who will not renounce the world and the things in the
     world,
and will not deny his soul and body,
90   and the whole of him become dead to all sensation,
seeing nothing of the pleasures of life emotionally,[4]
desiring nothing of the affairs of the world,
and will not be charmed by the words of any human person,
one who does not become senseless and blind to the things of
     the world,
95   to its affairs and customs, to its practices and words,
seeing as much as the eye is able to see by nature,
but from within allowing nothing to penetrate in the heart
     (Mt 15.17)
‹nor allowing the heart› to ask about the types and forms of
     these things,
and hearing as much as the human ear receives,
100 yet remaining like a lifeless and insensitive stone,
not recalling the sound nor the meaning of speech,
such a one is not able to offer purely the mystical and bloodless
sacrifice to God who is pure by nature.
For when one senses that they do these things in truth,
     (Jn 3.21; 4.24)
105 one has been separated from all the world, and the things of
     the world,
and he shall know and believe me, what I again intend to write.
The dark air that David called a wall, (Ps 17.12, 30)
and the Fathers named the sea of life,[5]

---

[4]ἐμπαθῶς.

[5]Some patristic uses of this expression include St. Basil, *Homilia* 12.5; PG 31:417B; John Chrysostom, *In Genesim Sermo* 9.2; PG 54:623A; Origen, *In Jeremiam homilia* 18.5; PG 13:472C.

one has stepped over, one has passed through, one has gone
    into the haven,
110 in which all who arrive there find all good.
For there is the paradise, there the tree of life,[6]
there the sweet bread, there the divine drink,[7]
there the inexhaustible wealth of gifts.
There is the bush that burns without being consumed,
115 and immediately the sandals of my feet are loosened; (Ex 3.5)
there the sea is rent and I walk through alone,[8]
and in the waters I see enemies plunged into the sea;[9]
there I see the wood thrown into my heart
and transforming all bitter things, (Ex 15.25)
120 there we gather honey flowing from the rock, (Deut 32.13)
and from thence my soul shares not in affliction,
there I found Christ who gave these things to me,
and I followed him with all my heart; (Mk 12.30)
there I ate manna and the bread of angels, (Jn 6)
125 and I desired nothing of human things any longer;
there Aaron's dry staff blossoming forth. (Num 17.8)
I saw and I marveled at the wonder working miracles of God;
there I saw my barren soul bearing fruit,
and how the dry wood makes beautiful fruit;
130 there I saw that my muddy and profligate heart
was pure, and guiltless, and virgin,
and I heard: "Hail, highly favored one,
for the Lord is with you and in you forever!" (Lk 1.28)
There I heard: "Bathe yourself in a bath of tears!" (Jn 9.7)
135 And having done so I believed and looked upon the vision.
There I was buried in a tomb in ultimate humiliation,
and Christ was present with immeasurable mercy,
and from there he lifted the heavy stone of my wickedness,

---

[6]Gen 2.8–9; Rev 2.7.
[7]Ex 16.15; Wis 16.20.
[8]Ex 14.21; Ps 77.13.
[9]Ps 77.53; Ex 15.4.

and said: "Come here, come out of the world as out of a grave."
    (Jn 11.43)
140 There I saw how my God suffered dispassionately,[10]
and how, though he was immortal, he became dead,
and he arose from the tomb without breaking the seal.
There I saw the future life and incorruption
that Christ generously gives to those who seek him, (Rom 2.7)
145 and the kingdom of heaven I found within me, (Lk 17.21)
that is the Father, the Son, and the Spirit,
the inseparable divinity in three persons.
I found that those who do not honor it above all the world,
and regard it a glory, and an honor, and a wealth
150 to worship, to preside at the liturgy, and to be present,
such people are not worthy of the immaculate divinity,
not worthy of the pleasure, nor the joy, nor any goods
of which they will have no part without repentance,
if, as we said, they do not learn and acquire everything,
155 and they do not do with zeal everything that my God has said.
Let anyone, if God should so order, touch the sacred things
with toil, and much fear, and reverence.
For it is not permissible for everyone to minister to such
    things,
for even if one receives every grace of the Spirit,
160 and one is pure of sin from their mother's ‹womb›,
unless it is by God's command and his choice
that assures and illuminates their soul with divinity,
and inflames their soul with the desire of divine love, then
it does not seem to me reasonable for them to minister divine
    things,
165 and to touch the untouchable and awesome mysteries,
to which is fitting glory, and honor, and all worship
now and always through all, unto all ages.

[10]ἔμπαθεν . . . ἀπαθῶς.

Hymn 20

*Thanksgiving and confession with theology; also concerning the gift
and participation of the Holy Spirit.*

For my sake you were seen on earth, ‹born› of a virgin,
you who are invisible before the ages,
and you became flesh, and you were manifested as a human
      being, (Jn 1.14)
you who are wrapped in unapproachable light. (1 Tim 6.16)
5 Everyone supposed that you were limited,
you who cannot be contained by anything,
all speech is not able to tell of you,
and a mind that is compelled ‹tries to› grasp with yearning,[1]
yet is not able to seize you when it is humbled by fear,
10 and again, burning within, it searches for you.
When you have appeared briefly in your luster,
the seeker is sent away with trembling, and rejoices with joy.
For human nature cannot bear
to contemplate all of you clearly, my Christ,
15 even if we believe that we receive the whole of you
from the Spirit whom you give, my God,
and from your immaculate body and blood, (Heb 2.14)
of which we have a share, and by which we confess that we
      grasp
and we eat you without separation, my God,
20 and without mixing. For you do not share in
our corruption or filth, but you give to me
your incorruptible purity, O Logos,
and you wash out the filth of my vices, (Is 4.4)
and you chase out the gloom of my sins,
25 and you cleanse the shame of my heart,
and you diminish the thickness of my wickedness,

---

[1]νοῦς δὲ βιαζόμενος δράσσεται πόθῳ. Perhaps: "a mind compelled by yearning
grasps."

and you make me a light, I who was darkened,
and in two respects you put me in my prime:
You shine around me with a ray of immortality,
30 and I am both stupefied and burning within,
yearning to fall down and worship you yourself.
And when I, the wretched one, reflect on this,
Oh marvel that I find you
remaining in me, moving, speaking,
35 and then rendering me voiceless
by the amazement of your unapproachable glory.
And so astonishment holds me, and perplexity,
because I see that the one who holds all things
in his palm is held in my heart. (Wis 1.7)
40 But, my Christ, what is this strangeness about your mercy,
what is your infinite condescension, O Logos?
Why have you come to my poverty,
and how did you come into my filthy house,
you who dwell in unapproachable light, my God? (1 Tim 6.16)
45 But how do you keep my house unburned
when the fire is unendurable for mortal nature?
And what shall I do that is worthy of your glory,
and what shall I find in proportion to such great love?
What shall I bring to you, you who have glorified me
50 the unworthy with such glory and honor?
For people deem me unworthy to see,
and they do not wish to speak or to feast
with me, the all-wretched.
You who sustain every breath and nature,
55 you who are unapproachable even for the seraphim,
the creator of all, the author, and master,
not only do you see, and speak to me, and nourish me,
but you have deigned me essentially worthy
to take and to eat even your flesh,
60 and to drink your all-holy blood,

which was poured out for my sake when you were slain.²
And you appointed me deacon, and minister, and one initiated
    in
these mysteries, I whom you know,
you who knew all things before you created the ages,
65 and before you made any of the visible things
—for it was afterward that you made visible things—,
me the sinner, the profligate, the publican, (Mt 11.19)
the bandit, becoming a murderer of myself,
a deceiver of the good, a worker of lawlessness,³
70 and a transgressor of all your commandments. (Mt 15.3)
And so you know these things are true:
how would I be seen before you, O my Christ,
how would I approach your table? (Lk 22.30)
How would I take your immaculate body
75 when I have hands completely stained?
How would I sing your praises, how would I intercede for
    others
since I lack the faith and good works
to have affection and frankness before you?⁴
But I myself am in debt, as you know,
80 for many talents, for many unlawful deeds. (Mt 25.15)
My mind is at a loss, my tongue is feeble,
and no word is found for me, O Savior,
to announce your works of goodness
that you have done for me, your slave.
85 And my interior burns as from fire, (Jer 20.9)
and I cannot bear to keep silent
about the great weight of your many gifts.
You, who have made the birds speak with a voice, (Eccl 12.4)
give also to me a word, to me the all-wretched,

²Mt 26.28; Jn 6.53; Rev 5.9.
³Ps 6.9; Lk 13.27.
⁴"affection" = ἀγαπήσεως; "frankness" = παρρησία.

90   so that to everyone, by written and unwritten means,
      I may explain in full the things you have done for me
      through your boundless mercy, O my God,
      and through your benevolence alone!
      For they are frightful and great, beyond the mind,
95   what you provide for me, the stranger,
      the unlearned, the beggar, who cannot speak freely,
      who has been rejected by every person.
      Parents did not turn to me with natural love,
      my brothers and friends were all mocking me,
100   for when they said that they love me they only lied.
      My relatives, strangers, the princes of the world
      did not so much as turn to me and bear to see me,
      except to destroy me by their ungodliness.
      Often I blamelessly yearned for glory,
105   and I have not yet found it in the present life.
      For glory, worldly glory, I am well assured,
      even without other action, is sin.
      How often I yearned for people to love me,
      and to have the intimacy of friendly relations with them,
110   and no one among those who think good things would tolerate
          me,
      but others wanted even more to see me and to know me,
      but I fled such types as workers of wickedness.
      And so all these things, Master, and more besides,
      I have not the means to say nor to recount, things that
115   you have accomplished for me, the profligate, in your
          providence,
      in order to drag me from the depth, and from worldly
          darkness,
      and from the terrible deceit of life's pleasures.
      The good fled from me on account of my outward appearance,[5]
      but I took flight from worthless folk by my own free will.

      [5]Cf. *Catechesis* 22.25–29; SC 104:367; deCatanzaro, *Discourses*, 244.

120 For I used to love, as was said, glory, and wealth of the world,
and the appearance of clothing, and habits of laziness.
I do not know what I shall say aloud, I do not know what I can
    say to you,
for I am afraid to either speak or to write such things
lest I should fall and sin by my words,
125 and what has been falsely written shall be indelible.
When anyone would invite me to the works of madness
and sin of this deceiving world, truly,
my heart completely gathered itself within,
and it hid itself as though ashamed,
130 wholly and invisibly held together by your divine hand.
And I used to love all other things of life,
whatever delights the eyes, and smoothes the throat,
and beautifies this corrupted body.
But the abominable practices and licentious yearnings,
135 you banished them from my heart, my God, (Is 44.22)
and put hatred toward them in my soul,
even if I was attached to them by my own free choice,
both desire without action and actions without desire,
you made me have the more—an utterly great marvel—
140 and by your divine plan you separated me from
all kings, princes, and riches of the world.
Often when I and many others wished for these things,
you yourself did not permit the will of anyone to stand among
    these things.
I felt hatred, Master, a hatred from the heart
145 toward others who said that I was seeking glory and wealth in
    my life
so that I never initiated an encounter with such people,
and enraged, they also beat me rather violently with sticks,
and others would revile me in front of everyone with abusive
    remarks,
saying that I was a worker of every transgression;

150   they wish to pervert me from the straight path. (Acts 13.10)
     For I fled from actions lest I be reviled,
     but they reviled me, as though I had come to such practices,
     as if I also desired the praise of human beings,
     those who spoke continued to revile me always,
155   until I would go along with their proud designs.
     But to those who say that they give the glory of the world,
     you have granted, my Savior, that I refute them:
     "If you possessed all the glory of the world," I would say,
     "and the crown of the kingdom was on your head,
160   and your feet were shod in scarlet,[6]
     and if at once you made me lord of all this,
     and you yourself stood as a common citizen, wishing to be my
        slave,
     I would not at all share in your wickedness and
     your proud designs, or go along with you in this life."
165   What sort of paper could contain your benefits
     and the many bounteous things that you have worked for me?
     For even if myriads of tongues and hands were given to me,
     I would not be able to proclaim or to write about all of them.
     For they are certainly an abyss in their infinite multitude;
170   they are incomprehensible by the magnitude of their glory.
     My reason is feeble, my heart is distressed
     because I am not able to tell about you, my God.
     For when I reflect on the things I, the wretched, have done,
     on how much you have come to my aid, from what you have
        pulled me out of,
175   from how many evils, O Savior, you benevolently rescued me,
     and you have not remembered the evils that I have committed,
     but as if I have done many and great goods,

---

[6]A crown and scarlet boots are part of the emperor's regalia. A note in the edition suggests that this passage refers to Symeon's reluctance to enter court service as a teenager (SC 174:122n1). But it would more likely refer to the period of Symeon's conversion to monastic life at age twenty-seven.

and as though I remain pure from the holy mother—the
     baptismal font—
thus also you embraced me, thus you honored me,
180 thus you adorned me with the apparel of the kingdom.
I am wholly seized by trembling and astonished with joy.
I stand still and speechless, and I am exceedingly faint
because you, God, are given to me, you the creator of the
     world,
to me who had already become a very loathsome person,
185 and abominable to all humans and demons,
and surpassed even the latter in the practice of unnatural acts.
Alas for me the shameful and filthy, how do I say it?
You were made one with me, O Benevolent One, by your
     immeasurable compassion.
You who are great in purity, even greater in holiness,
190 incomparable in power, and like no other in glory.
And you descended from above, from immeasurable height
down to the last gate of the hell of my sins,
and of the darkness of my poverty and collapsed house.[7]
As a result of many lawless deeds and great negligence,
195 my house was utterly neglected and filthy.
You first of all stood me up when I was lying down,
and you stood me on the rock of your divine commands,
     (Ps 39.3)
and you washed and purified me from the mud of my wicked
     deeds,
and you dressed me in a garment white beyond snow, (Ps 50.9)
200 and you swept my defiled house, (Lk 15.8)
and entering you dwelt there, O Trinity, O my God.
And thus you rendered me a throne of your divine divinity,
and a home of your unapproachable glory and kingdom,
and an earthen jar bearing manna, manna of immortality[8]

[7]Mt 11.23; Lk 6.48.
[8]Heb 9.4; Ex 16.33.

205 and a lamp holding divine and unquenchable light within,
and truly a wooden box for the beautiful pearl, (Mt 13.45)
and a field in which was hidden the treasure of the world,
    (Mt 13.44)
a fountain from which those who drink shall no longer thirst,[9]
the fountain that bubbles up abundant water tenfold,
210 and it renders immortal everyone who drinks in faith,
a paradise that has a new tree of life in its middle,[10]
and a land that covers all round the One who is uncontainable
    to all.
‹I mean› you whom I sought at the same time from the whole
    of my heart,
and I always desired to hear a word about you,
215 and I wished to keep the memory of you in my soul,
and to hear and to talk about you very often.
For even if at an earlier stage my mind was not able
to form an image of you clearly,
nor could my eyes contemplate you nor my ear hear,
220 nor my heart receive divine ascents,
but then by hearing alone my soul was utterly struck down
    with amazement,
and humbled by fear and trembling.
But now, seeing you within herself, my soul is driven out of her
    senses,
and reflecting on you, insofar as you grant for her to,
225 you who are wholly in the whole of everything, and wholly
    outside the universe,
and again she contemplates you inside herself,
you who are wholly incomprehensible in your divine divinity,
invisible and hidden from everyone,
you, the unapproachable, and approachable only to whom you
    have wished,

[9]Rev 21.6; Jn 6.35.
[10]Rev 2.7; cf. *Hymn* 47.1–18.

230 because you have benevolently wanted to reveal
    yourself as approachable among human beings,
    you who are unapproachable to seraphim, and cherubim, and
        to all the angels,
    and fearful in just a gleam of your divine nature.
    ‹My soul› is utterly beside herself, and all the more astonished
235 at your goodness and benevolence
    because you purify defiled souls, and enlighten the mind,
    and you grasp the earthy and material essence,
    and you kindle a large flame of divine affection,
    and like a fire you cast into me a passionate love of divine
        longing,[11]
240 and you prepare me to progress as far as third heaven,
    and, Savior, you have me snatched away to paradise,
    where I hear strange and secret sayings,
    which are not permitted for mortals to speak or to explain in
        words. (2 Cor 12.2–3)
    And to you is fitting honor, glory, and majesty,
245 eternal power, Christ, to the Master of the universe,
    with the Father and Spirit all-holy by nature,
    now, and always, and forever and ever. Amen.

Hymn 21

*A letter to a monk who asked: "How do you separate the Son from the
Father—hypothetically or actually?"[1] In which you will find a wealth
of theology refuting his blasphemy.*

    You gave light, you revealed the light of glory,
    the unapproachable light of your essence, O Savior,
    and you enlightened a darkened soul,

---

[11]"affection" = ἀγαπήσεως; "longing" = πόθου; "passionate love" = ἔρωτα.
[1]ἐπινοίᾳ . . . πράγματι. Here in this hymn Ἐπίνοια is translated "hypothetically"
or "hypothesis," and πράγμα as "actuality," "actually," or "actual fact."

rather, it *was* darkness from sin, (Eph 5.8)

5   since she had lost her natural beauty,
you brought up this soul lying in hell,
and you granted her to see the light of a divine day,
and to be enlightened by the rays of the sun,
and for the soul herself to become light. O great marvel!

10 They do not believe, those who have not despised
the glory of human beings, as you have commanded, (Jn 12.43)
for they have not tasted the divine glory
which you have given and you also give now, my God,
to those who with their soul, with their whole attitude

15 have sought you, the Eternal Glory, (1 Pet 5.10)
you the God truly glorified.
Seeing you is the zenith of glory.
And one who has been deemed worthy always to see you
has certainly received an angelic dignity,

20 even if still bound to the flesh according to nature.
And if you have consented to remain with someone
and if you have willed that someone remain in you, (Jn 15.4)
you have fulfilled your divine plan
and you have rendered a perishable being God like yourself.

25 You are the God who coexists[2] by nature,
who is before all eternity,[3] with the coeternal[4] God,
your Son and Logos who was begotten from you,[5]
who is not hypothetically separated from you,
but being in actuality inseparable from you.

30 But even if he is separated from you, it is not by nature,
but rather by his hypostasis or person,[6]
for saying "in actuality" belongs to the ungodly and the
   atheists,

[2]συνυπάρχων.
[3]προάναρχος.
[4]συνανάρχῳ.
[5]Jn 1.13 in some texts.
[6]ὑποστάσει δε μᾶλλον, εἴτ᾽ οὖν προσώπῳ.

and "hypothetically" belongs to those in utter darkness.
For the mind has a word[7] it has begotten
35   truly, unceasingly, and in a way separated.
And if it is begotten and truly comes forth
and was separated by a word that has independent existence,[8]
but also remains within the begetting mind,
which must also be considered a paternal bosom, (Jn 1.18)
40   and it goes throughout the entire cosmos,
and fills all things wholly without the Father, (Eph 4.10)
and is itself wholly with the Father.
And certainly by the energies he comes among others
and by illumination is he considered to cross over.
45   For you have heard the expressions: He walks, and remains,[9]
he turns his face, and looks, (Ps 9.32)
he descends, and again goes up,[10]
he is present, and flies away again,
and many other things ‹concerning› the divine energies,
50   of which all the divine Scriptures speak rhetorically,
of which the Spirit proclaimed,
the All-Holy Spirit, inexpressibly proceeding from the Father,
and sent by the Son to the human beings.
But not to the faithless, nor to those who love glory,
55   not to the orators, nor to the philosophers,
not to those who study the writings of the Greeks,
not to those who are ignorant of Scriptures within our
      tradition,
nor to those who are practiced in theatrical life,
nor to those who speak smoothly and at length,
60   not to those who have been granted great names,
not to those who are loved by the famous,

---

[7]νοῦς . . . λόγον.
[8]ἐνυποστάτῳ λόγῳ.
[9]Gen 3.8; 18.3.
[10]Gen 11.5; 17.22.

not to those who illegally take part in crimes,
not to those who summon, nor to those who are summoned,
and not to those who entertain; nor to those who are
    entertained,
65 but to those who are poor in spirit and in life, (Mt 5.3)
to those who are pure of heart and body, (Mt 5.8)
to those of simple speech and more simple life,
and to those who have simpler thought,
to those who flee glory like the fire of Gehenna,
70 and who from their soul flee the flatterers
(for the Spirit does not receive flatteries
nor bear to hear what is not),
to those who look only to the glory of the soul,
and the salvation of all the brethren, (2 Macc 12.25)
75 and not even by a tiny movement of the heart
do they have feelings toward any worldly thing,
like praises or human glory, (1 Thess 2.6)
or all the other pleasures and passions.
For such as these are as dead while living by truth,
80 because they are true but ‹considered› deceivers. (2 Cor 6.8–9)
These are humble of spirit and of heart, (Mt 11.29)
they are meek and zealous for the Lord. (Acts 22.3)
They are ungodly to the ungodly,
but the scent of life to the Lord's chosen. (2 Cor 2.16)
85 They are unchaste to the unchaste at heart,
but like angels to those with virgin souls.
They are humbled amidst glory,
and in poverty they are glorified.
They regard thrift as a kingdom,
90 and a kingdom as poverty.
When nibbling they are in self-control,
and when fasting they are filled in every way.
They do not have dealings with injustice,
nor can they disregard one who is afflicted and

95   oppressed by the rich.
They do not stand in awe before the face of humans, (Mt 22.16)
for they see the face of the Lord.
They are not broken-hearted over gifts,
nor do they disregard the law of justice, (Rom 9.31)
100   for they have inviolate wealth
and they reckon all things of the world as dung.
They have the Spirit as their teacher;
they do not need education from human beings,
but, enlightened by the light of this Spirit,
105   they look at the Son, they see the Father, (Jn 14.9)
and they fall down and worship the Trinity in Three persons,
the One God inexplicably united in nature.
They are again initiated into the mystery from the Father,
that the Son is begotten indivisible,
110   as he alone knows, for I am unable to say.
For if I were able, the world would certainly
have to tell things beyond words and thoughts,
and all things above would have to be below.
For if the creature fully understood the Creator
115   and what nature he is, it would perceive the whole of him.
And if the creature were also able to tell and write this in a
       word,
that would be a work greater than the Creator himself.
Stop, human, tremble, ‹you who are› mortal by nature,
and consider that you were brought forth from non-being,
120   and stooping from the maternal womb
you saw the world that was created before you!
And if you were able to know the heights of heaven, (Ps 102.11)
or to mark out the essence
of the sun, and moon, and of the stars,
125   how they are attached, and how they move about,
though lifeless and without sensation they are moved,

or the essence of the earth herself, from whence you yourself
    were taken,
her limits and measures, area and magnitude, (Job 38.5)
and if you have seen what she is carried upon,
130 and again what is that support, or where does she have a base,
if you knew these things and one at a time you have found the
    end,
and if you have counted the sand of the sea,[11]
and if you have discerned your own nature,
and interpret the work of wisdom,
135 then you shall perceive the Creator himself,
how in the Trinity is the Unity without confusion,
and the Unity is the undivided Trinity.
Seek the Spirit, be outside the world!
Do not give total sleep to your eyes,
140 do not be concerned about the present life!
Weep, mourn for the time you have ruined! (Jas 4.9)
Equally God may console you, (Mt 5.4)
and just as he already granted you to see the world,
and the sun, and the light of day,
145 so also shall he deign to illuminate things of the present day
and to show to you the rational world,[12]
and to enlighten you by light, by the Triple Sun,
whom if you will see, then you shall know what I say,
then you shall know the grace of the Spirit.
150 Because even when absent he is present by his power,
and when present he is not seen in his divine nature,
but he is both everywhere and nowhere.
For if you will seek to see him in a sensible manner,
where will you find him? "Nowhere," you would certainly say.
155 But if you will be able to contemplate him mentally,[13]

[11]Gen 32.12; 22.17.
[12]τὸν νοερόν σοι κόσμον.
[13]νοερῶς.

or rather he shall enlighten your mind,
and open the pupils of your heart,
then you shall no longer deny that he is everywhere.
But through him you shall be taught everything, (Jn 14.26)
160 even if you are an uneducated peasant.
But if you do not know that the eye
of your intellect has been opened and is seeing the light,
if you have not the sweetness of the divine,
if you have not been enlightened by the divine Spirit,
165 if you have not wept tears painlessly,
if you have not seen your mind cleansed,
if you have not known your heart was purified, (Mt 5.8)
and was shining bright reflections,
and you have not found Christ within you even when unhoped
        for,
170 and you were not astounded on seeing the divine beauty,
and did not forget human nature,
seeing yourself entirely transformed,
tell me, how do you not tremble to speak about God?
How dare you, you who are yourself all flesh,
175 and have not yet become spirit like Paul, (Rom 8)
to speak or to philosophize about the Spirit?
You hear that he does not dwell in such persons
because they are flesh, according to the saying. (Rom 8.9)
But I have written this so that you may know how I believe.
180 And if you wish, you may trust me and be sorrowful.
For if you truly do not have the treasure, (Mk 10.21)
which the world cannot contain, (Jn 14.17)
if you have not yet received the glory of the fishermen,
which those who receive truly received God,
185 you shall leave the world and the things in the world, (1 Jn 2.15)
you shall hasten, you shall run before the gates of life
and the gates of the theater here below close on you, (Mt 25.10)
and before the market is dispersed, alas,

and the sun darkens, and the stars,[14]

190 and the earth passes away, and hell is opened, (Mt 24.35)
and all shall become darkness and chaos,
and then you shall know, beloved soul, and learn
that those who do not have the divine Spirit
shining in their intellect like a torch,

195 and dwelling in their heart inexpressibly,
are sent away to eternal darkness. (Jude 13)
For the Spirit also is Lord,
and the Spirit is God, Father of the Lord, (Jn 4.24)
certainly the Spirit is one, for he is not divided. (1 Cor 12.12, 23)

200 One who possesses him truly has the three,
but without confusion, if also without division.
For he is the Father, how will he be the Son?
For he is unbegotten according to essence,
there is the Son, how would he become the Spirit?

205 The Spirit is Spirit, how would he be revealed as Father?
The Father is Father because always the begetter.
But how does this begetting always happen?
Because he is not at all separated from the Father,
and inexplicably all of him proceeds.

210 He always remains in the paternal bosom, (Jn 1.18)
and always comes forth ineffably.
The Son is seen everlastingly in the Father.
He is begotten, but united,
for even in the Son the Father is beheld (Jn 14.9)

215 inseparably, indivisibly, without separation.
The Son is the Son because he is always begotten,
and before the ages he is begotten,
coming forth without being cut off from his root,
but he is even apart without being parted,

220 and wholly united to the Father who is living.

[14]Mt 24.29; Joel 2.10.

He himself is life, and provides life to all.[15]
Whatever the Father is, so also is the Son; (Jn 17.10)
whatever the Son is, likewise the Father.
I see the Son, I also see the Father, (Jn 14.9)
225 The Father is seen through the Son unchangeably,
except the One begets and the Other is continually begotten.
What is apart from the Father that also exists?
What is there? Say it, point it out to all human beings!
God is without beginning and maker of all things,
230 anything that has been or is destined to be.
God equal to the Father both by essence
and by nature, and by authority,
and truly by form, and by species,
and by time never apart from the Father.
235 How does he come forth? Like a word from a mind.
How is he separated? Like a voice from a word.
How is he embodied? Like a written word.
From the heights I have been brought down to lowly things
and arrived at myself grieving,
240 and I wept over the race of human beings
because they seek strange paradigms,
hypotheses, and actual facts, and sayings
they introduce from human things,
believing they represent the divine nature,
245 nature that none of the angels nor humans
are able to look upon or to name.
For what would one call the Creator of all?
For names, and facts, and sayings
all happen by the command of God.
250 For he established names for his works,
to each fact its own appellation,
but he did not name them all himself, rather he granted to
‹some› works in turn

[15]Jn 14.6; 10.28.

to arrange names for his other works, (Gen 2.19–20)
one calls, and another is called.
255   But *his* name has not yet been made known to us,
except as "the God who is inexpressible," as he said. (Ex 3.14)
And so if inexpressible, if he does not have a name,
if invisible, if concealed,
if unapproachable, if unique beyond any word,
260   not only beyond mortal thought,
but even beyond that of immaterial minds.
For he also established darkness as a hiding place, (Ps 17.12)
and all other things hence are of darkness,
only he is like a light out of darkness.
265   How do you introduce an hypothesis about him,
or see him separated in actual fact?
Whence and how have you penetrated the darkness,
and how have you alone of all creatures been set apart?
But if these things are not yours, but another's,
270   I wonder whose, and I ask you in order to learn,
from an angel or one of the immaterial beings?
And do you not even know that they keep both
their faces and feet reverently and discreetly covered
with their divine wings (Is 6.2)
275   —if you would understand these wings at all—
and that they cannot endure the unapproachableness of God's
        Glory?
For it is not the God's nature they see, but the glory of glory.
To what sort of person dare you say ‹this insight› belongs?
To John or to the great Paul?
280   But the former shouts and proclaims to all
that he is not even worthy to loosen
the strap or lace of his sandals. (Lk 3.16)
And the latter, after he ascended to third heaven,
and after that was lifted into paradise, (2 Cor 12.2–4)
285   surely he did not say something private to you alone

that you hid and you now wish to proclaim?
For we have heard him saying nothing in writing
concerning such things,
but even Paul himself says with a great voice:
290 "I heard words that I cannot say." (2 Cor 12.4)
And God dwells in "unapproachable light." (1 Tim 6.16)
And so John does not loosen his laces,
nor is he even competent to loosen his strap.
And Paul was not able to express the words
295 that he heard, saying they are inexpressible. (2 Cor 12.4)
And who, having thus examined God,
remained unburned by the unapproachable light,
and arrived in the middle of his dwelling,
and contemplated the very nature of the Master,
300 so that this miserable person would dare to say
anything more than John and Paul?
For who would not tremble, and who would not mourn
the blindness and darkness of those now speaking
and renewing a truly strange riddle[16]
305 that hurls down into one pit all
who ask it and are asked?
For if they separate the Logos by an hypothesis
or by actual fact thoughtlessly, they err,
falling into heresy on both sides.
310 For to suppose "by actual fact" makes a splitting of the Logos,
and "by hypothesis" a confusion as though they are not at all
    distinguished.
Tremble, O human being, at least know thyself.
Speak about yourself, speak and say whatever you wish!
Perhaps, like David, you will call out
315 saying: "Your wisdom is marveled at,

---

[16]Symeon plays on the word αἵρεσις, which can mean either choice or heresy. Here it is translated as "riddle" to better refer to Stephen's question to which this *Hymn* is a response. In verse 21.309 Symeon uses the word αἵρεσις to mean heresy.

and your knowledge beyond me, O my God!" (Ps 138.6)
Yes, leave behind your meddling,
and put away the blasphemy of your sayings!
And first of all say: "How may we be saved?"

320 And afterward say also how you yourself were saved,
so that you are not revealed as teaching us just by your word,
but also making us more zealous by your work!
That is, if you do not intend to pass judgment against
and condemn yourself for not practicing what you preach,

325 and thereby transgress your own words,
as though you never made a beginning in these things.
Set the rock as the first of your foundations, (Lk 6.48)
for a house is not built in the air!
Do the commandments of Christ the Rock,

330 the Builder of the divine Church,
of the new people, of the rational flock!
Practice and speak building on rock,
even more, let yourself be built by the Rock!
He is a shepherd, he is also an architect.[17]

335 May he also be the foundation of life for you.
For what use is a roof before the foundations?
First the structure and then the roof, (1 Cor 3.9)
practice in knowledge and thus contemplation!
Why do you want to drink the wine before the harvest?

340 For it is not contained in old wineskins. (Mt 9.17)
Why expect to gather sheaves before the planting,
and to distribute to others in vain?
If you wish, come here, may you not fall from the path,
but teach us about the depths of judgments, (Rom 11.33)

345 of judgments about us, how some run successfully
though they are sinners who have not known God,
how others who have known God are unfortunate,
and are known by God alone, (Gal 4.9)

[17]Jn 10.11; 1 Cor 3.10.

how others suffer yet give thanks equally,
350 and others bear being poor thankfully,
but others, though rich, act wickedly and unfairly,
and the rest by stealing and doing wrong
believe they serve God by these things,
and many other things that you see each day.
355 Because mortals act and suffer in turns,
and God the creator of all sustains them, (2 Macc 1.24)
would he not be considered unjust by the lawless,
or by those who are fainthearted like me?
Speak, teach about divine judgment,
360 about that hour and that day,
in which we shall all be placed naked near
the judgment seat of my God and Savior. (Rom 14.10)
We shall receive the rewards of our
actions and our words here below, of our discussions
　　　(1 Cor 3.8)
365 along with our considerations, rewards according to our
　　　worthiness.
Tell me, who *there* will speak boldly, (1 Jn 4.17)
and who in turn will be put to shame?
You have to speak endlessly about these things.
And after these examine also creation,
370 for you shall find in it another abyss!
Behold the sky, sun, and the stars.
Look at the earth established by a command,
becoming the mother and tomb of us all! (Sir 40.1)
And having gone there speak about death,
375 philosophize many necessary and
useful things, useful to friends together with relatives,
as also to the rich and to the famous!
And while you explain among everyone, there will be enough
for you to speak about
380 unto death . . .

and that shall benefit you after death.
Then behold the earthly world,
the species of animals of all kinds in it,
the multicolored visions of feathered creatures,
385 together with the voices of the common sparrows,
wonder at the surface, and magnitude, and boundaries of the
        sea,
be astounded, and declare vehemently:
"O the depth of wealth and knowledge of the Divine,
O your wisdom, my all-merciful God." (Rom 11.33)
390 Come here and draw yourself in from external things,
collect your mind, understand yourself,
rather, philosophize on yourself and what you have,
and whatever you look at, in each thing seen,
may you find for yourself a teacher of virtue.
395 Or imagine a passion of wickedness,
so that from the magnitude and beauty of creatures,
the incomprehensible wisdom of God,
and the intelligible combat you may learn
what the Sculptor of all has prefigured.
400 And by all means may you acquire prudence like the serpent,
        (Mt 10.16)
but may you vomit the poison of wickedness!
Like the horse, may you run in the righteous path,
but may you not neigh at the female at all! (Jer 5.8)
May you become a cat watching for the mental mouse,
405 but certainly not snatching a neighbor's property,
nor stealing your brother's portion.
But also, by the mouse, may you drive away from your house
all mice that are against you!
But do not become a wolf, and may you flee wolves.
410 Rather, may you become the Master's dog,
and breathe the whole of your anger against them,
and may you trace the paths of your Master

until you discover, until you attain,
the divine gate. May you not turn back[18]
415 and become the prey of the mental beasts!
Imitate the hare, if you cannot imitate the dog.
Gain the rock that is Christ as your refuge[19]
and be hidden where there is no fear.
Or like the deer, climb the mountains, (Ps 103.18)
420 escape the hands of the hunters,
or fly like the beautiful bird[20]
and pass over all the traps!
Understand that the wings are holy love, (Ps 54.7)
without which you would pass nowhere.
425 Imitate the foal carrying the Creator, (Mk 11.7)
become also the ox pulling a divine plough
and cutting the sweet furrow of the word!
Imitate all without the contraries!
Bad fox, living by hypocrisy,
430 being one thing and appearing another;
it pretends to be dead in order to catch something.
The terrible bear, for if she receives ‹a blow› from a sword
she does not stop scratching the wound
until she dies from it.
435 The wicked pig eating insatiably;
wicked, the asp, for it even plugs its ears. (Ps 57.5)
Wicked, the wicked beasts, that if you wish to examine them,
you shall also hasten to flee them, beloved soul,
in this you shall certainly find true wisdom. (Sir 6.18)
440 For walking the path you shall come to what is better,
and with all, you shall understand yourself,
and when I ask, you shall certainly declare:
"The word that you speak, I also receive it!

---

[18]Jn 10.7; Mk 13.16.
[19]Ps 103.18; 1 Cor 10.4.
[20]Ps 10.1; 54.7; 123.7.

And it is in you, and it crosses over to me."
445 Or does it leave you empty of the word?
You shall say: "I know that the word also came to me,
and is wholly with you as before."
So how, having separated from you, has the word come to me
and remains whole in you without separating from you?
450 Tell me this and now leave God alone,
lest all creation tremble and fall,
and crush your thick flesh,
and beat your fleshy soul,
and with fire burn your mind
455 that vainly steps into nothing useful!
For neither actually nor hypothetically
is the indivisible divided from the Logos.
For one who is shut up inside the house,
but has their mind wandering about outside,
460 is not left mindless in the house,
but the mind is both with him and certainly outside.
So what do you call this separation?
Will you say it is an actual fact or will you say an hypothesis?
If ‹you say› an hypothesis, how is it fully outside,
465 and if a fact, how is it within the house?
And indeed, what is this example
to the Logos who is beyond mind and thought?
For, having been sent from the Father, the Logos descended
        (Jn 10.36)
and dwelt entirely in the womb of the virgin,
470 and he was wholly in the Father and wholly in the womb,
and wholly in the universe, being uncontainable.
Not reduced, not diminished at all, he went entirely in
and remained unchanged. He took the form of a slave
and having been begotten he became human in every way.
        (Phil 2.7)

₄₇₅ The whole of him went through the womb and he came into
          the world;
      again he was taken up from whence he was not separated. (Mk
          16.19)
      And so would you really dare to say these things
      happened according to hypothesis or actual fact,
      things that are secret to all angels, archangels, and to all created
          nature?
₄₈₀ For he is truly perceived, but not fully expressed,
      and he is by no means perfectly comprehended by the mind.
      And so how is he God and human, and also human-God,
      and also Son of the Father, whole and inseparable from him,
      and how did he also become ‹child› of the virgin and come
          forth in the world,
₄₈₅ and yet he remained incomprehensible, as was said, to all?
      By hypothesis or actual fact? Tell me! Certainly now you are
          silent.
      For even if you wanted to speak, your mind would not provide
          a word,
      and your talkative tongue would remain idle.
      But if you would wish to say the divine nature is actuality,
₄₉₀ by all means may you say also what sort, for I do not know.
      Glory to you, Father, and Son, and the Holy Spirit.
      Boundless Divinity, indivisible by nature,
      prostrate, we all worship you in the Holy Spirit,
      we who have your Spirit, as we have received from you.[21]
₄₉₅ And seeing your glory we are not curious about sundry things,
      but in the Spirit we see you, the unbegotten Father,
      and the begotten Logos, proceeding from you,
      and so indivisible, without confusion, Trinity to whom we
          prostrate in worship,
      One divinity, and dominion, and power. Amen.

[21] 1 Cor 7.40; 2.12.

Hymn 22

Thanksgiving and theology concerning how the divine grace of the Spirit is named through his energies.

What is the new mystery, Master of all things,
that you have shown to me the profligate fornicator?
What is this great marvel perceived within me,
and not fully understood but still hidden?
5   For it is seen by me like a star rising from afar, (Num 24.17)
and again it becomes like a great sun
not having measure, nor weight, nor limit in magnitude,
and it becomes a little ray, and then a flame is seen
in the middle of my heart and viscera,
10   often turning around, and burning
all things within my guts, and making them into light.
And so it uttered and taught in a friendly way
to one who was entirely without means and seeking to learn:
"I am the sweet star whom you once heard (Num 24.17)
15   is to rise from Jacob, it is I, do not doubt,
and I reveal myself to you as a sun rising from afar,
to be an unapproachable light for all the just,
in the existence to come and in life eternal. (Ps 96.11)
I also reveal myself as a ray and I am seen as a light by you,
20   burning yet not consuming the passions of your heart,
washing away your filth with the dew of sweetness (Is 4.4)
and my divine grace, and utterly quenching
the coals of your body, sins of pleasures,
and doing all by my benevolence,
25   what I have also done of old in all the saints."
Have mercy on the suffering one, pity the afflicted,
may you not get angry at me, for again I wish to speak!
How are you a star from Jacob, you who are utterly
        incomprehensible? (Num 24.17)

How is it that you are and you become, for everyone unto the
     present day?
30   And how do you also reveal yourself as a rising sun,
you who are nowhere, and everywhere, and above all creation,
and also proclaimed as invisible to all?
And how do you also become a ray, and a flame seen by me,
and how do you burn matter, being in essence immaterial?
35   How do you bedew and wash the filth of my body,
being entirely unapproachable fire, and unendurable to angels?
How do you envelop yourself with the corruptible essence of
     my body,
and how, without confusion, do you mix with a human soul?
How, through this soul, in the whole body without confusion,
40   do you, the intangible, deify me completely?
Tell me, and may you not send me away, me the hateful and
     afflicted one!
"O audacity, O recklessness, O words of folly!
How do you not shudder to ask these things so abruptly?
And how do you not perceive that you ask what you already
     know,
45   but you dare to speak with God like one who tempts,
and what you know, as though ignorant, you pretend to ask
     me,
and you want to write openly your knowledge to everyone?
But nevertheless I endure you since I am benevolent,
and again I teach you, saying these things to you:
50   By nature I am inexpressible, infinite,
without need, unapproachable, invisible to all,
intangible, unfeelable, immutable by essence,
alone in the unique All, and all one with everyone
who recognizes me in the darkness of life,
55   I am outside all the world, outside visible things,
outside of the sensible light of sun and of darkness,
of the place of punishments, and of terrible condemnation,

in which the arrogant servants fell, those who
wickedly raised their heads against me, the Master.

60 I am immovable; for where am I not,
so that I could depart and take possession of another place?
I am also ever-moving without limit,
where would you go to search for me in order to find me
    there?
At my word the sky was brought forth like nothing,

65 the sun, the stars, and the earth, like a little afterthought,
came to be and likewise the other things that you see.
The angels, having been introduced by me before the world,
look at the glory of my glory from afar, but not my nature itself.
For I merely thought to bring about the powers

70 and instantly they were present, singing the praises of my
    mastery.
But you who reside below in exile,
where all the first transgressors fell,
where Adam and with him Eve your proto-mother,
and the wicked devil who deceived them, (Gen 3.13)

75 where there is deep darkness, where there is a huge pit,
where snakes are always biting your heels, (Gen 3.15)
where there is lamentation, woe, and endless remorse,
where every desperation, anxiety, and sorrow,
both death and destruction, overpower you all,

80 how can you sit idle? How do you remain unconcerned? How
    can you be negligent?
Tell me! How do you not worry about the evils that you have
    done in the world?
And ‹how do you not› value repentance alone,
and hasten to demonstrate sincere repentance,
and to enquire about it with much entreaty,

85 and to investigate carefully how you may accomplish it,
so that you may be able, through repentance and by my
    benevolence,

to receive great forgiveness of your crimes?
But abandoning this repentance you seek things above nature,
you enquire about things in the heavens, but not even those,
90 rather you search out my nature, as was said,
I who made heaven and all things as nothing,
and you desire to learn things concerning me, as no one else
    knows.
Oh the wonder, O the ambition of a human![1]
For even if I found fault with you, still again I shall praise you,
95 because you also are my work and creation.
How you were formed from earth, from clay, from dust,
    (Gen 2.7)
how you live with dust and you are conquered in it,
do you reckon it all as nothing, do you regard it like a shadow,
and do you disregard all and seek only me?
100 You wish to speak about me, to describe on my account,
to see me, if possible, through the whole of your life,
and not to taste sleep, or eat, or drink,
or to be concerned about clothing of the body in general.
    (Mt 6.28)
But as if they were trees and wood standing along the road,
105 so do you reckon all honors of the world,
and you disregard them as nothing in the path of life,
not turning the vision of your intellect,[2]
nor allowing the eyes of your soul to look toward these things,
but you imagine and call to mind only me,
110 and you love me like none of those living with you. (Jn 21.15)
For who, by my name, gladdens their heart
and immediately rises to love or desire?
Who, often hearing my remembrance spoken,
has taken only me to heart and wept from their soul?

---

[1]ὦ τοῦ θαύματος, ὦ πρόθεσις. The former is a genitive of exclamation, the latter
a vocative, hence the two spellings, Oh and O.
[2]διανοίας.

115 And who has sought to learn and to keep
my divine words or my commandments with zeal?
        (Ps 118.73, 100)
Who like you considered me God above all,
and promptly desired to serve me, and
on account of this has disregarded parents, and brothers, and
        home, (Mk 10.21)
120 and likewise relatives, and neighbors,
and friends, and so has come to me,
as though not seeing any of them, ‹as though›
not having discovered on earth any person in the world,
but like a stranger treading a foreign country or city that
125 has barbarians and everyone speaking a foreign tongue,
thus among living companions, acquaintances, and friends,
private citizens, and princes, and the wealthy of the world,
and happens to be settled, and living in their midst?
But to the insensitive these are small and bare sayings,
130 but for me, their overseer, they are great and sublime.
Who among the great ones of the earth, of the authorities and
        thrones,
or of those who claim to govern and to reign through me,
or those who appear to hold the place of my divine apostles,
who has either considered this or been able to keep it,
135 so that in the time of keeping my commandments and law,
        (1 Cor 7.19)
they see one person just like all: relatives and strangers,
wealthy and poor alike, famous and obscure,
and all the powerful along with the common?
Who is the one who has judged dispassionately, looking upon
        them evenly?
140 If I should find a soul keeping these things in the world,
especially in the present day and generation,
I shall glorify them equal to my apostles and prophets,
and they shall sit with me in my advent, (Mt 19.28)

for then they shall judge justly like the apostles did on earth,
145   and they will gain the glory of the judge of the dead and the
        living. (Acts 10.42)
That is what is good to seek, and to observe the rest with them,
and as much as one can, to keep them meticulously,
and it is better not to search out my nature, son of man,
nor the energies of my Holy Spirit,
150   how he is revealed as a sun, how he is seen as a star
from afar where being revealed, and passing over the
        mountains,
and being hidden from your eyes, (Acts 1.9)
procuring for you inconsolable affliction and suffering,
and when you think he will no longer be seen by you,
155   he is found within, somewhere in your heart,
and apportioning astonishment and joy for you unexpectedly.
Because he shows himself to you as a flame, and he is seen as a
        ray and a fire,
do not be amazed nor examine him, for this is not good for
        you!
And so believe that I am utterly formless light,
160   completely simple, uncompounded, indivisible by nature,
at the same time inscrutable, inaccessibly accessible.
For I am truly seen, I am benevolently shown
according to the receptivity of each human being.
When I change form, it is not I who experience the change,
165   but those who see are deemed worthy to see me in this way.
For otherwise they are not able to see me nor do they receive
        any more,
and because of this they sometimes contemplate
a sun when they have a purified mind,
and sometimes a star when they find themselves
170   under the gloom and night of this body.
And the boiling over of love makes me a fire and a ray.
For when the charcoal of affection has been enflamed,

then I also see the eagerness of your heart,
I am found united to it and I provide light,
175 and I am revealed as a fire, I who created the fire by a word.
For the virtues of the soul lie underneath like firewood,
the divine light of the Spirit takes hold in these virtues,
and is named according to the underlying of the firewood,
for the light has no particular name among humans.
180 And so when a person is stung with compunction and weeps,
then ‹the Spirit› is also called water, for he also cleanses,
he is united to the tears, he washes away all filth.
And when remorse quenches the rage of the heart
with his cooperation, he is called meekness.
185 But again when one is enflamed against impiety,
this too comes about through him, it is called zeal.
And again peace, and joy, and kindness, it is said, (Gal 5.22)
because each is given to the one who mourns
and he makes joy bubble up in the heart like a fountain.
190 From this, all sympathy and mercy
is poured out, flowing from the soul to everyone,
most of all to those who wish to repent and to be saved.
For he has mercy on all, but with the latter he concurs,
and co-operates with, and unifies, and suffers with them in all
        things,
195 being united in their soul by free will,
and he judges, by the mind, the beauty of their repentance.
He attains a most true love toward them.
And he is called humility, as all things of the world,
even the soul herself and one's own body,
200 and all practice they believe become as nothing
when a person has tasted his sweetness,
and looked upon the impossible beauty of his light.
Having seen these things, may you no longer beg of me
to speak or to explain fully about such things to you!
205 For they are by nature inexpressible, utterly unspeakable,

and forbidden to humans, unknowable even to angels,
and wholly incomprehensible to any other created essence at
    all.[3]
But may you know only things about yourself, or much better,
    know thyself,
and then you shall know that since I am by all means
    unattainable,
210 I interact with and I love only those who love me, (Prov 8.17)
and those who always remember fervently my
    commandments,
and those who never prefer anything else that flows their way,
I shall live and converse with them now and forever." Amen.

Hymn 23

Precise theology concerning the incomprehensible and uncircum-
scribed divinity; and that the divine nature, being uncircumscribed, is
neither interior nor exterior to the universe, yet it is also both interior
and exterior as the cause of the whole of creation; and that the divine
is inapprehensibly grasped by a human only according to the mind, like
the rays of the sun by the eyes.

O Trinity, O Creator of all,
O my God alone for the alone,
uncircumscribed by nature,
incomprehensible in glory,
5   inexplicable in works,
immutable in essence!
O God, life of all things,
O God above all splendors,
O source of the Logos without beginning.

---

[3]καὶ κτιστῇ πάσῃ ἄλλῃ τινὶ οὐσίᾳ ὅλως ἀκατανόητα. This line is in prose, con-
taining twenty syllables rather than fifteen as in the rest of this poem; it was perhaps
left unfinished by Symeon.

10   My God beyond all eternity,
you who have never come into being,
but you were without a beginning!
How shall I find you entirely,
you who carry me about within you?

15   Who will give me possession of you,
you whom I carry around within me?
How are you both outside all creatures,
and again within them?
Yet neither within nor without?[1]

20   Since I am inapprehensible, I am not within,
but as I am apprehendable, I am exterior,
and being uncircumscribed,
I am neither inside nor outside.
For what is the Creator inside of,

25   and what sort of thing, tell me, is he outside of?
I carry around all things within me
as I hold together all creation.
And I am outside of everything,
being separated from everything.

30   For the Creator of creatures,
how shall he not be outside of everything?
And being before all things, (Col 1.17)
and filling all as I am filled, (Eph 1.23)
having created them, how shall I

35   not be in all my creatures?
For I was everywhere,
in the whole universe as beyond fullness,
and I fill everything that I have created. (Eph 4.10)
Understand what I say to you!

---

[1]This *Hymn* changes voice at line 20 from that of Symeon to that of God. A dialogue style with changes in speaker or addressee is common in the *Hymns*. In *Hymn* 23 it is not always clear where one speaker ends and another begins. There seem to be two dialogues: The first one is between Symeon and God (23.1–53?), the second is between Symeon and a disciple (23.54ff.).

40   Having created, I did not change place,
      nor was I united to things that were created,
      and being uncircumscribable,
      where then would you say that I am?
      (I do not speak to you bodily,
45   but understand me intellectually.)
      And seeking me spiritually,
      you shall find me uncircumscribable,
      yet because of this I am
      neither inside nor outside,
50   and if I am both everywhere, and in everything
      dispassionately, and without confusion,
      and accordingly outside of everything
      because I was before everything. (Col 1.17)
      But let us dismiss this whole
55   creation that you see,
      because it has no share in reason,[2]
      and rightly has no kindred
      with the Logos,
      having been deprived of all mind!
60   So let us grant that the living one is intimate
      with the word[3] of wisdom,
      so that—as mind is to Wisdom,
      and as reason[4] is to the Logos—
      by having more intimacy and kinship,
65   the creature also may well have
      communion with the Creator,
      since this living one was created according to the image
      and likeness of its Creator! (Gen 1.26)
      Of what nature is this living one I speak of?
70   It is truly a human being I say to you,

[2] λόγου.
[3] λόγον.
[4] λόγος.

a rational being among the irrational creatures,
as though double, composed of each,
of the perceptible and of the intellectual.[5]
This creature is in the middle of creation,
75 the only one who knows God, (Rom 1.21)
and only to the rational creature is God
inapprehensibly graspable by the mind,
or is God invisibly contemplated,
and unseizably seized.

80 How graspable and how inapprehensible?
And how mixing without confusion?
How? Tell me, explain these things!
How shall I explain to you the ineffable?
How can I say to you what cannot be spoken?
85 Nevertheless, pay attention and I shall speak.
The sun makes its rays to shine
(I speak to you of this sensible sun,
for the other you have not yet seen)
at any rate you see its rays
90 and they are perceptible to your eyes.
But the light of your eyes
is united to your eyes.
Now speak to one asking:
How is the light of your eyes
95 united to the rays?
Is it in an interaction without mixing
or are they mixed with each other?
I know you will say without mixing,
and you also will agree that they are mixed.
100 And you will tell me the light is apprehended
when the eyes are open
and have been well purified.
But this light, if you close your eyes,

[5]νοουμένων.

      is at once inapprehensible,
105   it is not present to the blind,
      but it *is* present to those who see.
      And when it sets, it abandons them
      like the blind.
      For in the night the eyes
110   of humans do not see.
      So also the soul, through the eyes,
      stoops to see the light,
      and when the light is not present,
      the soul is as in complete darkness.
115   And when it rises,
      then you see the light first,
      and in the light also you see all things,
      but having the light you do not possess it,
      for you have it in that you see,
120   but you are not able to possess
      nor to hold it in your hands.
      It seems to you that you do not have anything at all;
      you spread your palms,
      the sun shines on them,
125   and you suppose that you grasp it.
      It is this I say that you have.
      Suddenly you tighten again your grip,
      and the light is ungraspable,
      thus again you have nothing.
130   Simple things are simply grasped,
      and seizable without being gripped tight,
      for if this light is thought to be
      a body by nature
      when the sun is seen,
135   still it is also indivisible.
      And so, tell me, how do you
      bring it into your house?

And how will you be able to possess it,
how will you grasp the inapprehensible,
140 and how will you acquire the whole of it,
piecemeal or entirely?
But how will you take a piece of it
and hide it in your pocket?
You will tell me that certainly
145 it would in no way be possible!
So if the sun which, by word
and command, the Creator
set as a lamp
to shine on all those in the world
150 you are unable to speak of
or completely explain its nature,
how is it also a body?
For it is certainly not incorporeal.[6]
How is it inapprehensibly apprehended?
155 How does it mix without confusion?
How is it seen by rays
and illuminate you with them?
Yet if you would look upon it directly
it would instead blind you completely.
160 But you are at a loss to explain to me
even the light of your eyes,
how ‹when it is› apart from the light
it cannot see at all,
and how it unites with every light
165 and as light it sees everything.
And ‹the light of your eyes› remains completely unaffected,
distinguished from the lights,
and in like manner it is light
fully united to light.

---

[6]Lines 146 to 153 are a rather weak rhetorical question that is made more obscure
by the parenthetic definition in lines 149 to 151.

170 And the union is ineffable,
    not mixing with these ‹external› lights,
    and the distinction likewise
    is not comprehended.
    So how would you examine fully the nature
175 of the Creator of all things?
    Again, how do you claim
    to explain his energies?
    How, tell me how to recount them,
    and how in a word to compare them?
180 Accept everything by faith?
    For faith does not doubt,
    faith in no way hesitates,
    moreover everything is as I say.
    I say everything to you openly.
185 The Creator of the universe
    is the divine nature and wisdom,
    and he is in no way a thing among everything
    nor in everything (for how would it be
    that, being nothing among all creatures,
190 he is the cause of all things?)
    he is everywhere and in everything,
    and fills everything completely
    by his essence, by nature,
    likewise by his hypostasis.
195 God is everywhere
    as life-giving life.
    For what has ever been created
    that he himself has not produced?
    Understand me, even down to the gnat
200 and the spider's web!
    For from whence, tell me, is so much thread
    provided for the spider?
    The spider does not spin, but she

untiringly weaves every day.

205 She is more clever than fishermen,
than all fowlers;
extending her threads,
she ties them together at the ends,
and finally at the center of them

210 she weaves her snare
like a net in the air.
And seating herself,
she awaits her prey,
if some winged creature falls therein,

215 then it shall be caught.
And so he who by his providence
extends unto all these details,
how is he not in everything?
How is he not with everything?

220 Yes, he is in the middle of everything,
yes, he is also outside of everything,
yes, he himself is the rational[7] light
illuminating souls,
yes, he also never sets.

225 Where would he hide, he who fills the universe? (Eph 4.10)
And if you do not see him,
know that you are blind,
and in the middle of light
you are filled entirely with darkness.

230 For he is seen by those who are worthy.
They do not see him complete,
but he is seen invisibly
as a single ray of sun,
and is graspable to them,

235 being inapprehensible in essence.
On the one hand the ray is seen,

[7] νοητόν.

    but the sun itself blinds,
    and its ray is graspable to you,
    as we said, inapprehensibly.
240 So on that account I say:
    Who shall give to me what I have?
    Obviously, who will show me
    all this that I see?
    Furthermore I see the ray,
245 but the sun I do not see.
    Surely the ray seems to you and is seen
    by you not like the sun.
    Seeing this ray, I desire
    to see entirely its begetter.
250 Seeing thus, I say again,
    who will show me what I see?
    Moreover, having the rays
    wholly within my home,
    I say again, where shall I find
255 the source of the rays?
    But the ray in turn is plainly
    another source in me.
    O strange marvel!
    The sun shines above,
260 and again the ray of the sun
    on earth appears to me
    as another sun, and shines brightly.
    The second is truly
    similar to the first.
265 Having the ray, I say I have ‹the sun›,
    but seeing the sun far from me,
    I likewise cry out:
    Who shall give to me what I have?
    For they are not cut off from each other,
270 and they are not wholly separated,

and they stand apart ineffable.
As for the whole, how much do I possess?
One grain or a spark!
And I seek to take the whole,
275 even if I have the whole by all means.
How do you have the whole? What do you say to me?
Do you jest as to the foolish?
Stop playing with me, do not say:
"No, but I have the whole,
280 if I have nothing at all."
How or what do you say? I am amazed.
Listen and again I shall say:
Consider for me a large open ocean
and seas of seas;
285 again, picture in your mind
an abyss of abysses!
So if you stand near these,
the shore of these oceans,
by all means you would rightly say to me
290 that you see the water,
though not seeing the whole of it completely.
For how would you see the entirety,
it is boundless to your eyes,
and unmanageable for your hands?
295 Certainly you see as much as you see.
And if someone were to ask you:
"Do you see the whole of the seas?"
You would answer: "By no means."
"Do you hold all in your palm?"
300 "No," you would say, "for how could I?"
And if one were to ask again:
"Do you not see them at all?"
You say: "Yes, I see a small bit
and I hold some water from the sea."

305   So by whatever water you have
      while you keep your hand submerged in water,
      you keep all the abyss
      united to your hand
      (because your hand, the water, and abyss are not separated)
310   even if you do not hold all the abyss, but rather a little bit.
      And so compared to all the seas, how much do you have?
      "Like one drop," you will say.
      But the whole, you do not have.
      Yet you hold it united to your hands.
315   At any rate, I also say to you,
      that having nothing, I have,
      and I am poor yet I see
      wealth laid away for me.
      When I am satiated, I hunger,
320   and when I am needy, I am rich.
      When I drink, I also thirst.
      And the drink is very sweet,
      one taste stops all
      the thirst of myriads,
325   and I always thirst to drink,
      drinking way beyond my fill.
      I desire to have the whole
      and to drink, if possible,
      all the abysses at once.
330   This being impossible,
      I tell you that I always thirst
      even though in my mouth
      there is always water
      flowing, bubbling up, splashing all around.
335   But seeing the abysses
      it seems like I don't drink at all.
      ‹For› I desire to have the entirety.
      And again, having abundantly

the whole completely in my hand,
340 I am always a beggar.
United to a small part,
I certainly have the entirety.
And so the sea to the drop,
and again the abysses of abysses
345 are united to this drop.
And so having one drop,
I have all united to it.
And again the drop itself,
which I tell you I possess,
350 is wholly indivisible,
untouchable, inapprehensible,
likewise uncircumscribed,
very difficult to see,
that which is entirely God!
355 And so if such is to me
a divine drop,
what do I seem to fully possess?
Certainly, in having, I have nothing.
I shall say this again another way:
360 The sun shines from above,
advancing by its rays,
or rather I seize a ray;
I ascend running up
to approach the sun.
365 But when I shall well approach,
and I would seem to touch it,
the ray escapes through my hand,
and immediately I am blinded,
and I fall out of both
370 the sun and the rays.
And so I fall from the heights.
I sit, and again I weep,

and I seek the ray as before.
So in this condition,
375 the ray, having split for me
all the gloom of the night,
descends like a rope
from heavenly heights.
Quickly I grab it,
380 I grip it as though to seize the graspable,
and it is unseizable.
But I seize it inapprehensibly,
and I ascend.
And thus going up
385 the rays ascend with me,
I surpass the heavens, (Ps 148.4)
and the heavens of heavens.
And again I see the sun
above them all.
390 And if it flees, I do not know,
and if it stands firm, I know not.
While I walk, even as I run,
still I cannot overtake it.
And I surpass the height of height,
395 and when I have arrived
beyond all height, as I seem to,
the rays with the sun
vanish from my hands,
and at once I am carried down
400 to the calamity of hell, a wretch.
This work, this practice,
is for the spiritual,
up down, down up,
their race without rest,
405 whenever one falls, then they run,
whenever one runs, one stands still.

Reclined all the way down,
then being all the way up,
wandering around the heavens,
410 and again fixed to the earth below,
and the beginning of the course is the end,
but the end is the beginning.
Perfection without end,
then again the beginning is the end.
415 How is it the end? As Gregory
the Theologian has said,
illumination is the end
of all those who desire,
and the divine light is
420 the repose of all contemplation.[8]
One who manages to see this
retires from and separates themself
from all creatures,
because they see their Creator.
425 One who sees him outside of all things,
is alone with the Alone,
and sees nothing of all
visible or intellectual things;
one sees only the Trinity.
430 Let such a one keep silent.
For things in the Trinity are seen dimly,
and are understood only so much.
And so you have been astonished hearing
things within the visible realm?
435 But if you have been astonished at that,
how shall I not seem a storyteller
in revealing to you things beyond the visible?
For divine things are certainly
unspeakable and beyond telling.

[8]The reference is not certain, perhaps *In sancta lumina*, PG 36:344A.

440 Certainly, so also are the things within them,
    even if a word is somehow
    forced out from desire to speak
    about divine and human realities.
    But leaving divine things aside
445 and saying something of our own matters,
    I will show to you in a word
    the path and then I shall stop.
    Know that you are double
    and you possess two pairs of eyes:
450 perceptible and rational,[9]
    as there are double suns,
    there is likewise two-fold light:
    perceptible and rational,[10]
    if you see them you shall be a human
455 such as you were originally created to be.
    And if you see the perceptible sun,
    but in no way the rational sun,
    you are certainly half dead. (Lk 10.30)
    One who is half dead is also a corpse,
460 in all things inactive.
    For if one who does not see physically[11]
    is someone without activity,
    by how much more is one who does not see
    the rational light of the world (Jn 8.12)
465 a corpse and worse than dead?
    A corpse has no sense perception,
    but having died in its senses,
    how much suffering it will have!
    What is more, it shall be as though
470 dying painfully forever.

---

[9]αἰσθητοὺς . . . νοερούς.
[10]αἰσθητοῦ . . . νοητοῦ.
[11]αἰσθητῶς.

But those who see the Creator,
how shall they not live outside all things?
Yes, they live outside all things,
and they are in the midst of all,
475 and they are seen by everyone,
but by everyone they are not seen
in perception of present things.
On the one hand they are in the midst of all,
on the other hand beyond perception of all.
480 They become outside of all things,
united to immaterial ‹realities›,
they perceive not perceptible things.
For even their eyes see
in an imperceptible sensation.
485 —How? Tell me.—I shall tell you at once.
Just like when you see a fire you are not burned,
so also I see without feeling.[12]
You see the fire, what nature,
and by all means you see the flame,
490 but you do not feel pain,
but you are outside of it,
and seeing you are not consumed
by feeling imperceptibly.[13]
Or how else would you say it?
495 For you do not burn without feeling,
but in a feeling you see fully.
Understand me, one who sees spiritually
also experiences this,
for the mind contemplating all things
500 also distinguishes dispassionately.
One sees such a seasonable beauty,
but outside desire.

[12]ἀναισθήτως.
[13]ἀναισθήτως ἐν αἰσθήσει.

And so the fire is the beauty,
the touch[14] is the desire.

505 If you do not touch the fire,
how would you feel the pain?
By no means! And again the mind,
before it will desire wickedly,
when seeing gold,

510 will certainly look upon it as so much mud, (Zech 9.3)
and see glory not as glory,
but as a mere image of phantasms
appearing in the air,
and shall reckon wealth as

515 wood in the desert,
a bed of leaves lying on the ground.
Why do I try to expound on
and to explain everything?
If you would not comprehend by experience,

520 you cannot know these things!
And being at a loss to know you will say:
"Alas, how do I not know that,
alas, how far I am from
these beautiful things in my ignorance!"

525 And you will hasten to know these things,
so that you will at least be called knowledgeable.
For if you do not know yourself,
what nature you are, what sort you are,
how shall you know the Creator?

530 How shall you be called faithful?
How shall you be called a human being
when you are an ox or a wild beast?
Or you will be like some irrational animal
or even worse than them,

535 not knowing the one who created you. (Is 1.3)

---

[14]ἀφή also means enkindling.

Who, not knowing the Creator,
would dare to claim that they
are rational! They are not!
For how, since one is deprived of reason?[15]
540 And one who is deprived of reason
is ranked as an irrational beast,
and being shepherded by humans,
one will certainly be saved,
but if they do not wish it, but if
545 they approach mountains and chasms,
they shall be the food of beasts (Ezek 34.5)
like a lost lamb. (Lk 15.6)
Practice and achieve these things,
may you not drift away my child!

Hymn 24

By confession in this present work, Symeon shows the depth of his humility, and further on he teaches humility to one driving toward a measure of perfection and deigned worthy of such things in contemplative revelations; by this Symeon imitates Paul the divine, who called himself a sinner and unworthy of being called an apostle.

Grant to me, Christ, to kiss your feet! (Lk 7.38)
Grant that I may embrace your hands,
your hands that brought me forth with a word,
your hands that without toil created all things!
5   Grant that I may insatiably take my fill of these,
grant that I may see your face, O Logos, (Ex 33.18, 20)
and enjoy your unspeakable beauty,
and perceive and indulge in your vision,
a mysterious vision, an invisible vision,
10   an awful vision; grant that I may tell fully

[15]λόγου.

this vision's energies, not its essence!
For you are above nature, above all essence,
you, your whole self, are my God and creator.
But the radiance of your divine glory (Heb 1.3)
15 is a simple light to us, seen as a sweet light,
light reveals itself, light unites all of itself,
as I suppose, to the whole of us your slaves,
light is seen spiritually from afar,
light is suddenly discovered within us,
20 light gushing forth like water, and burning like fire
in the heart which it utterly lays hold of. (Ex 24.17)
My Savior, I have known that by this fire
my humbled and wretched soul has been seized,
and burned, and consumed. (Jer 20.9)
25 For when fire takes an essence like twigs,
how would it not burn, how would it not consume,
how would it not produce inescapable suffering within?
Having enkindled me, grant that I may speak, Savior,
it shows an inexpressible vision of seasonable beauty, (Ps 44.2)
30 and gladdens me, and makes an unbearable
flame of desire. And how shall I bear it,
how would I endure, and how shall I fully tolerate,
or how shall I express this great marvel,
that is happening in me the profligate?
35 For I do not bear to keep silent, my God,
or to bury your works in the depths of oblivion, (Wis 16.11)
works that you have done and you do each day
with those who always seek you fervently,
and those who by repentance flee to you for refuge,
40 lest I also, like the worthless servant
who hid his talent, be condemned justly, (Mt 25.25–27)
but I speak, disclosing these things to everyone,
and I pass them on in writing, and I fully describe
things concerning your compassion

45 for generations to come, O my God, (Ps 47.13)
    so that learning your bountiful mercy
    —mercy that you have pointed out and you show
    toward me the profligate, alone impure,
    sinning more than all others—
50 ‹so that› no one may hesitate, but rather desire,
    lest they be afraid, and they may approach rejoicing,
    and not be frightened, but rather have confidence,
    seeing the ocean of your benevolence,
    and they may run to you, and fall down, and weep, (Lk 15)
55 and they shall receive deliverance from their failures,
    saying in themselves sincerely, my God:
    "If the creator has had mercy on this
    utterly wicked, wholly depraved, and utterly profligate,[1]
    one who sins beyond all other humans,
60 how would he not even more greatly have mercy on me,
    who have failed only sparingly
    and have not transgressed all the commandments?"
    And so they may know also the multitude of my evils,
    I would like to tell them here, certainly not all, O Logos,
65 for they are innumerable beyond the stars, (Gen 22.17)
    beyond the drops of rain, and the sand
    of the sea, beyond the multitude of surging waves.
    I will tell only what the book of my conscience bears,
    and the storehouses of my memory contain,
70 but the others, you alone know the sum.
    I had become a murderer—listen everyone
    so that you may weep sympathetically—but the manner
    ‹of murder› I leave aside, begging too long a speech.
    Alas, I had also become an adulterer at heart, (Mt 5.28)
75 and a sodomite in deed and by free choice.
    I became a philanderer, a wizard, and a corrupter of boys,
        (1 Cor 6.9, 10)

---

[1]πανάσωτον; or perhaps: "morally abandoned wretch."

a perjurer, a blasphemer, a money grabber,
a thief, and a liar, shameless and rapacious—Woe is me!
abusive, brother hating, exceedingly jealous,
80 and money-loving, reckless, and also every
other form of wickedness I have committed.
Yes, trust me, I say these things truly,
and not in imagery, not in clever metaphor!
So who, having heard these things, would not be shocked,
85 would not marvel at your long-suffering,
O Benevolent One, who would not be astonished and say:
"How is it that the earth did not split open, refusing to bear
or to endure this wretch on its surface,
and how did it not take him alive down into hell? (Num 16.33)
90 How is it that a thunderbolt from above was not brought
down to destroy this transgressor? (Prov 23.28)
And how is it the sky did not collapse and
at the same time the sun and stars be extinguished
on this one who has despised you? (Mt 24.29)
95 Oh your forbearance," one would say, "and,
Savior, your goodness and mercy!
For surely the deeds of this all-wretched sinner
are beyond all pardon."
When hearing of this each one shall cry out:
100 "Has justice allowed this one to live?
And how, being just, has God really allowed
him to be in the land of the living?"
But if one should suppose that I am probably writing lies,
grant them forgiveness since you are merciful. (Lk 6.36)
105 For they know not your long-suffering, Savior,
and the abyss of your benevolence,
and having heard the disgusting details of my works,
they have justly borne this judgment.
One might say: "If your justice leaves
110 this man guiltless, then there is no judgment hereafter."

But most certainly it is because you are going to judge later
that you are now patient, my God.
For by all means you wish the salvation of everyone,
    (1 Tim 2.4)
you await their repentance, (Wis 11.24)
115 the repentance of works, by your just forbearance. (Rom 3.26)
For it is proper for justice not to strike the fallen,
but rather to stretch out a hand to them,
which you do, my good Master, and
you have not failed nor shall you ever cease to do.
120 For the life of all human being is combat,[2]
and all humans are your slaves, of you the creator.
And we, small and great alike, have
sworn enemies, the princes of darkness. (Eph 6.12)
So if you did not stretch out your hand,
125 rather you permitted them to overpower us,
where would your justice be? Where your benevolence?
For we have been made slaves of the evil one
by our personal judgment, by our own free will,
but you yourself have come and redeemed us
130 by your immaculate and precious blood, (1 Pet 1.19)
and you have offered us, my God, as a gift to your Father.
So when the enemy sees us he cannot endure it at all,
he cannot bear the jealousy that he has,
but he roars against us like a lion,
135 and prowling about, and gnashing his teeth,
he cruelly seeks whomever he may devour. (1 Pet 5.8)
And so those who by this savage beast
are wounded, and receiving blows,
and lying wounded, O my Christ,
140 shall you not have mercy on them, or rather sympathize?
And will you not await their sanity?
But would you chastise, but would you crush utterly,

[2]Job 7.1; Eph 6.12.

and finally would you execute such as these?
For that is just, yes even *I* say this,
145 because they are not overpowered unwillingly,
but they surrender themselves voluntarily.
This savage and complex beast is equally
clever in villainy, and the master of wickedness,
and so he feigns friendliness, like a friend
150 seeking to hunt and to catch me whole,
showing to me the life that is visible,
it separates me from the intellectual life.[3]
By the sensation of things now present he robs me,
and steals away the wealth to come.
155 He appears one thing on an external view,
but hidden within he is another thing, O Savior!
But if humans who have studied him
can fashion treacheries by hypocrisy,
what will the inventor of evil not do? (Rom 1.30)
160 How will he not mislead especially the young, (Rev 12.9)
and how will he not trick those who are innocent,
completely inexperienced, utterly guileless,
he who is both Satan and villain by choice,
and who can skillfully find every deception?
165 He tricks and wounds everyone equally,
no one has escaped from under his hand,
nor has passed through his missiles unharmed
without tasting the poison in them.
We have all sinned and we fail to obtain (Rom 3.23)
170 your glory, and your mysterious divinity, O Christ,
and we importune you for the gift of salvation,
and to justify us by your grace and mercy,
which you have now poured out upon me abundantly,
     (Titus 3.6)
concerning which I shall not hesitate to speak and to write.

---

[3]"visible . . . intellectual" = ὁρωμένην . . . νοουμένης.

175 For how could I bear in silence
the things that happen hourly, O my God,
and are accomplished in me the wretched one?
For in truth they are inexpressible,
incomprehensible, above the mind, beyond speech,
180 and how do I express them or how do I recount?
But therefore, not bearing to be silent, I now shall speak:
You alone are God without beginning, uncreated,
in the Son and Spirit Holy Trinity,
you are incomprehensible, unapproachable.
185 Creator of the visible and of intelligible creation,
and you are Lord and Master, (Jude 4)
above the heavens, and all things (Eph 4.10)
in heaven, you alone are maker
of heaven, alone wielding power,
190 alone bearing the universe by your command,
and holding everything together by your will alone. (Wis 1.7)
You have myriads of angels around you,
and a thousand thousands of archangels, (Rev 5.11)
thrones, dominions without number, (Col 1.16)
195 you have powers, cherubim and seraphim
that have many eyes, sovereignties and authorities,
and more numerous other ministers and friends. (Ps 103.4)
You have the glory exceedingly glorified,
such that some among them dare not freely
200 look intently on it, O my God,
nor can they bear the flashing radiance
of your face when it is revealed.
For how shall the creature be able to fully contemplate,
to fully understand, its creator?
205 I suppose this is in no way possible,
but the maker, as much as he so wills it,
is manifested and seen, by those whom he wants,
and he is known, and he knows the creature,

and he is contemplated and he sees as much
210   as the maker will give to see.
      For if they are brought into existence by you,
      my God, they have being from you, and seeing,
      and ability to minister to you blamelessly.
      But you are up beyond all sovereignties, (Eph 1.21)
215   but then again, they are around you, my God,
      but we are below, in the lowest pit, (Ps 87.7)
      —by "pit," I do not mean the visible world,
      but certainly the darkness of sin—
      in a grievous pit, a darkened pit,
220   in a pit and grave, in the very lowest place,
      where the sun has not illuminated.
      For it is outside the seen world,
      and the world to come, the night of sin,
      and those who foolishly fall into it,
225   it holds them now and likewise it shall keep
      the dead chained forever and ever,
      of whom I am the first, O my Christ,
      having been embraced and brought down into it,
      and having been found in its lowest bottom,
230   I shouted: "Have mercy on me!"
      when I attained knowledge of my evils,
      for I had learned to where I was brought down because of
            them.
      On account of this I cried out, I laboriously brought down
      a rainstorm of tears from my eyes,
235   I repented from the whole of my heart, (Joel 2.12)
      and I cried out with inexpressible cries.
      And from untold heights you listened
      to me lying in the very bottom,
      at the end of the boundless, endless darkness,
240   and having abandoned the powers around you,
      passing by all visible things,

you descended there where I was lying.
At once you shone, you chased away the darkness,
    (2 Sam 22.29)
you woke me with your divine breath,
245 you stood me on the feet of your commands,
you enchanted me by your beauty, and wounded
me with love. You completely changed all of me. (Song 2.5)
I saw your face and I was frightened,
and yet it appeared to me kindly and approachable,
250 and your beauty utterly changed me,
and astonished me, O Trinity my God!
For one character in each of the three,
and the three are one face,[4] my God,
that is called the Spirit, God of all things.
255 And so you become visible to me, the all-wretched.
How would I not tremble, and dare
to make myself lower than where I was,
and cover myself again with darkness,
in order to hide from you who are unendurable to all?
260 But on the one hand I did this out of cowardice,
on the other hand you, my God, enfold me the more,
you embrace me more, to take me in your arms even more,
in the bosom of your glory, my God,
in the hem of your garments, (Mt 14.36)
265 you lead all of me in, and cover me with your light,
and make me unmindful of visible things,
and of terrible things that recently held me.
Oh depth of mysteries, O summit of glory,
O ascension, O deification, O wealth,
270 O unspeakable splendor of your words!
Who will comprehend in words,

---

[4]Πρόσωπον could also be translated as countenance, expression, appearance, or person. But the latter would be heresy in this context. This is a strange expression, cf. *Hymn* 12.23; see also *Hymn* 31.17ff.; SC 174:386.

    or understand the magnitude of your glory?
    For one who has not seen what eye has not seen,
    nor heard what the ear has not heard, (1 Cor 2.9)
275 and has not ascended into the heart of the human,
    how shall they believe someone writing about these things?
    And even if one would believe, how shall they be able
    to see what the eye has not seen?
    How shall one worthily grasp through hearing
280 what the ear of humans has never heard,
    in order to think properly concerning them,
    and to be able to arrive at the genius,
    the beauty of which is impossible to those who see it,
    and the form is formless,
285 and, in order to tell you again,
    it is beyond understanding for all to whom it appears?
    Who, by inventing these things with reasoning,
    would not fall out far from the truth,
    and would not be led astray by imagery and fantasies,
290 seeing and inquiring about false images
    of their own mind's personal suppositions?
    For just as hell and the punishments therein
    appear as each person might wish,
    although no one at all knows how they really are,
295 so also, understand me, the good things there
    in heaven are incomprehensible and
    invisible to all; but these things are known
    and visible to only those to whom God shall disclose
    according to the measure of each person's worthiness: (Eph 4.7)
300 the measure of faith, hope, and love,
    the measure of their keeping of the Lord's commandments.
    But the measure of spiritual poverty is another thing,
    the perfect measure is neither small nor large. (Deut 25.14)
    For God hates these extremes not unjustly,
305 but justly, as they are certainly not righteous.

For on the one hand small spiritual poverty falls short of justice
by its indifference or even contempt,
and remains useless, that is reasonable and just.
But spiritual poverty that is not small, but large,
310 brings the one possessing it to madness,
and harms all others who deal with them.
The just measure of humility is
neither to despair completely of oneself, (Deut 25.15)
nor to suppose there is anyone in the world
315 worse than oneself in disgusting deeds,
and because of this one always cries and wails,
and despises all visible things.
For this is the sure sign of remorse
that concerns God, that comes from the soul.
320 But if one is attached to something from the visible world,
and has not known oneself in their feelings,[5]
nor had fear of divine judgment
and eternal fire in their heart, (Mt 25.41)
and not acquired perfect humility,
325 and because of this they are deprived of both
the vision and the gift of these goods,
of which the eye of no human has seen. (1 Cor 2.9)
Let us all hasten to find humility,
this nameless grace of our souls,
330 that does not have a name, but by experience
it becomes named for those who acquire it!
Christ is meek, humble of heart. (Mt 11.29)
One who possesses him dwelling within knows
that they have humility because of him,
335 or rather he himself is the humility.
The soul seeking glory from humans (1 Thess 2.6)
does not at all know this humility.

[5] ἐν αἰσθήσει usually translated as senses or perception.

But one who possesses even a little self-conceit,
how shall they have humility within themselves?
340 Certainly by no means! Alas for me the all-wretched,
vainglorious, and arrogant,
not possessing even one virtue,
and senselessly disregarding all
my days in the present life!
345 Who would not weep for me, who would not grieve deeply,
because I fled the world, and the things in the world, (1 Jn 2.15)
and yet I am not separated from the world in my senses?[6]
I have put on the habit of monks,
yet I love the things in the world just like the worldly:
350 glory, wealth, both pleasures and enjoyments.
I bear the cross of Christ on my shoulders, (Lk 23.26)
yet I completely refuse to also endure the disgraces
of the cross; I do not want it at all, (Heb 13.13)
but instead I put myself among the famous,
355 and with them I wish to be glorified.
Oh the misfortune! Oh the insensitivity!
I am worthy of double punishment;
for having failed much in my earlier life,
I promised to repent thoroughly,
360 but now I am revealed to be an arrogant transgressor
of all the blessings that God has provided,
and I am shown to be a denier of my promises,
and unworthy of all benevolence.
But, O my God, O you alone who are all-merciful,
365 hasten, anticipate, turn me again
to repentance, to tears, to remorse,
so that I may be washed, and purified, and see[7]
your glory shining clearly in me,
the glory you give to me now and unto the ages,

[6]τῇ αἰσθήσει.
[7]2 Kg 5.10; Jn 9.15.

370   to me glorifying you with unceasing exclamations,
    the maker and master of the ages!

Hymn 25

Concerning the contemplation of the divine light that occurred in
Symeon, and how the divine light is not comprehended by darkness.
And in this he is dumbfounded by the excess of revelations; he recalls
human weakness and condemns himself.

How shall I describe, Master, the vision of your face,
how shall I tell the unutterable contemplation of your beauty?
How shall the sound of a tongue contain what the world does
    not contain,
how could anyone express your benevolence?
5   For sitting with the light of a lamp shining on me,
and illuminating the gloom and darkness of the night,
I seemed to be occupied with reading in the light,
as though I were examining the sayings and considering the
    syntax.
And so as I began, Master, meditating on these things,
10   suddenly you appeared from above, much greater than the sun,
and you shone from the heavens down as far as my heart,
    (2 Cor 4.6)
but all other things I saw as being in the depths of darkness,
but in the middle was a shining pillar, splitting the air
    completely, (Ex 13.21)
extending from the heavens all the way to me, wretched one.
15   Immediately I forgot the light of the lamp;
I was not aware that I was in the house;
it seemed I was sitting in the air of darkness.
Moreover, I was utterly oblivious even of my body;
I was saying to you and now I say from the depths of my heart:

20 Have mercy on me, Master, you alone, have mercy on me,
        (Ps 56.2)
    I who have never served you at all, Savior,
    but I have provoked your anger from my youth,
    I pursued every wickedness of flesh and soul,
    and committed innumerable sins, disgusting
25 beyond all human beings, beyond all irrational beasts;
    I surpassed reptiles and all wild animals.
    It is necessary that you show mercy to me;
    I have sinned foolishly beyond all.
    For you yourself have said that the healthy do not
30 need treatment, Christ, but the sickly do, (Mt 9.12)
    on which account I am very sick and negligent,
    therefore pour much mercy upon me, O Logos! (Sir 18.11)
    But what exultation of light! Oh but the movements of fire,
    oh but the swirling flame in me, the wretch,
35 light that operates by you and by your glory!
    I understand and I say that the glory is your Spirit,
    the Holy, of the same nature and honor, O Logos,
    the same race, the same glory, the same essence, alone
    with the Father and you, Christ, God of all things. (Eph 4.6)
40 Prostrating in worship I give thanks, because you have deigned
        me worthy
    to know somewhat the power of your divinity.
    I give thanks because when I was sitting in darkness[1]
    you were revealed to me, you illuminated me, having deemed
        me worthy
    to see the light of your face which is unendurable to all.
45 I remained seated in the middle of the darkness, I know,
        (Mic 7.8)
    while I was in its middle, covered by darkness,
    you appeared to me as light, illuminating all of me with all
        your light,

[1]Ps 106.10; Is 9.2.

and I became light in the night, though I was in the middle of
    darkness.
And the darkness did not entirely overcome the light, (Jn 1.5)
50 nor did the light drive away the visible darkness,
but promiscuously unmixed, wholly divided
into parts far from each other, in truth, not wholly mixed,
but yet in this place they filled all things, as I reckon.
Thus I am in the light, though in the middle of darkness,
55 thus in darkness but again living in the middle of the light,
and behold the middle of light, behold also the middle of
    darkness,
and I say: Who shall grant that I may find light in the middle of
    darkness
which cannot contain the light it receives? For how shall
    darkness contain (2 Cor 6.14)
light within it and not flee, but instead the darkness
60 remains in the middle of light? Oh awesome wonder seen
doubly with the double eyes of both body and soul!
Now listen, I tell you the awesome things of the double God,
and the things that happened to me as to a double person!
He took up my flesh, and gave to me his Spirit,
65 and even I myself have become God by divine grace,
moreover I am a son of God by adoption. Oh what dignity! Oh
    the glory! (Rom 8.15)
Like a sorrowing person I consider myself wretched,
    (Rom 7.24)
and I consider my weakness, and I groan,
I am utterly unworthy to live, as I well know.
70 But taking courage in his grace, and considering
the beauty that he has given to me, seeing this I rejoice.
So on the one hand as a human I know that I see nothing of the
    divine,
since I am completely separated from invisible things,
but by the adoption I have become God,

75   and I perceive, and I become a participant in sacred realities.
As a human I have nothing of the sublime and divine,
but since now I have been shown mercy by God's kindness,
I have Christ, the Lord, the benefactor of all. (Acts 10.38)
For this reason again, Master, I prostrate in worship begging
80   that I may not at all fail in the hopes I have in you,
nor fail in my way of life, and honor, glory, and kingdom.
But since now you have deigned me worthy to see, Savior,
so also provide for me to see you after death!
I do not say how much, Compassionate One, but abundantly,
     compassionately,
85   by your kindly vision, as even now you look upon me,
and you fill me with your joy and divine sweetness.
Yes, my maker and sculptor, protect me with your hand,
     (Ex 33.22)
and may you not abandon me, no, nor bear a grudge!
May you not measure my great arrogance, Master,
90   but deign also that I march untiringly unto
the end by your light, and by the way of your commands,
     (Ps 118.32)
and place my spirit in the light of your hands,
All-merciful One, release me from my enemies,[2]
from darkness, from fire, from eternal punishments, O Logos!
95   Yes, you who are abundant in pity, inexpressible in mercy,
deign that my soul be given into your hands,
as even now I am in your hand, O Savior!
And so let not sin obstruct my path,
nor cut me off, nor tear me from your hand.
100   But may the terrible prince and destroyer of souls be put to
     shame
when he sees me in your palm, O Master,
as even now he dares to come near me,
for he sees me sheltered by your grace!

[2]Ps 105.10; Lk 23.46.

May you not condemn me, Christ, do not banish me to hell,
105   may you not drive my soul down to the depths of death,
because I dare to pronounce your name,
I who am filthy, defiled, utterly impure.
May the earth not open up and swallow me, the transgressor,
        O Logos. (Ps 105.17)
I am completely unworthy to live or to speak!
110   May fire not descend upon me and suddenly absorb me
        (1 Kg 18.38)
as though I have not been granted to say: Lord have mercy!
May you who are abundant in pity, benevolent by nature,
not wish to enter into judgment with me! (Ps 142.2)
For certainly what shall I cry out, since I am sin.
115   And so, having been condemned, what, pray tell, can I say,
I who from my mother's lap have failed you immeasurably,
        (Acts 3.2)
and even unto now I remain insensitive to your patience,
I who was brought down to the depth of hell ten thousand
        times,
and have been pulled up from hell by your divine goodness,
120   I who have defiled the members of my flesh, my soul,
and my body, as no one else among the living,
a frantic, shameless lover of pleasures,
both lecherous and deceitful in my soul's wickedness,
I who have not kept even one of your commands, O Christ?
        (Mt 5.19)
125   What is my apology to you? What shall I answer to you?
        (Jer 12.1)
By what nature of soul shall I bear your cross-examinations,
        O my God?
If you should lay bare my lawlessness and deeds,
O immortal King, may you not show them to everyone,
because I tremble when I consider the works of my youth,
        (Ps 24.7)

130   and to speak of them makes me shudder and fills me with
              shame.
       For if you should wish to reveal these things to everyone,
       my shame would be worse than every punishment.
       For who, seeing my licentiousness, and my wretched deeds,
       who, seeing my impure embraces, my shameful practices,
135   in which I am even now defiled when I call them to mind,
       who will not be dumbfounded, seeing fully, who would not
              shudder,
       who would not cry out, and immediately turn their eyes
       and say: "Take away, Master, this utterly filthy person!
       Command that the hands and feet of this wretch be tied up,
              (Mt 22.13)
140   and that he be quickly thrown into the dark fire, (Lk 12.5)
       lest he be seen by us your genuine servants!"
       Truly, worthily, Master, truly, justly shall all
       these people say this loudly, and you yourself shall do this,
       and I, the profligate and perverse, shall be thrown into the fire.
145   But you who have come down to save the profligate and
              perverse, (Mt 18.11)
       may you not put me to shame, Christ, in the day of judgment
              (Ps 118.31)
       when you shall place your sheep at your right,
       and me and the goats on your left, (Mt 25.32)
       but may the immaculate light, the light of your face,
150   cover my works and the nudity of my soul, (Ps 84.2)
       and clothe me joyously, so that in frankness,
       unashamedly I may be chosen with the sheep on the right,
       and with them I shall glorify you forever and ever! Amen.

Hymn 26

That insofar as one lives in ignorance of God one remains dead among those who live in the knowledge of God; and that the divine body and blood of the Lord becomes incomprehensible to those who partake unworthily of the mysteries.

Now, O Master, I am as one dead among the living,
and among the dead I am as though living, wretched beyond
all human beings upon the earth, whom you have created, my
        God.[1]
The fact that I am a corpse among those who live according to
        you
5   shows that I am certainly worse than those who have not been
        created;
to live this irrational life like the beasts among the dead
is certainly like the life of those who have not known you as
        God.
For how is it not similar, and how is it not equal?
Even if I seem to know you, even if I seem to believe,
10   even if I seem to praise you and to call upon you—
for if even my mouth speaks the words that I have learned,
and I chant hymns and prayers that the ancients (Eph 5.19)
who had received your Holy Spirit set out in writing—
        (Acts 19.2)
and I say these things, and I seem to have accomplished
        something great,
15   still I am insensitive[2] and ignorant, because just as
learning children do not know the power of words,
so also by my prayers, and psalms, and hymns (Eph 5.19)
I persist, and praise you alone, the compassionate one,
still I do not receive perception of your glory and light,

---

[1]Tob 5.10, LXX.
[2]ἀναισθητῶ: unfeeling, stupid.

20 and just like the heretics who have studied much
think that they know you, think that they understand you,
these all-wretched heretics suppose that they even see you, my
    God,
so also when I say many prayers and many psalmodies
with only my tongue, and perhaps also my heart, (Eph 5.19)
25 because of these I believe that I have the summit of faith,
because of these I imagine that I have received
all knowledge of truth and need nothing more, (Titus 1.1)
and because of these I say that I see you, the light of the world,
    Savior, (Jn 8.12)
and because of these I say that I possess you and I am united
    with you,
30 and I think that I share in your divine nature, (2 Pet 1.4)
and concerning myself I search, I examine parables
and words, I cite the Scriptures, and I say:
The Lord said that those who eat his flesh
and those who drink his blood remain in him,
35 but also the Master dwells in them. (Jn 6.57)
And so saying this I proclaim that the incomprehensible is
    within reach,
the incomprehensible ‹Lord› is in the comprehensible body,
and the utterly intangible is held and seen.
And I, unfortunate one, do not perceive that in those whom
    you wish,
40 —in the perceptible, tangible, and visible beings—
you the creator are perceptible, tangible, and visible.
But in the unclean like me, and even more the unworthy,
    (1 Cor 11.27)
you deify your perceptible body and blood,
and without change you transform the absolutely intangible,
45 and utterly incomprehensible. But what is more, in truth
you remake them spiritual, invisible. Just as of old when
you went in and out of the closed doors (Jn 20.19)

and became invisible to the eyes of the disciples
in the breaking of the bread, so also now
50   you fulfil the bread and make it your spiritual body.[3]
And I seem to possess you, whether you wish, whether you do
          not wish,
and I have a share of your body, and I suppose that I partake of
          you,
and I am considered holy, my Christ,
and an heir of God, and your co-heir, (Rom 8.17)
55   and your brother, and a participant in eternal glory.
So by this I am rendered completely insensitive,[4]
by this it is revealed that I am ignorant of what
I sing, and what I say, and what I always practice and chant.
For if I knew fully, I would certainly have known
60   that you became human immutably, my God,
so that when you assumed me, you fully deified me,
but not in order for you to remain human in heaviness
and be seized by mortality, you who are God, completely
unseizable, incorruptible, and incomprehensible by nature.
65   Now that I know this, I believe that your divine body
and your holy blood have become inapprehensible,
and truly an unapproachable fire for me the unworthy,
with shivering and fear, with trembling will I partake of these,
I will purify myself in advance with tears and groaning.
70   But now I sit in darkness and I am led astray by ignorance,[5]
I am a wretch overcome by a perfect insensitivity.
But I wholly beseech you, I persistently beg you,
prostrating, and calling for help, and seeking your mercy,
look upon me now as always, my absolute monarch,
75   show your compassion, show your sympathy,
show no grudge toward me the publican,

[3]Lk 24.30; 1 Cor 10.3.
[4]ἀναισθητῶν.
[5]Ps 106.10; Mt 22.29.

the utterly profligate one who has sinned
against you beyond all rational and irrational nature!
For even if in life I have committed every crime,
80 still I admit that you are God, creator of all things.
I worship you Son of God, the same essence of God,
begotten from him before all ages,
and in the last times, from the holy virgin
Mary the mother of God, you were begotten like an infant,
85 and became human, you suffered for my sake,
and you were crucified, and, Savior, you surrendered to burial,
and rose up from the dead after the third day,
and you went up in the flesh, to the place from whence you
        were never separated.
So thus I believe, thus I prostrate worshipping you,
90 and I hope you will come again both to judge everyone
and to render to each what is due, Christ, (Mt 16.27)
may my faith be reckoned before my works, my God,
and may you not look for works that fully justify me, (Jas 2.24)
rather let this faith suffice for me in place of all. (Rom 3.28)
95 This faith shall speak in defense, it will justify me,
it will render me a participant in your eternal glory. (1 Pet 5.1)
"For one who has faith in me," you have said, O my Christ,
"shall live forever and shall not see death." (Jn 11.25–26)
And so if faith in you saves those who have despaired,
        (Mt 9.22)
100 then behold, I have faith, save me, shine your divine light upon
        me,
and when you appear, Master, may you enlighten my
soul that is held fast in darkness and the shadow of death![6]
May you also give to me compunction, your drink of life,
a drink that cheers the senses of my flesh and soul,
105 a drink that always delights me and provides life for me.

---

[6]Is 9.2; Ps 106.10.

May you not deprive me of it, Christ, I am a humble stranger,
I place all my hopes on you! (Ps 77.7)

Hymn 27

What sort of person a monk must be; what is his practice, progress, and ascent.

Render the house of your soul a palace,
make it a settlement for the Christ and King of the universe
    (Eph 3.17)
by crying your tears, by crying aloud, and by laments,
and by bending your knees, and by a multitude of groans,
5   if truly, O monk, you wish to be alone.
And then you are not really alone, for you are with the King,
and you are alone with respect to us, since you are away from
    us,
and separated from the whole world, this is complete solitude.
You are not solitary when united to God and King,
10 but you have become numbered among all the saints,
    (Eph 2.19)
living with angels, and dwelling with the just,
and truly a co-heir with everyone in heaven.
And so how is someone alone when they have citizenship
    there, (Phil 3.20)
where there is the assembly of the martyrs and the pious,
15 there is the chorus of prophets and divine apostles,
there is the innumerable crowd of the just, (Rev 7.9)
of high priests, patriarchs, and of the rest of the saints?
But when one has Christ dwelling within, (2 Cor 6.16)
how, tell me, can it be said that one is alone?
20 For both the Father and the Spirit are united to my Christ,
and how is one alone when united to the three as to the one?

One who has been united to God is not alone even if they are
    solitary, (Jn 8.16)
even if one is settled in the desert, even if one is in a cave.
But if one has not found him, if one does not know him,
25   if one has not received the whole incarnate
Logos God, then, alas, one has not become a monk at all.
Hence this one who has been separated from God is alone.
But each one of us, we are certainly
separated from other human beings,
30   and we are all orphans living alone,
even if we seem to have union by virtue of our cohabitation,
and by mixing with each other in the gathering of so many.
For we are separated in body and soul,
which even death shows to be true,
35   death separates each person from relatives and friends,
and makes one forget all whom they now love.
Just like night, and sleep, and practices in life
does death dissolve the union of the many.
But one who has made their own cell a heaven through virtue,
40   sees and contemplates the creator
of heaven and earth settled in their cell,
and they prostrate in worship, and are always united to the
    unsinking light,
to the never-setting light, to the unapproachable light
    (1 Tim 6.16)
from which one is by no means separated nor at all removed,
45   neither in the day nor night, nor in food, nor drink,
but neither in sleep, nor on the road, nor a migration from
    one's place,
but as one lives, so one dies, rather, put more clearly,
the light is wholly and eternally united to one's soul.
For how can the bride be separated from the bridegroom,
    (Jn 3.29)

50   or the man from the woman to whom he is united once and for
           all? (1 Cor 7.10)
      Tell me, shall the lawgiver not abide by the law?
      He who has said: "The two shall be made one flesh,"[1]
      how shall he not be utterly one spirit with her? (1 Cor 6.17)
      For in the man is the woman, and in the woman is the man,
55   and the soul is in God, and God in the soul, (Jn 14.20)
      and he is united, and known in all the saints.
      Thus are they united to God, those who purify
      their souls through repentance in this world,
      and they are appointed monks who are apart from others.
60   Those who take on the mind of Christ, which is also a mouth
           (1 Cor 2.16)
      and tongue truly without deceit, with which they converse
      with the all-powerful Father, with which they always cry:
      "O Father, O Absolute Monarch, O Creator of all things!"[2]
      Their cell is a heaven, and they are a sun,
65   and the light is in them, the divine and never-setting light
      that enlightens every human who comes into the world,
           (Jn 1.9)
      and the light comes from the Holy Spirit. (Mt 1.20)
      And so night is not in them; I cannot tell you how. (Rev 22.5)
      For I shiver when I write this for you and tremble when I think
           about it.
70   But I teach you how they live and in what manner
      they serve God, and sought him alone
      before all else, and they found him alone,
      and loved him alone, and were united to him alone,
      and became monks alone with the Alone,
75   even if they were received among a multitudinous people.
      For truly these are monks and solitaries living alone,
      these who are alone with God alone, and in God,

[1]Mt 19.5; Gen 2.24.
[2]Rev 4.8; Eph 3.9.

stripped of considerations and all sorts of thoughts,
seeing God alone in their mind without thoughts,
80 in a mind fixed on the light like an arrow stuck in a wall,
or like a star in heaven, or how I cannot say.
Equally, they inhabit their cells like another
shining bridal chamber and believe they live in heaven,
or truly so do they live. Look, do not doubt it!
85 For they are not on earth, even if they are held by the earth,
but they pass their life in the light of the age to come,
in which the angels dwell, and where they walk about,
by which sovereignties and authorities are plundered,
and thrones, and all dominions are strengthened.
90 For even if God rests among the saints,
still the saints live and move in God, (Acts 17.28)
walking in the light as on the ground.
O marvel, like angels and like children of the Most High[3]
shall they be after death, gods united to God,
95 by adoption they are made like him who is God by nature.
        (1 Jn 3.2)
But they are lacking these things now only because they are
        held
by the body, and sheltered, and covered, alas, (2 Cor 5.6)
like prisoners under guard, seeing the sun
and its rays entering through a hole,
100 and not being able to perceive it fully,
nor to look upon it after having come out of the jail,
nor glance at it to see it clearly in the open air.
And this is what distresses them, that they
do not contemplate the whole Christ, even if they see the
        whole,
105 for they cannot strip off the shackles of the body,
even if they are set free of the passions and every attraction,
but having been set free of many passions they are held by one.

[3]Mt 22.30; Lk 6.35.

For one who has been bound in many fetters
does not hope to find release from the many,
110 but one who has been able to cut through most of the fetters,
but remains held by one, is more distressed than the others,
and is eager, and always seeks release from it,
in order to appear free, to walk rejoicing,
so to go in haste toward their desire,
115 on this account one seeks deliverance from this fetter.
Accordingly, let us all seek him who alone
is able to free us from the fetters!
And let us desire him, him the beauty of whom
astounds all thought, astonishes all feeling,[4]
120 wounds every soul, and makes her fly to love,
glues and unites souls everlastingly to God. (Ps 72.28)
Yes, my brothers, run to him by works,
yes, friends, rise up, yes, do not be left behind,
yes, do not speak against us and deceive yourselves!
125 Do not say: "It is impossible to receive the Holy Spirit."
Do not say: "Without him it is possible to be saved." (Acts 4.12)
And so do not say that one can possess him without knowing!
Do not say that God is not seen by humans.[5]
Do not say: "Human beings do not see divine light,"
130 or that it is impossible in the present times!
This is never impossible, friends,
but it is very possible for those who wish it,
but only for as many as life has provided with purification of
      the passions,
and has made pure the eye of their intellect.[6]
135 But for others, true blindness, the filth of sins,
shall deprive them of divine light, both here and hereafter,

[4] φρένα.
[5] 1 Tim 6.16; Jn 1.18.
[6] διανοίας.

and do not be misled, it will send them away to the fire and
    darkness. (Mt 8.12)
See, friends, how beautiful is the Master!
Yes, do not close your mind by looking toward the earth,
140 yes, do not, by concern for wealth and worldly affairs, and
by desire for glory, be overpowered and leave
him behind, the light of eternal life! (Jn 8.12)
Yes, friends, come with me, lift yourselves up with me,
not by the body, but by the mind, and soul, and heart,[7]
145 cry out in humility to the good Master,
the merciful God, who alone is benevolent!
And by all means he shall heed, and certainly he will have
    mercy,
and certainly he will be revealed, and certainly he shall display
and give a glimpse of his joyous light to us.
150 Why do you humble folk shrink back, why are you careless,
why do you prefer relaxation of the body, and glory
that is unworthy and without glory, empty, and vain?
Why do you say that a life free of care is virtuous?
It is not so, brothers, it is not, be not led astray,
155 but just as those who have a life, and a wife, and children,
and longing for wealth and temporal glory,
they hasten and run to fulfill their fantasy,
so also everyone who repents and everyone who serves God
ought to hasten and always be anxious,
160 thus one's repentance shall be acceptable,
and one's well-pleasing service become perfect, (Rom 14.18)
and then having been made wholly a friend of God by these
    virtues, (Eph 2.19)
the whole person is united and sees him face to face,
    (1 Cor 13.12)
and receives confidence to speak freely before him in
    proportion (1 Jn 3.21)

[7]νοῖ . . . ψυχῇ . . . καρδίᾳ.

165 to how much one hastens to fulfill his will.
     May we also be deemed worthy to do likewise,
     and to share his mercy with all the saints, (1 Thess 3.13)
     now insofar as it is accessible in this age,
     but then we shall receive the whole Christ,
170 the whole Spirit, in the Father forever and ever. Amen.

Hymn 28

Concerning the intelligible[1] revelation of the energies of the divine light, and the rational[2] and divine activity of the virtuous life.

     Let me be confined alone in my cell, (Mt 6.6)
     leave me alone with the benevolent God alone,
     keep far away, remove yourself to a distance, leave me alone
     to die in the presence of the God who fashioned me!
5   May no one knock on the door, may no one release their voice,
     let none of my relatives or friends visit me,
     may no one draw my thought and tear me away
     from the contemplation of the good and beautiful Master,
     may no one give food to me, nor provide me with drink!
10   For it will be sufficient for me to die in the presence of my God,
     before the merciful God, the benevolent God
     who descended to earth in order to call sinners, (Mt 9.13)
     and to lead them to divine life with him.
     Hereafter I do not wish to look upon the light of this world,
          (Jn 11.9)
15   nor the sun itself, nor the things in the world.
     For I see my Master, I see the King,
     I see him who is truly light and creator of all light,
     I see the fountain of all good, I see the cause of all things,

[1] νοητῆς.
[2] νοερᾶς.

I see the beginning without beginning, from which all things
     were made,
20   through which everything lives and is filled with nourishment.
It is by his choice they happen and are seen,
and by his will all things cease to be.
And so how would I go out of my cell and leave him behind?
Leave me, I shall mourn and weep day
25   and night for what I lost when looking at this world,
seeing this sun, seeing the light of this world,
both perceptible and dark, it does not illuminate the soul.
The blind without eyes, living in the world, after they
have departed from it will also be the same as those who see
     now.
30   I also was led astray in the world, the whole of me was
     rejoicing,
I reckoned that there was no other light at all,
no light that is also life, like I said, and the cause (Jn 1.4)
of being, whatever is or shall be,
and I was like an atheist, not knowing my God. (Eph 2.12)
35   But now, by his ineffable compassion, he was well pleased
to appear to me, the wretch, and to be revealed.[3]
I saw and I knew that he is truly God of all things,
God, whom no one among all human beings in the world has
     seen. (1 Tim 6.16)
For he is outside the world, outside light and darkness,
40   outside the air, and mind, and all senses.
And that is why when I saw him I found myself beyond the
     senses.
And so you who are dominated by the senses, allow me
not only to close my cell and sit inside, (Mt 6.6)
but also to dig a pit underground and to hide there.
45   And passing my life there I shall be outside the whole world.
And seeing my immortal Master and Creator,

[3]Gal 1.15; 1 Cor 15.8.

I shall prefer to die of yearning, seeing that I shall not die.
>   (Ps 117.17)
And so what profit is there for me who am outside the world,
but then, what do they who are in the world now gain?
>   (Mt 16.26)
50   Truly nothing, but they dwell naked in tombs, (Ps 67.7)
and they shall be raised up naked, and all shall be judged.
>   (Jn 5.28)
Because they have ignored the true life, the light of the world,
>   (Jn 8.12)
Christ I say, they loved the darkness, (Jn 3.19)
and they all chose to walk in it, (Jn 12.35)
55   they have not received the light shining in the world, (Jn 9.5)
whom the world can neither contain nor see.
On that account, leave me and let me alone,
I beseech, so I can weep and seek him out,
for him to be given to me abundantly, and to be seen by me
>   copiously.
60   For not only is he looked upon, not only is he contemplated,
but he even shares himself, and dwells, and remains,
and is like a treasure hidden in the bosom.[4]
One who carries him is delighted and rejoices when they see
>   him,
and they imagine that everyone sees him hidden within.
65   But he is not seen by all, nor felt by all,
a thief is not able to steal him, nor is a brigand able
to carry him off, even if he were to kill the one carrying him.
>   (Mt 6.19)
Or if a thief wished to separate them, in vain would he toil
>   (Ps 126.1)
by searching their pouch, searching their clothes,
70   loosening their belt, thoroughly examining them.

---

[4]Mt 13.44; Job 23.12.

Even if the brigand were to cut open one's gut, and even feel
     around
the bowels, he would not at all be able to find or to take Christ
     from them.
For he is invisible, beyond the hand's grasp
and at the same time both tangible and utterly felt.
75 And then he is wholly held in the hands of those who are
     worthy.
But withdraw from the unworthy and he lies in your palm.
What is this? O Marvel! What is it not? For it has no name.
So having been astonished and longing to possess it,
squeezing my hand I imagined that I grabbed and held it,
80 but it ran through my hand, it was not at all restrained.
I was distressed and I opened the fist of my hand,
and I saw again in my hand what I saw before.
O unspeakable wonder! Oh strange mystery!
Why do we trouble ourselves in vain? Why do we all deceive
     ourselves? (Ps 38.7)
85 Why do we continue to gape before the light, the imperceptible
     light,
we who have been honored with intellectual reason in our
     sense perception?[5]
Why do we look to the material, to these perishing things,
when we have an immaterial and wholly immortal soul?
Why do we marvel at these things? Utterly insensitive, why do
90 we also prefer—like the blind—the heaviness of iron
and the magnitude of its mass over a little gold,
or instead of a precious pearl as if it were worthless?
     (Mt 13.45ff)
And why do we not seek the little grain of mustard
that is more precious than all visible things,

---

[5]οἱ ἐν αἰσθήσει νοερῷ τετιμημένοι λόγῳ. "Sense perception," αἴσθησις, might also be rendered as "consciousness." This term usually carries a sense of felt experience.

95 greater than creatures and invisible things?
    Why do we not give everything to receive it,
    and why do we even want to live without possessing it?
    Believe me, it is better to die many times, if it were possible,
    and possess only this, I mean the little mustard grain!
100 Alas for those who do not have it planted
    in the bosom of their soul, for they shall greatly hunger!
    Alas for those who do not see it growing
    because they shall stand naked like trees without leaves!
    Alas for those who do not believe in the word of the Lord,
105 that this grain becomes a tree and sends out shoots, (Mt 13.32)
    and they do not seek out the growth of this little
    grain in haste and vigilance of their mind each day,
    they shall suffer the loss of its work,
    like the servant who foolishly buried his talent. (Mt 25.18)
110 Truly I myself am also one of these, careless every day.
    But, O indivisible Trinity, O unity without mixing,
    O light of three persons, Father, Son, and Spirit,
    O first cause without beginning, O power of dominion,
    O light that has no name, for it is so utterly nameless,
115 O light, again having many names since you operate all things,
    O one glory and dominion, power, and kingdom,
    O light as one will, purpose, wish, and strength,
    have mercy, have pity on me the afflicted!
    For how would I not be afflicted, how would I not be grieved,
120 I who despise and neglect your so very great kindness,
    your great mercy, I the wretch who ignorantly and
    frivolously walk the way of your commands? (Ps 118.32)
    But even now have compassion, and now have mercy on me,
    and rekindle the fervor of my heart, my Christ,
125 which lets loose my miserable flesh, in
    sleep, and filling my stomach, and drinking much wine!
    These things also utterly quenched the flame of my soul,
    and dried up the fountain, the fount of tears,

for fervor begets fire, and the fire also begets fervor,

130   and from both, a flame is kindled, a fount of tears.
The flame grows streams, and the streams grow flames,
in which talk of divine things has taken me up,
and also concern for your commands and ordinances,
     (Ps 118.143)
vigilance takes repentance as a co-worker,

135   and they stood me in the middle of things present and future,
from whence suddenly I came outside visible things.
I fell in fear when I saw whence I had been rescued.
I saw the things to come, from afar but certainly real,
and when I desired to grasp these things, a fire of yearning was
     kindled,

140   and little by little a flame was ineffably seen,
at first in my mind, but then in my heart,
and tears gushed forth, the flame of divine yearning,
and the flame gave to me unspeakable sweetness with them.
And so having taken confidence in myself, as though it would
     never

145   be extinguished, for it burns well, I said, and I became
     negligent
in sleep and in filling my stomach. I was foolishly enslaved,
I lowered my guard and I desired wine more abundantly.
Though not intoxicated, satisfied nonetheless, immediately this
awesome wonder was quenched, desire in my heart,

150   this flame overtook even as far as heaven, and was burning
strongly within me, but not consuming
the essence of my organs like grass. (Is 40.6)
But—Oh the marvel!—it transformed the whole into flame,
and when the grass touched the flame it was not at all burned.
     (Ex 3.2)

155   What is more, the fire surrounding the grass
united with it and kept it entirely indestructible.
Oh power of divine fire, oh strange energy!

O you who shatter rocks and hills by fear alone,
and by your face, O Christ, my God.[6]

160 How do you mix grass with utterly divine essence,
my God who dwells in utterly unendurable light?
How, remaining unchanged, utterly unapproachable,
do you keep the essence of grass unburned?
And how do you change it completely yet keep it unchanged?

165 Though it remains grass, how is it light? But the light is not
        grass.
But you, the light, unite yourself to the grass without mixing,
and grass becomes light, immutably changed.
I can not bear to hide your marvel in silence, (Acts 4.20)
nor can I refrain from telling your divine plan,

170 the plan you have made with me, the profligate and lecherous.
And I cannot bear not to describe the inexhaustible wealth
of your benevolence fully to all, my redeemer![7]
For I want all the world to receive from your benevolence,
and that no one at all be left empty of it.

175 But first, O absolute monarch, shine again in me, (2 Cor 4.6)
abide in and illuminate my humble soul,
show to me clearly the face of your divinity,[8]
and reveal to me all of yourself invisibly, O my God!
For you are not wholly seen by me, but you are wholly revealed
        to me,

180 though you are inapprehensible, you also want to become
        entirely within my reach,
you are limitless to all, truly you become small,
both in my hand and on my lips
you are seen as a sweet and radiant breast,
flashing like lightning and turning. Oh strange mystery!

185 Give yourself to me so also now, so I may take my fill of you,

[6]Jdt 16.18; Ps 113.6–7.
[7]Eph 2.7; Ps 65.16.
[8]Ex 33.18; Ps 79.4.

so I may kiss you and embrace your
unspeakable glory, the light of your face, (Ps 4.7)
and I may be filled, and then give a share to all the others,
and having been transported I may come to you wholly
      glorified,
190 and by your light I also may become light and stand before
      you,
and then I shall be unconcerned about these many evils,
I shall be released from fear, and not turn away again.
Yes, give this to me, Master, yes, generously bestow this on me
you who have given freely everything else to me, the unworthy!
      (Rev 21.6)
195 For ‹I have› great need of this, and this is everything:
for if even now you are seen by me, if even now you are moved
      with compassion,
for if even now you illuminate and mysteriously teach me,
and you both shelter and protect me with your mighty hand,
      (Ex 33.22)
and you are present, and you chase away and destroy the
      demons,
200 and you subject all things to me, and provide me with
      everything,
and you fill me with all good things, O my God,
but none of this is of use to me, if you will not grant that
I pass the gates of death without shame.
If the prince of darkness were to come and he did not
205 see your glory with me, and he were not utterly ashamed,
if the dark one were not burned up by your unapproachable
      light,
and all the opposing powers with him
were not turned away when they see the sign of your seal,
      (Rev 9.4)
and I also were not to pass through with confidence in your
      grace, whole and

210 without trembling, and I were not to approach and to prostrate
          myself before you,
      of what use to me are the things that now happen in me?
      Truly none, but they kindle the fire for me all the more.
      For I am hoping to be both your servant and friend
      by participation in your goods and eternal glory.
215 If I were deprived of all these and at the same time I lost you
          yourself, my Christ,
      would not the suffering be worse for me than that of the
          unfaithful, (1 Tim 5.8)
      of those who have not known you, of those who have not seen
      your radiant light, and have not taken their fill of your
          sweetness?
      But if it should happen that the fulfilment of these pledges are
          for me, (Eph 1.14)
220 and I should receive the prizes, Savior,
      that you have promised to those, Christ, who believe in you,
          (Jn 7.38)
      then I also shall be happy and I will praise
      you, the Father, and Son, and the Holy Spirit,
      truly one God forever and ever. Amen.

Hymn 29

*That the divine realities appear only to those to whom God has been
wholly united through participation of the Holy Spirit.*

      From where do you come, how do you enter,
      I mean into my cell
      which is secured on all sides? (Jn 20.19)
      For this is strange,
5   and beyond words, and beyond my mind,
      that you happen within me, (Lk 17.21)
      suddenly whole and shining forth,

and seen radiant,
like a moon all of light.
10   This takes my understanding
and renders me speechless, my God.
I know that you are the one
who comes in order to enlighten
those who sit in darkness, (Lk 1.79)
15   and I am beside myself, and I am rendered
outside my senses[1] and beyond words,
because I see a strange wonder
surpassing all creation,
every nature, every world.
20   Nevertheless, now I shall tell everyone
what you oblige me to say:
O entire race of human beings,
of kings and of princes,
both wealthy and poor,
25   both monks and laity,
every tongue of the earthborn
hear me speaking now,
now I describe in full
the greatness of God's benevolence!
30   I sinned against him like no
other human being in the world.
Let not anyone suppose that
I say these things by humility.
For in truth I sinned
35   beyond all human beings.
To put it briefly,
I have committed every act
of sin and wickedness.
But still he has called me, I know,
40   and I obeyed at once.

[1]φρενῶν.

But where did you suppose
that I mean he called me to?
Did he call me to the glory of the world, (Mt 4.8)
or to pleasures, or to relaxation,
45   or then was it to wealth,
or the friendship of princes,
or to something else among visible things
here in this life?
Away with such blasphemy!
50   Rather, I said that he
called me to repentance,
and immediately I followed
the Master who called me. (Mt 4.21–22)
And so when he ran, I left in haste,
55   and so when he fled, I gave chase
like a dog pursuing a hare.
But when the Savior was removed
and hiding far away from me,
I myself did not despair,
60   nor did I turn backwards
as though having lost him. (Mt 24.18)
But in the place I found myself
I sat and wailed, (Ps 136.1)
crying and in turn inviting
65   the hidden Master to me.
And so thus he was seen by me when I was
rolling about and screaming;
he drew near to me.
When I saw him I leaped up,
70   and I rushed headlong to grasp him,
he quickly fled,
I myself ran vigorously,
and so often I ran and
overtook the hem of his garment.

75 He stood still a bit,
    I myself greatly rejoiced,
    and he flew away, and again
    I pursued, and thus
    going away, coming,
80 hiding himself, appearing,
    I did not turn back. (Lk 9.62)
    I did not shrink back at all,
    I did not give up running,
    I did not suppose that he was leading me astray,
85 or that he was thoroughly testing me, (Jas 1.13)
    but with all my strength, (Lk 10.27)
    but with all my power,
    I sought the One not seen,
    I looked round the roads
90 and fences where he might appear.
    And I was filled with tears,
    and I asked everyone
    if they ever saw him. (Song 3.1–3)
    But whom do you suppose
95 I mean that I asked?
    The wise of this world, (1 Cor 1.20, 27)
    or would you expect the learned?
    Indeed not, but the prophets,
    apostles, and fathers,
100 the wise in truth,
    those who possess
    this whole wisdom itself,
    this one who is himself
    Christ, the wisdom of God. (1 Cor 1.24)
105 And so with tears and
    and vehement yearning of my heart
    I asked them to tell me,
    wherever they saw him,

or in what sort of place,
110 or even in what manner.
     And when they told me
     I ran with all my power,
     I did not sleep at all,
     but I forced myself.
115 Thence when I saw my desire,
     he was seen just a bit by me.
     Seeing him, as I said before,
     I pursued him vigorously. (Phil 3.12)
     Therefore he saw that I
120 regarded all things as nothing, (Phil 3.8)
     that I reckoned from my soul
     that everything in the world,
     I mean with the world itself,
     and everyone in the world
125 was nonexistent in my perception,
     and when he saw me separated from
     the world by such a disposition,
     then he was entirely seen by all of me,
     he was wholly united to all of me,
130 he who is outside the world,
     and who carries the world
     with everything in the world,
     and holding together the visible
     with the invisible, using only his hand.
135 Therefore—listen to me—
     he meets me and lets himself be found.
     Whence or how he comes, I do not know.
     For how would I know (Jn 3.8)
     from whence he came, he whom no one
140 among humans has ever seen, (1 Tim 6.16)
     nor known where he is,
     where he shepherds, where he lies down? (Song 1.6)

For he is not wholly contemplated,
he is not understood fully,

145 and he dwells in unapproachable
light, and he is light, (1 Tim 6.16)
in three persons inexpressibly,
in uncircumscribable places,
my uncircumscribed God,

150 one Father, likewise the Son
with the divine Spirit,
one is the three and the three
are one God inexplicably.
For a word is not able

155 to express the inexpressible,
nor can the mind clearly understand.
For the things in us I can
scarcely express at all.
But to explain to you these things,

160 neither I nor any other
would be at all able to do so.
How is God outside everything,
in essence and nature,
in power and glory,

165 and how is he everywhere and in everything,
and how does he abide in the saints
in a manner more special than these
and, in a conscious way, does he pitch his tent in them?
        (Jn 1.14)
And how in essence is he

170 altogether beyond essence?
How is he embraced in their entrails,
he who holds together all creation?
And how does he shine in the heart, (2 Cor 4.6)
their fleshy and thick heart?

175 And how is he both within it

and also outside all things,
yet he fills all things, (Eph 4.10)
in night and in day
he shines, and is not seen?
180 Tell me, shall a human mind
understand all these things
or be able to tell them to you?
Indeed not, neither an angel
nor archangel could explain to you,
185 one could not expound
them with words.
And so only the Spirit of God
who is divine, knows these things, (1 Cor 2.11)
and understands since he alone is
190 naturally enthroned with
and coeternal with
the Son and the Father.
Therefore, for whom he will shine,
and to whom he would be richly united,
195 he shows all things inexpressibly, (Jn 14.26)
I tell you, he shows them by his work.
For just like the blind, if they will see,
at first they see the light,
and then all creation,
200 which is in the light—O wonder!—
so also one who is enlightened by the
divine Spirit in their soul at once
comes into participation
and contemplation of the light,
205 the light of God, and most certainly God,
who also shows everything,
or rather, whatever he commands,
whatever he wishes, whatever he wants.
Those whom he shall enlighten by his illumination, (2 Cor 4.6)

210   to *these* he will give to see
       things in the divine light.
       In proportion to their love, (Jn 14.15)
       and their keeping of the commandments
       do the enlightened ones see,

215   and they are initiated into the depth
       of divine and secret mysteries.
       Just as if one were to go into
       a dark house holding
       a torch in their hand,

220   or another were leading the way
       and holding the light,
       one would then see the things
       inside the house, so also
       the one who is illuminated

225   by the rays of the rational sun
       brightly sees things unknown
       to everyone else, and tells
       —though not all—whatever
       they can express in words

230   For who could ever reveal
       the things of the other world:
       what nature, how many, and what sort,
       things that are incomprehensible
       and invisible to everyone?

235   For the form of formless things,
       the size of things without measure,
       the beauty of things inconceivable,
       who shall know, how shall one measure,
       how shall one be able to tell fully?

240   And how would one sketch out with words
       the shapes of shapeless things?
       "Absolutely no way," you will tell me.
       But only those who contemplate

know these things.
245 On which account not by words, but by works
let us hasten to seek out,
to see, and to be taught
the wealth of divine mysteries (Col 1.27)
that the Master gives
250 to those who search diligently,
and who manifestly acquire
forgetfulness of the whole world
and of the affairs in the world.
Because one who seeks the divine things
255 by free choice of their entire soul, (Deut 4.29)
how shall they not truly
be unmindful of all things,
and acquire a mind naked
of all these, and at once
260 find themselves alone outside
everything? Those whom God alone sees
become solitary on his account,
and they renounce the world
and everything of the world.
265 The Alone having found the alone,
unites himself to them.
Oh awesome plan of salvation,
oh unspeakable kindness!
But do not talk about things hereafter,
270 do not inquire after nor seek them out!
For if the multitude of the stars, (Ps 146.4)
or if all the drops of rain,
or if the sand no one will be able to count, (Sir 1.2)
and also the other creatures'
275 magnitudes and beauties,
or their natures and arrangements,
or their causes, such as they are,

no one could be able
either to tell or to understand,
280 how would anyone be able
to express the Creator's compassion
that he displays to holy souls
with whom he is united?
For by all means he also deifies them
285 in a personal union.
Accordingly, one who wishes to speak
of the characters or the nature
of this deified soul,
her disposition, her thought,
290 or to describe to you everything
concerning her, one knows not how,
one would be attempting to present
to you through words the nature of God himself.
But it is not permitted
295 to seek out such things,
for those in the world
or living according to the flesh,
but only for those who receive them by faith alone (Heb 13.7)
and who imitate exactly the lives of all the saints
300 by tears, and by repentance,
and by the rest of the austerity,
by long-suffering of temptations,
and by running in order to transcend
the world, as was said by me,
305 and they shall find, like I said,
everything without exception.
And when they find, then they shall be dumbfounded,
and they will marvel and even
pray for me the wretched one,
310 that I may not be driven away from them,
rather that I may obtain these graces

which they also yearned to obtain,
and I also desire. And by yearning may
I impair and make blunt the yearning.
315 Have you ever heard such a thing?
For yearning ignites yearning,
and the fire increases the flame.
But in me it is not so,
but—I do not know how to say it—
320 the excess of passionate love[2]
quenches my passionate love.
For I do not passionately love, as much as I want,
but I reckon that I possess
no passionate love of God at all.
325 But seeking insatiably
to love passionately as much as I wish,
I destroy even what passionate love
of God that I have. O marvel!
It is like someone who has a treasure
330 and who is greedy; because
they do not possess everything
they think that they do not possess anything at all,
even if they possess much gold.
So also I suppose that I suffer.
335 I am miserable in this
because I do not yearn[3] as I wish, (Rom 7.15)
no matter how much I wish
I do not believe that I yearn at all.
And so to yearn as much as I wish
340 is a yearning beyond yearning,
and I force my nature
to love[4] beyond its nature.

[2] ἔρωτος.
[3] ποθῶ.
[4] ἀγαπῆσαι.

But when my nature becomes weak
it is also deprived of the strength
345   that it had acquired,
and paradoxically the passionate love
is mortified while living even more,
for it lives and flourishes in me.
How do I tell you that it flourishes?
350   I am at a loss for examples.
Only this shall I declare to you,
that everyone is incapable of
expressing such things in a word.
May God give such gifts to all
355   who seek them with repentance, (Jas 1.5)
may God who alone is truly
the giver of such graces
grant also to those who
mourn and wail,
360   and to those who well purify themselves
to enjoy such graces,
to those who come into participation
henceforth even in their senses,
and may they go to the hereafter with these graces, (2 Cor 5.8)
365   and rest in them,
and enjoy eternal life,
and through them be
found sharers of
unspeakable glory! Amen. (1 Pet 5.1)

Hymn 30

To one of his disciples. That the divine fire of the Spirit touches the souls purified by tears and repentance, and grasps them, and purifies them even more. The fire illuminates their members darkened by sin, and by cleaning their wounds, brings them to perfect healing so as to make them shine with divine beauty.

There is truly a divine fire,
the Master said that
he came in order to throw this fire
upon earth. Tell me, what sort of earth? (Lk 12.49)
5   Certainly upon the human beings,
upon those who think earthly things,
the fire he wanted and still desires
to ignite in everyone.
Listen and learn, child,
10   the depth of divine mysteries!
This divine fire therefore,
what type do you reckon it is?
Do you suppose it is visible,
or created, or graspable?
15   Indeed not. For you also are
an initiate of such fire,
and you certainly know that
it is ungraspable,
uncreated, and invisible,
20   without beginning, and immaterial,
utterly immutable,
likewise uncircumscribed,
inextinguishable, immortal,
in every way without limit,
25   outside of all creation,
things both material and immaterial,

visible and invisible, (Col 1.16)
bodiless and incarnate,
terrestrial, celestial, (Phil 2.10)
30   it is outside of all these
by its nature, by its essence,
yes, and even by its authority.
And so, tell me, in what kind of matter
shall this fire be thrown?
35   In souls who have
the most abundant mercy,
and before this, and along with it,
these souls obtain faith, and their
works make firm their faith.
40   The Master casts fire into these souls (Mt 25.1ff)
as though upon a lamp full
of oil and hemp,[1]
thus is that fire which the world
does not and cannot see.
45   (I mean by "the world" those who are in the world
and who think worldly thoughts.) (Phil 3,19)
And just as a lamp catches fire
—I speak to you in images perceptible to the senses—
when it touches the fire,
50   so also—understand that I speak spiritually—
the divine fire touches
and ignites souls.[2]
If it does not first touch, how will the fire ignite?
And if it is not thrown, how shall it touch?
55   Certainly and by all means impossible.
But when the lamp catches fire,
and clearly illuminates everyone, (Lk 11.33)

---

[1]Cf. *Hymn* 33.118ff.
[2]Lines 40 to 52 are a difficult construction made even more cumbersome by the parenthetic phrases.

and the oil should fail,
will not the lamp be extinguished?

60 Look at me, and another more important thing
that frightens me more than anything!
When my lamp burned brightly
in an abundance of oil,
with plenty of hemp,

65 a rat or some other animal came
and either overturned the lamp,
or little by little licked
and drank the oil,
and it ate the hemp,

70 and the lamp was extinguished.
And this is something most marvelous,
that the whole hemp
which is called a wick,
when it falls into the oil,

75 at once the fire is quenched,
and for me the lamp is
dark, not shining at all. (Lk 11.34–36)
Understand that the lamp is my soul,
and the oil is virtues,

80 and my mind is the wick,
and in it the divine fire
shines and illuminates
my soul, and at the same time illuminates
the whole house of my whole soul,

85 and all thoughts and considerations
in this house. (Mt 5.15)
Thus when this lamp shines,
if jealousy were to creep in,
or the passion of resentment,

90 or passionate love of vainglory,
or any other desire

for some pleasure or passion,
and it overturns the lamp
—that is to say, the intention of my soul—
95   or if it were to absorb the oil
—I mean the oil of virtues—
or otherwise ‹consume› the wick
which is my mind, as I said,
and possesses in itself the divine
100   light shining strongly, then
it may consume the wick with perverse thoughts,
or throw it all
into the oil within;
that is to say, into the consideration
105   of its acts of virtue,
and thence, falling into
self-conceit, the mind would be blinded.
And if because of these things
or perhaps because of something else
110   it happens that my lamp is extinguished, (Mt 25.8)
where then would you say to me that the fire
has gone or what does it become?
Does the fire remain in the lamp
or is it separated from the lamp?
115   What ignorance! What madness!
How is it possible that the lamp
burns without the fire,
or that the fire remains in the lamp
away from the fuel material?
120   The fire always yearns
and wishes to grasp the fuel material,
but it is our part by all means
to prepare the material in advance
and to supply them very eagerly,
125   and for us to equip ourselves

as lamps with mercy
and all sorts of virtues,
and to adjust properly
the wick of the mind
130   in order to touch the fire,
and to ignite it little by little,
and thus the wick remains
with those who have acquired the fire.
For otherwise—may no one be misled—
135   the fire is not seen, it is not seized,
it is not held together at all.
For, just as I said, the fire is
outside all creation,
but it becomes comprehensible by incomprehensible means
140   by a secret union,
and likewise circumscribed
in an uncircumscribed manner.
But do not seek these things at all,
neither by words nor theories,[3]
145   rather beg to receive fire
that teaches and shows all these
mysteries manifestly to those who
possess it, as well as things that are
inexpressibly more mysterious than these. (Jn 14.26)
150   If you wish, child, hear even
greater mysteries than these!
When the fire shines, as I said,
and it chases away the swarm
of passions, and it purifies
155   the house of your soul,
then the fire mingles with her without mixing,
and unites inexpressibly,
and unites essentially to the essence

[3]ἐπινοίαις.

of this soul, the whole by all means to the whole,
160   and little by little illuminates the soul;
     it utterly consumes and enlightens her,
     and—I do not know how to express it—
     the two become one,
     the soul with her Creator,
165   and in the soul the Creator
     is completely alone with the alone,
     he who embraces all creation
     in his palm.
     Do not doubt, this is the one who
170   with the Father and the Spirit
     is completely contained in one soul,
     and within himself God
     envelops the whole soul.
     Think, see, contemplate these things!
175   For I told you that the light is unendurable,
     unapproachable even for angels.
     This light that possesses the soul within itself,
     and yet dwells in the soul,
     and does not burn it completely.
180   Do you know the depth of mystery?
     A human being is small
     among visible creation, shadow and dust,
     yet can have all of God within,
     God, on whose finger
185   creation is suspended,
     and from whom everything has
     both life and movement, (Acts 17.28)
     every mind, soul, and reason[4]
     of all rational beings has existence from him.
190   But also the breath of irrational beasts
     and likewise the breath of all living creatures,

[4]λόγος.

of the rational and the perceptible,[5]
all have their being in him.
Those who possess him, whosoever shall possess him,
195 and bear him within them, (Lk 11.27)
and see his beauty,
how shall they endure the flame of desire,
how would they bear the fire of love,
how shall they not drop hot tears
200 from their heart,
how would they express these wonders,
and how shall they number these things
that are accomplished in them?
And yet, how shall one keep totally silent
205 when compelled to speak?
For one sees oneself in hell, (Lk 16.23)
I mean compared to the brilliance of the light,
for none of those
who sit there in hell
210 rather than in the shining divine light,
know themselves,
but they are in ignorance
of the gloom in which they are seized,
ignorant of their destruction, and of their death.
215 Nevertheless I say that this soul
sees the light shine within,
and perceives that it was
in a most terrible darkness,
and a most secure prison
220 of the deepest ignorance.
Then she sees where she lies,
where she is confined,
a place that is all mud,
a place filled full of unclean

[5]rational . . . perceptible = νοερῶν . . . αἰσθητῶν.

225 and poisonous reptiles,
and herself bound
and restrained with fetters,
both hands and feet, (Mt 22.13)
both squalid and filthy,
230 at the same time the soul has been wounded
by the bites of the reptiles
and her flesh swells,
and bears at the same time
with a multitude of worms.
235 Seeing these things, how shall the soul not tremble,
how will she not weep, how will she not cry out,
and fervently repent,
and beg to be rescued
from these most terrible fetters?
240 Thus everyone who sees these terrors
will groan, and lament,
and will want to fall in with
Christ who makes the light shine forth!
Therefore one who does these things, as I said,
245 and prostrates before him who gives light
—Pay close attention to what I shall say!—
he who enlightens me touches my fetters
and wounds with his hands,
and where his hand touches
250 or wherever his finger approaches
the fetters at once are released,
the worms are killed,
and the wounds vanish,
the filth disappears with them,
255 and the defilement of my flesh
becomes small, and there is complete healing
all at once on my flesh,
such that no one sees a scar

at all in any place,
260 rather God renders the spot
all resplendent
like the divine hand.
Strange marvel, my flesh,
I mean the essence of my soul,
265 yes, and of my body,
participates in divine glory
and flashes forth divine radiance. (1 Pet 5.1)
When I see this accomplished
in a member of my body,
270 how shall I not desire
and beseech that the whole of my body
be released from evils,
and likewise possess
the health and glory such as I said?
275 While I was doing so
with even greater fervor,
and I was dumbfounded
in proportion to these marvels,
the good Master himself
280 shifts his hand and goes around
the rest of my body,
and I see,
in the manner I mentioned before,
the rest of my body purified and
285 dressed in divine glory.
And so straight away, having been purified
and released from chains,
he gives to me his divine hand,
he raises me from the mud.
290 All of him enfolds me,
he falls upon my neck (Lk 15.20)
—Alas, how shall I bear these things?—

and he kisses me many times.
And when I had fainted
295 and lost all my strength
—Woe is me! How shall I write this?—
he lifted me upon his shoulder (Lk 15.5)
—O love, O kindness!
and he leads me out of hell, (Ps 29.4)
300 out of this place of nether-gloom,
and he leads me to another place,
whether to the world or the air,
I simply cannot say.
This I know: that a light
305 carries me, and holds me together,
and leads me to a great light,
this great, divine marvel,
not even the angels can describe
or speak of to each other
310 at all, so it seems to me.
And having arrived there,
he then shows me other things,
things in the light, I tell you,
rather, things from the light.
315 He gives to me a strange
renewal to contemplate,
a reformation to which he himself has reformed me,
and he released me from destruction,
and from death in my sense perception.
320 He set all of me free,
and gave to me immortal life,
and separated me
from the perishable world,
and everything in the world.
325 He dressed me in an
immaterial and radiant robe, (Lk 15.22)

likewise sandals,
and a ring, and a crown
incorruptible, and eternal,
330   and all foreign to things here below.
He made me intangible,
untouchable, O marvel,
and likewise invisible,
united to invisible things.
335   And so after having
rendered me like this, the Creator
led me into
a perceptible and bodily tent, (2 Cor 5.4)
and he enclosed me in it,
340   and he locked me up,
and having led me down into
the perceptible and visible world,
and he determined that I should live
and be with those in darkness,
345   I who had been released from darkness,
and that I should be confined with them,
I mean those who are in the mud.
Moreover, I am to teach them
and lead them to a knowledge
350   of the wounds that cover them,
and the chains that restrain them.
Having thus commanded, he went away.
And so having been left alone,
I mean in the darkness as before,
355   I was not satiated with the very things
that I said he gave to me,
the unutterable goods;
he had completely restored me,
made me completely immortal,
360   made me completely divine

    and rendered me Christ.
    But the deprivation of him
    made me forget all
    the blessings of which I had spoken,
365 and then seemed to have been deprived of.
    Because of this I was distressed
    as though stuck in my former evils.
    And sitting in the middle
    of my tent, as though enclosed
370 in a basket or in a jar, (Ex 2.6)
    I cried, I wailed very much,
    not at all looking outside.
    For I was seeking him,
    him whom I desired, (Song 3.1)
375 for whom I had passionate love, by whose
    youthful beauty I was wounded.[6]
    I was enflamed and burning,
    all of me set on fire.
    And so was I living thus,
380 thus also I wept,
    and at the same time melting away,
    and flogged terribly,
    and crying out in anguish,
    he heard my screaming
385 from incomparable heights,
    he stooped down and saw me. (Ps 101.20)
    He had compassion on me, and again
    deemed me worthy to behold
    that which is invisible to everyone,
390 to see as much as is accessible for a human being.
    Seeing him I was amazed,
    having been confined in my house,
    and shut up in a jar,

[6]Ps 44.2; Song 5.8.

and being in the middle of darkness,
395 I say to you, between heaven and earth.
I use a sensual[7] term when I call these things
darkness because they heavily cover
all human beings
who are in them,
400 the darkness covers even their minds,
minds that are mingled with sensual things.
Nevertheless, while in these things I saw
him who preexists, as I said,
and who is now spiritually[8] outside everything,
405 and I was amazed, I was astonished,
I was frightened, and I rejoiced,
and understood the wonder,
how he is outside everything,
while I am within everything.
410 Alone I see him seeing me,
I do not discern where he is,
how great he is, or what nature,
or what kind, or whom I see,
or how I see, or what I see.
415 Yet seeing what I have seen,
and wailing because I cannot
know this manner,
nor understand fully,
nor can I perceive just a bit,
420 how the one whom I see sees me.
Again I saw him within
my house and within my earthen jar
where suddenly he became whole,
ineffably united to me,
425 unspeakably joined,

[7]αἰσθητῶς.
[8]νοερῶς.

and mixed in me without mixing,
like the fire in the iron itself,
and the light in the crystal,
and he made me like a fire,
430   and made me like light,
and I became that
which I had seen before
and had contemplated from afar,
and I do not know how to explain to you
435   the paradox of his manner,
for I was not able to know,
nor do I know now by any means,
how he entered, how he was united.
And the one who was united, how shall I tell you
440   who is it who was united to me,
and to whom was I myself united?
I tremble and I am frightened, lest perchance
if I tell you, you may doubt, and then
you might fall into blasphemy
445   because of ignorance, and you might destroy
your soul, my brother.
Nevertheless, I and he
to whom I was united, have become one,
so what shall I call myself?
450   The God who is double in nature,
who is one hypostasis,
has rendered me double.
And having made me double,
he has supplied for me
455   also a double name, as you see.
See the distinction!
I am a human being by nature,
and God by grace.
See what sort of grace I mean,

460 a union with him,
      both perceptibly, and rationally,
      both essentially, and spiritually!
      On the one hand, I have expressed
      the rational union in different and
465 manifold ways, but I say the perceptible
      union belongs to the mysteries.
      For having been purified by repentance,
      and by rivers of tears,
      and having partaken of the deified
470 body as God himself,
      I myself become God
      by this ineffable union.
      See the mystery!
      Therefore the soul and the body
475 to say it again
      out of great joy,
      are one in two essences.
      Therefore body and soul are one and two
      partaking of Christ
480 and drinking his blood,
      united to both essences,
      and likewise to both
      natures of my God;
      they become God by participation,
485 and they are called by the same name,
      by his name;
      they have participated in God's essence.[9]
      And so it is said that charcoal is fire,
      and iron is black;
490 when it is burned it looks like fire.
      So if it appears as such,
      it would also be called as such,

[9] οὗ οὐσιωδῶς μετέσχον, literally: "of whom they have partaken essentially."

seen as fire, it is called fire.
If you have not known yourself
495   as such, do not doubt those who
tell you about such things,
but seek from the whole
of your heart and you shall receive
a pearl or a drop, (Mt 13.45)
500   or like a grain of mustard, (Mt 13.31)
a seed like a divine spark. (Lk 8.5)
How shall you seek what I tell you?
Listen and practice with haste,
and you shall find in no time.
505   Take a clear image for me,
the image of stone and iron,
for certainly there is in them
the nature of fire,
but it is not seen at all.
510   But yet, when they are struck together
they continually send out
sparks of fire and they are
immediately seen by everyone.
Nevertheless, they do not burn
515   unless they take hold of wood.
But when one little spark out of them
unites with the wood, little by little
it enkindles the whole wood,
and the flame is raised upward,
520   and it illuminates the house,
and chases out the darkness,
and makes everyone see,
everyone who is in the house. (Mt 5.15)
Have you seen the marvel? Then tell me.
525   Before being continually struck,
how will they send out sparks?

And without a spark, how
will the wood ignite of itself?
Before it ignites, how will it illuminate,
530 how will it chase out the darkness,
how will it provide for you to see?
"No way," you will certainly say to me,
"can that ever happen."
Therefore may you also be eager
535 to do likewise, and you shall receive
—What do I tell you that you shall receive?—
a spark of divine nature
that the creator compared
to a priceless pearl,
540 and to a grain of mustard.
And what do I tell you to do?
Listen carefully my child.
Let your soul and body take
the place of the stone and the iron,
545 but let the mind, like a master
of the passions, meditate on
virtuous practices
and thoughts pleasing to God.
And grasping the body like stone
550 and the soul like iron
in his rational hands,
let him draw and lead
them to deeds with violence.
For the kingdom of heaven
555 is also subject to violence. (Mt 11.12)
What sort of deeds do I tell you about?
Vigilance and fasting,
ardent repentance,
rainstorms of tears, and remorse,
560 continual remembering of death,

and unceasing prayer,
and patient endurance of all sorts
of trials that come upon you.
Before all these, silence,
565 and deep humility,
and perfect obedience,
and cutting out one's own will.
And so the meditating soul
by always embracing
570 these and other such virtues
makes your mind at first
receive illuminations,
but this is quickly extinguished
because it has not yet been threshed
575 in order to ignite quickly.
But when the divine darts
also ignite the heart,
then it illuminates the heart,
and purifies the mind,
580 and raises it to the heights,
and leads it up to heaven,
and unites it to the divine light.
How, tell me, will you be purified
before you do what I have told you?
585 And before you have been purified,
how will your mind receive
the divine illuminations?
And how, tell me, from whence,
from what other means shall the divine fire, (Lk 12.49)
590 by falling into your heart,
light up and
ignite it, and burn,
and unite it, and join,
and make the creature

595   inseparable with the creator?
       "Absolutely never," you will say to me,
       "shall this be possible
       for anyone of those born
       or yet to be begotten."
600   But do not ask me about the things hereafter!
       For if you have been united to the light,
       the light itself shall teach you all things, (Jn 14.26)
       and shall reveal all,
       and shall give a glimpse,
605   as much as is fitting for you to learn.
       Besides, it is impossible
       for you to learn these things by words.
       Glory to the Lord forever. Amen.

Hymn 31

Concerning theology, and that the divine nature is unfathomable and by all means incomprehensible to human beings.

       Lord, our God, Father, Son, and Spirit,
       you are without visible shape in your form, and all-beautiful in
            appearance,
       your impossible beauty obscuring all vision,
       for you are beautiful beyond the sight of all things.
5   You are seen as measureless in size by those whom you wish,
       in essence beyond essence, unknown even to angels.
       That you are, they know from your energies,
       thence you called yourself God, the one truly being. (Ex 3.14)
       We say that this is your essence, we call this hypostasis.[1]

---

[1]"your οὐσία, we call this ὑπόστασις." Prior to the Arian controversy ὑπόστασις was synonymous with οὐσία, but was then given a technical meaning akin to πρόσωπον—that is "person" or "personal reality." Because of its technical sense, and to distinguish ὑπόστασις from πρόσωπον, I have chosen to transliterate ὑπόστασις

10   For that which has neither essence nor hypostasis does not
          really exist,
      because of this we boldly say that you have essence,
      we say that you have hypostasis,[2] which no one has ever seen,
          (Jn 1.18)
      God in three hypostases, one origin without beginning.
      But otherwise how dare we to call you essence
15   or to glorify three distinct hypostases in you?
      But who will understand fully what sort of union ‹you have›
      if the Father is in you and you are in your Father, (Jn 17.21)
      and from him your Holy Spirit proceeds, (Jn 15.26)
      and you yourself, the Lord, are your Spirit,
20   and my Lord and my God, you are called Spirit,[3]
      and your Father both is and is called Spirit? (Jn 4.24)
      And none of the angels or human beings has ever seen you,
          (1 Tim 6.16)
      no one has contemplated these things, or knows the way,
      how would one say, and how would one express, how would
          one dare to proclaim
25   division, or union, or confusion, or mixing, or even combining,
      how say the one is three, or the three is one?
      So on account of this, Master, from what you said, one believes,
      from what you taught, every believer praises your power,
      since everything concerning you is in every way ungraspable,
30   unknowable, and not to be revealed to all who were created by
          you.
      For even your existence is incomprehensible,
      because by nature you are uncreated, but likewise you have
          begotten.
      And how shall a creature know the manner of your existence,

rather than translate it. In lines 9 and 10 Symeon seems to use οὐσία and ὑπόστασις as
synonyms, then in line 15 he begins to use ὑπόστασις in the sense of "person."
      [2]ἐνυπόστατον λέγομεν. That is: "we say [that you are] self-existent." The point
being that we say God has existence even though it is unlike any existence we know.
      [3]2 Cor 3.17; Jn 20.28.

or the begetting of your Son, God and Logos,
35   or the procession of your divine Spirit,
in order to know also your union, and to look upon your
          separation,
and to clearly understand the form of your essence?
No one has ever seen any of these mysteries of which I speak,
for it is not possible for another to become God by nature
40   in order to be able to examine also your nature,
essence, shape and form, likewise your hypostasis.
But you yourself are in yourself, you alone are Trinity God,
you alone know yourself, your Son and Spirit, (Mt 11.27)
and you are known by them alone since they share your
          nature.
45   But other beings, just as they see clearly the rays
of the perceptible sun and they perceive them brightly
when sitting in their house, they see the rays beaming in,
but they do not see the sun itself,
so also the light of your glory, so also your illuminations,
50   and those who seek you from their soul are deemed worthy to
          see
them in an enigma and with a purified mind. (1 Cor 13.12)
And you, what sort, what kind you are in essence,
or how you have once begotten and you continually beget,
yet you are not separated from the one who is begotten from
          you, but he is
55   whole in you, he who fills all things with his divinity,
          (Eph 4.10)
and you, Father, remain entirely in the Son himself,
and you have the divine Spirit processing from you,
‹the Spirit› who knows and fills all things, being God in
          essence,
and not separated from you, for he also gushes forth from you.
60   You are the fountain of good things, and your Son is all good,
he distributes the goods to all through the Spirit worthily,

compassionately, benevolently to both angels and human
>   beings.
None of the angels and no human being has ever seen
>   (1 Tim 6.16)
or known the nature of your existence, for you are not created.
65   But you have created all things by your commandment alone.
65a And so how can the things you created know you?
How you beget your Son, how you perpetually flow forth,
how your divine Spirit proceeds from you,
yet you do not ever beget ‹the Spirit›, having begotten ‹the Son›
>   once and for all,
and though you flow forth, how do you not suffer emptying or
>   diminishment?
70   For you remain beyond all fullness,
unceasing beyond all, whole in the whole world,
the visible, the rational,[4] yet again outside everything,
not receiving any addition, nor any defect at all.
You are entirely unmoved, remaining always thus.
75   Therefore by your energies you are in perpetual motion,
for you also possess, Father, incessant work. (Jn 5.17)
And your Son accomplishes the salvation of all,
and he provides, and perfects, and sustains, and nourishes,
he vivifies, and he preserves in the Holy Spirit.
80   For whatever the Son sees the Father doing, (Jn 5.19)
these things also the Son in like manner brings about, as he has
>   said.
And thus being unmoved, yet perpetually moving,
how is it that you are neither moved, nor standing, nor again
>   sitting,
but always sitting, always fully standing?
85   And while standing you are always being moved,
never changing place, for where would you go?
As was said, you fill all, you are beyond all,

[4]νοητῷ.

to what other sort of place or location would you move to?
But you do not stand, for you are bodiless.
90 You were simple, filling all things, in every way formless,
immaterial, uncircumscribed, completely inapprehensible.
And how would we say that you sit, or again that you stand,
and how shall we say that you sit, or on what kind of throne,
        (Is 66.1)
you who hold heaven and earth in your hand,
95 and you who rule all things under the earth by your power?
What sort of throne or what manner of house would contain
        you,
or how or where is it built, or on what kind of foundations,
and what sort of pillars is it raised, who shall fully understand?
Away with the human beings and all created nature
100 that would dare to enquire after such mysteries of God
before they are enlightened, before they are illuminated, before
        they see divine things
and become seers of the mysteries of Christ,
mysteries that when Paul saw them he was not able to express
        them at all, (2 Cor 12.2–4)
nor Elijah before him, nor the great Moses,[5]
105 but even Moses himself was deigned worthy to learn and
to express to others only the commandments and wishes of
        God.
But concerning God himself, he was deigned worthy to hear,
to learn, or to be taught nothing more at all,
except that God is he who is Creator of all things, (Ex 3.14)
110 maker and upholder of all that has been created.
And we, the all-wretched ones, who are confined by darkness,
and who are entirely darkness by our enjoyment of pleasures,
and we who are ignorant of ourselves, where and how we are
        overpowered,
we who are buried by passions, who are blind and dead,

[5] 1 Kgs 19.9ff.; Ex 19.1ff.

115 we who search out the one who is truly without beginning,
         uncreated God,
     who alone is immortal, invisible to all,
     we speak of God as though we saw him clearly,
     we who are separated from God.
     For if indeed they were united to him, they would never dare
120 to speak about him, seeing that everything of him
     is unspeakable and incomprehensible.
     But not only things about him, but even most
     of his works are unknown to everyone.
     For who would explain how from the beginning he moulded
         me,
125 or with what sort of hands did he, who is utterly bodiless, take
         up dust, (Gen 2.7)
     and, not having a mouth like us, how did he blow into me,
     and how did his breath become for me an immortal soul?
         (1 Cor 15.45)
     And from clay, tell me, how bones, and how nerves,
     how muscles, and how my veins, how skin, how hair,
130 how eyes, and how ears, how lips, how a tongue,
     how organs of speech, and hardness of teeth
     all clearly render an articulate word by the Spirit?[6]
     From matter both dry and moist, both hot and cold,[7]
     by a mixture of opposites he rendered me a living being.
135 And so how is the mind fettered to flesh, and how does the
         flesh adhere
     to the immaterial mind without mixing, without confusion?
     And without mingling, how do mind and soul bring forth the
         reason,[8]
     I refer to the immanent reason, and likewise
     they remain undivided, unchanged, utterly unmixed?

---

[6]"Spirit" (πνεύματι) in this context could be rendered "by the breath [of God]."
[7]These are the four elements of ancient physics.
[8]λόγον.

140 And so knowing these, brothers, to be unexplained
and incomprehensible to all, these things that pertain to us,
how do we not tremble before the one who made us this way
    out of non-being,
nor fear to consider, or to examine, or to speak of
things that are beyond our reason, beyond our mind?
145 But since we are creatures, from now on may we fear the
    Creator,
and search out his commandments alone,
and hasten to observe them with all our strength, (Jn 14.21)
if you would wish also to become heirs of life! (Titus 3.7)
But if you despise his ordinances,
150 and you disregard his wishes, as he has said,
and you disobey him in even one word, (Mt 5.19)
then neither glory, nor dignity, nor wealth of the world,
nor stupid knowledge of exterior learning,
nor organization, nor composition of eloquent language,
155 nor any other affairs and goods on earth
will then provide any help whatsoever,
when my God will judge everything and everyone.
But the word of the Master that was neglected by us
will then stand against the face of each one
160 and condemn everyone who has not kept it. (Jn 12.48)
For the word is not idle, but is the living word (Heb 4.12)
of the living God who remains forever and ever. (Is 40.8)
Hereafter the judgment shall be just as I said,
at once, alas, when the commandment comes
165 proving that one is unfaithful or by all means faithful,
that one is obedient[9] or disobedient to the Master's words,
that one has been attentive or negligent,
and thus the unjust will be separated from the just, (Mt 13.49)
the disobedient from those who truly submitted to Christ,

---

[9]πειθήνιον usually has an active sense, i.e. "persuasive." But it is taken here in the
passive sense to contrast ἀπειθῆ, "disobedient."

170 those who now love the world, from the friends of God,
and the heartless from the compassionate,
and at the same time the merciless from the merciful, and they
shall all stand
stripped of wealth, and honor, and power which they enjoyed
in the world, (Heb 4.13)
and, alas, they shall condemn themselves.
175 Having become self-condemned by their own works,
(Titus 3.11)
they shall hear: "Depart, both small and great,
you who have not obeyed me the benevolent master!"
Master, may we be rescued from this just condemnation
and may we possess the portion of your sheep, O Logos,
(Mt 25.33)
180 as a gift, since we have no hope of salvation
by works, we who are even now condemned forever!

Hymn 32

That the esteemed of the earth and the haughty in riches are led astray regarding the shadow of visible things. But those who have despised present things are in right participation of the divine Spirit.

Seeing me, Master, reviled by the faithful,
as one who both deceives and is led astray
because I say that I have received the Holy Spirit
by your benevolence and by the prayers of my father,[1]
5 have mercy and freely give reason, knowledge, and wisdom,
so that all who are set against me may know
that your divine Spirit speaks within me!
Grant that I may speak, as you have said, give also to me, as
you promised

---

[1] I.e., Symeon Eulabes.

Savior, ‹words› which no one will be able to contradict or
    oppose.[2]
10 For you are the giver of all good things.
Christ, even if they say I am deceived, I your servant
shall never be thus persuaded, when I see you my God,
and I look upon your immaculate and divine face,
and when I receive from it your divine illuminations,
15 and the eyes of my mind are illuminated in spirit.
Do not allow, O God, everyone who presently trusts
in you to wander the destructive wandering, that is the
    wandering
caused by not believing that even now you illuminate everyone
enlightening them with the rays of your divine divinity.
20 For you are rich in pity, we are rich in our sins.
You dwell in unapproachable light, but we all dwell in
    darkness. (1 Tim 6.16)
You are outside creation and we are within creation.
But most of us are outside creation,
for in their senses they are utterly lacking perception,
25 and being unnatural they are outside of everything,
seeing they do not see, looking they do not perceive, (Mt 13.13)
and they are not able to comprehend the marvels
of God in the senses of their minds,[3] but they are outside the
    world,
or rather in the world like corpses, and before death,
30 and before their departure, they are held down in lowest hell.
And so they are truly those of whom the Scripture speaks,
the famous, the wealthy, those who are haughty to everyone,
    (1 Cor 4.10)
and those who suppose that they are something among such
    types, (Gal 6.3)
yet at the same time they cannot see their own shame.

[2]Mt 10.20; Lk 21.15.
[3]senses of their minds = ἐν νοερᾷ αἰσθήσει.

35 For even if they possess the wisdom of the world within
         themselves, (1 Cor 1.20)
   and possess glory like a garment, they have set up their
   empty self-conceit like a tent for their deceived hearts,
   and indeed having dressed themselves in self-conceit, they
         dwell in it,
   as though sitting in the depths of deepest hell,
40 and they know not God, they know not the world,
   nor all the Creator's creations in the world. (Rom 1.20)
   For who will know the Creator before they see creation
   with reason like a rational person, and rationally in the mind,
   and observe the Creator rationally with their rational senses?[4]
45 Who? The one who contemplates spiritually through the divine
         Spirit,
   the one who is mystically enlightened and guided at the same
         time.
   Would such a one not come to a knowledge of their maker
         obscurely?
   For thus one shall be deemed worthy to receive
   the purified and more clear knowledge like all Scripture says.
         (Mt 5.8)
50 The impassioned, like I said, those who bear madness
   like a garment, having put on self-conceit like glory,
   take pleasure in laughing at the others.
   And they play in the shadows the way puppies do.
   If one throws to them a nut and it rattles as it rolls,
55 they leap upon it, grab it, take it in their mouth,
   and with it roll about, and frolic about.
   And if someone were to drag before their feet the cord of a
         whip,
   then they twist into a ball, and fall, and hold their feet up in the
         air,

---

[4]ἐν λόγῳ οἷα λογικός, ἐν νοῖ νοερῶς δέ, καὶ ἐν αἰσθήσει νοερᾷ νοερῶς κατο-
πτεύων.

and they become agents of laughter
60   for all the people who look at their falling.
So in this way these people also senselessly gladden
the demons in their personal actions and likewise in their
        dispositions.
Anyway, tell me when I ask, how, as you see it,
will such people as these explain the mysteries of God to
        others? (Ps 74.3)
65   And will they be enlightened at all, and how would they give a
        share
of the light of knowledge, or whether they
would offer a proper judgment justly in a true decision?
        (Hos 10.12)
I mean those who are vested in darkness like a garment,
who are out of touch with their senses, corpses in the middle
        of life.
70   But, O you lovers of God, listen to true
and wondrous sayings, which the mouth of the Lord
has spoken in anticipation and even now speaks to all!
If you do not reject glory, if you do not cast away wealth,
if you do not take off empty self-conceit completely,
75   if you do not become the last of all by your deeds,[5]
and even in your very thoughts, and better still in your
        intentions,
and believe yourself to be the last of all,
then you will not acquire streams of tears, nor purification of
        the flesh,
nor will you look at how these things are accomplished.
80   Henceforth, bewail yourselves, repent hereafter,
henceforth pour forth fervent tears daily,
so that you will clean out the rational eyes of your heart,
so that you may gaze upon the light shining in the world,

[5]Mt 19.30; Mk 10.44.

that shining cries out and shouts: "I am the light of the world.
   (Jn 8.12; 9.5)
85   I was, I am, and I shall be, and I want to be seen!
   For it is for this I have come bodily into the world, (Mk 1.38)
   I who am one, became double and likewise I remain one,
   so that those who faithfully prostrate and worship me, the
      visible God,
   and those who keep my commandments are
90   invisibly illuminated, and mentally[6] initiated into the glory
   of my awesome divinity, and of the flesh I have taken on,
   and they contemplate mystically the duality of my natures,
   and they may then praise me without doubt as the one God.
   For otherwise it is not possible to understand my divine plan
      properly,
95   nor to understand my condescension, nor to fear me,
   nor to prostrate and to worship me as God in the form of a
      human being, (Phil 2.7)
   and yet I remain inexpressibly God.
   I am the one who has become two, indivisible in hypostasis,
      not in nature.
   And so I myself am one God, and a perfect human being,
100   complete, perfect in all parts, flesh, soul, mind, and reason,
   entirely human and God in two essences,
   likewise double in natures, double in energies,
   and double in wills, in one hypostasis,
   at the same time both God and human, I am one of the Trinity.
105   Those who believe and who understand me to be thus
   by purifying themselves with zeal and repentance,
   and those who are able to contemplate with a pure heart,
      (Mt 5.8)
   and to be mentally initiated into my divine plan
   shall love me from their whole heart, (Mt 22.37)
110   and these also shall keep all of my commandments,

[6]νοερῶς.

astonished at my boundless compassion,
these shall be united with me and shall be partners in the glory
of my Father forever and ever." Amen. (1 Pet 5.1)

Hymn 33

*Concerning theology, that those who keep themselves according to the
divine image trample under foot the wicked powers of the prince of
darkness, but the others who have an impassioned life are conquered
and ruled by him.*

The Father is light, the Son is light, the Holy Spirit is light.
    (1 Jn 1.5)
Watch what you say, brother, watch lest you go astray!
For the Three are one light, one, not separated,
but united in three persons without confusion.
5   For God is wholly undivided by nature
and in essence he is truly beyond all essence.
He is not split in power, nor in form, nor in glory,
nor in appearance, for he is contemplated entirely as simple
    light.
In these the persons are one, the three hypostases are one.
10   For the Three are in the one, or rather the Three are one,
the Three are one power, the Three are one glory,
the Three are one nature, one essence, and one divinity.
And these are the one light that illuminates the world, (Jn 1.9;
    8.12)
not the world, perish the thought, not this visible world
15   —for the visible world has not known him, nor is it
able to know, nor can the friends of the world,
for the one who loves the world is an enemy of God,[1]
but we call "the world" that which God has made human
according to his image and likeness, (Gen 1.26)

---

[1]Jn 1.10; 1 Cor 2.14; Jas 4.4.

20   because one is adorned[2] with virtues, one rules terrestrial
         beings,
     just as God has authority over the universe,
     so also one reigns over the passions according to this image,
     and subjugates demons, the craftsmen of evils, (Lk 10.17)
     and tramples underfoot the dragon, the primeval, the huge[3]
25   dragon like a common sparrow. And how? Listen child!
     This fallen prince immediately found himself in darkness
     because he was deprived of the light; he is now in darkness
     with all those who fell with him from heaven; (Lk 10.18;
         Is 14.12)
     he reigns in it— certainly in the darkness I say—
30   over demons and humans who are held in the darkness.
     Every soul who does not see the light of life shining
     both in the day and night is punished by the prince of
         darkness:
     wounded, subdued, dragged, and enchained,
     and stabbed daily by the darts of pleasure.
35   Even if the soul seems to resist, even if she seems not to fall,
     but still she always has an irreconcilable war with him
     in much sweat, toil, trouble, and hardship.
     But every soul who contemplates the divine light,
     from whence the evil prince has fallen, despises the evil one,
40   and once enlightened by the unapproachable light itself,
     then the soul tramples underfoot the prince of darkness like a
         leaf
     fallen on the ground from a high tree.
     For she is in darkness where he has power and authority,
     but in the light he becomes an utterly dead corpse.
45   And when you hear the word light, note what kind of light that
         I tell you of,
     do not suppose that I mean the light of the sun!

---

[2]κοσμεῖται. This is a pun on κόσμος, "world."
[3]Ps 90.13; Rev 12.9.

For you also see in this light many human beings
sinning like me, terribly flogged,
falling, and foaming at midday,
50 and suffering invisibly from wicked spirits,
and while the sun shines, no more of it
is any help to those given over to the demons.
Therefore I do not speak to you of the light of the perceptible
          sun,
nor that of the day—far from it!—nor in any way of a lamp,
55 nor of the many stars, nor the light of the moon. (1 Cor 15.41)
I certainly do not insinuate to you that the effulgence
of any other visible light has such energy.
For perceptible lights enlighten only perceptible eyes,
and they illuminate and provide only to see
60 perceptible things, but not rational things.[4]
Therefore, all who see only perceptible things
are blind with respect to the rational eyes[5] of their heart.
And so the rational eyes of the rational heart
ought to be illuminated by a rational light.[6]
65 For if someone who has had the pupils of their body put out
is completely in the dark, not knowing where they are,
then how much more shall one be darkened who has
the eye of their soul blinded, and will they not be
almost dead in body, and in practice, and in spirit?
70 Then think precisely what sort of light I tell you of!
For I do not tell you of faith, I do not tell about
the practice of works, nor repentance, nor fasting by any
          means,
certainly not holy poverty, nor wisdom, nor knowledge,
not even teaching. For this light is none of these,
75 neither light nor efflux of light do I mean,

---

[4]τὰ νοητά.
[5]τὰ νοερὰ ὄμματα.
[6]rational = νοερὰ . . . νοερᾶς . . . νοερῷ.

nor external piety, nor a humble and
shabby appearance. For all these are practice
and fulfillment of the commandments, if they are perfected
and fulfilled well, as the Creator himself commands.

80 Tears are poured out in many ways
and they are either beneficial, or, more often, they do harm.
So tears of themselves are utterly unprofitable.
Keeping vigil certainly does not belong to monks alone,
but even the common people engage in works,

85 and weaving women, goldsmiths, and metal smiths
stay awake more than most monks,
and for this reason we say that none among
all of these virtuous practices is called the light.
And even if all these practices and virtues are brought together

90 without fail into one, still they are not the divine light.
For all human practices stand apart from the light,
and indeed when these practices are fulfilled by our own
    means
they are said to be light, according to us, for others
living in wickedness. These practices also lead others to good,

95 and what is darkness in me and what blinds me
becomes light for my neighbor and illuminates those who see.
And so that you will not suspect that I speak to you
    paradoxically,
listen and I shall tell you the solution of an enigmatic riddle.
Perhaps I fast on your account, so that I am seen to be fasting,
    (Mt 6.16)

100 and this is an incentive in my eyes,
and this is certainly a beam stuck into the middle of my eyes,
    (Mt 7.3)
and you are illuminated when you see me, if you do not
    condemn me,
rather if you blame yourself for gluttony.
For by this you are guided to self-control of the stomach,

105 and you learn to despise conspicuous wantonness.
    Again I put on cheap and ragged clothes, (Mk 6.9)
    and wearing only one tunic in every circumstance, I suppose as
        I walk around
    that I pursue glory and praise from all who see me,
    and by them I am seen as another new apostle,
110 and this becomes for me the cause of all damage,
    and certainly becomes darkness and a thick cloud in my soul.
    But this illuminates and teaches the crowds that see me
    to despise self-adornment, to despise also wealth,
    and to cling to worthless and rough clothing,
115 which is also truly the garment of apostles.
    And truly all the remaining practices of virtue
    are practices outside the light, works without splendor.
    For if all of them are brought together at one time, like I said,
    and the virtuous practices become one,
120 if it is possible for them all to occur in one human being,
    then they become like a lamp deprived of light.
    For as we do not say that fire is coals alone,
    nor again is the wood charcoal or flames,
    so also neither all faith, nor works, nor practices,
125 nor fulfilling the commandments are worthily said to be
    fire, flame, or divine light, for truly they are not.
    But we say that they are able to receive the fire, and to approach
        the light,
    and to be ignited by an unspeakable union,
    this is the praise and the fame of virtues.
130 And on account of this all askesis and all practices
    are accomplished by us so that we may share in
    the divine light like a lamp, like one candle
    the whole soul may cast her light before the unapproachable
        light. (1 Tim 6.16)
    Or rather, like a papyrus dipped into a candle
135 so a soul increasing in every virtue

is wholly ignited by the divine light, insofar as she will be able
    to see,
so will she contain as much light as she brings into her house,
and then the virtues are illuminated as they participate
in divine light, and they are called light,
140 or rather they are themselves light since they have been
       commingled with light.
And the light shines all around the soul herself and the body,
and truly shines on the one who first possessed it,
and then on all the rest who are in the darkness of life. (Lk 1.79)
Enlighten us, O Christ, in the All-Holy Spirit,
145 and make us heirs of the kingdom of heaven
with all your saints, now and unto the ages. Amen. (Jas 2.5)

Hymn 34

*That the union of the All-Holy Spirit with purified souls happens in
clear sense awareness—that is to say, in full knowledge, and the Holy
Spirit renders the purified souls in whom he dwells luminous like himself and makes them into light.*

The Invisible is by all means separate from the visible things,
and he who first made them is separate from his creatures,
the Imperishable from the perishable, and darkness from the
    Light,
but they were mixed when God came down.
5 For then my Savior united these extremes,
but the blind have not seen the union, and the dead
say that they have had no sensation[1] of this whatsoever,
and yet they suppose that they live and see—oh ultimate
    madness!—
and the unbelievers say: "No one has known

---

[1]αἴσθησιν.

10   or experienced this by experience, nor seen it with their
          senses,[2]
     but it happens only by report and by teaching of words alone."
     But, O my Christ, teach me to say something in answer to
          these remarks,
     and to draw these people from their great ignorance and
          faithlessness,
     and to give freely to see you, Light of the world! (Jn 8.12)
15   Listen and understand, fathers, the divine words,
     and know the union that happens in knowledge,
     and in full sense awareness, by experience, and by seeing![3]
     God is invisible, and certainly we are visible.
     And if God himself is united to the visible by his will,
20   then their union happens in knowledge.
     But if you would say that this happens unknowingly and
          without sense awareness,
     then certainly it is a union of the dead and not a union of Life
          to the living. (Jn 14.6)
     God is the creator of creatures, but we of course are creatures.
     And so if God who had created has come down and
25   united himself to the creature, then the creature becomes like
          the Creator.
     Certainly one would have sense awareness of true
          contemplation
     because the creature is ineffably united to the creator.
     But if we will not grant this, then our faith has utterly perished,
          (1 Cor 15.14)
     and our hope for things to come has utterly vanished,
30   and there shall be no resurrection nor general judgment.
     And since, as you say, the creatures without sense awareness
     are united to their Maker, knowingly understanding nothing,

[2] αἴσθησει.
[3] knowledge . . . sense-awareness . . . experience . . . seeing = γνώσει . . . αἰσθήσει
. . . πείρᾳ . . . ὁράσει.

and perhaps, according to you, God is not
life, nor does he provide life by uniting to us. (Jn 14.6; 17.2)
35 Again the creator is imperishable, but the creatures are
       perishable.
For those who have sinned bring not only their body,
but even their very souls to ruin,
and according to this reason we are perishable
in both body and soul, as we are all overpowered at once
40 by the destruction of mental[4] death and of sin.
And so if he who is imperishable by nature was united to me
       the perishable,
then truly there will be one of these possibilities of which I am
       about to tell you.
For either he will change me and make me imperishable,
or the Imperishable will be changed to corruption. And thus
45 it is possible that I would not know that he has suffered
and become like me. But if I have become wholly
imperishable and united to the Imperishable from my
       perishable condition,
then how would I not perceive it with my senses, how would I
       not see
by experience itself, nor know that I have changed to what I
       was not?
50 For to say that God is united to human beings and
that he does not give a share of his divine incorruptibility to
       them,
but rather he pulls himself down by their mortality,
by saying that one declares the destruction of the
       Indestructible,
and they blaspheme, and they utterly fall out of life. (Gal 5.4)
55 But if this is impossible, then it is better to accept the
       alternative
and hasten to participate in incorruption before your death!

[4]νοητοῦ.

God is the light, but we are in darkness,⁵
or to say more truly, we ourselves are the darkness. (Eph 5.8)
For God will not shine elsewhere—do not be led astray!—
60   if he does not shine in souls alone to whom he has been united
            before their death.
But to the others, even if they are shining heralds, like I said,
he shall appear to them as utterly unapproachable fire,
and he shall examine each one's sort of work, (1 Cor 3.13)
and again he shall be separated from these since they are
            unworthy,
65   and these shall receive the punishment they deserve.
Both here and hereafter God alone is the light of souls,
but we are darkness, having souls unenlightened,
and so if the Light of souls is united to my soul,
then either that Light will be extinguished and become
            darkness,
70   or my soul, having been illuminated, will be like the light.
For when the light has been kindled, immediately the darkness
            flees,
and that indeed is the work of perceptible light.
But if the created light does these things for you by its energy,
and enlightens your eyes, and gladdens your soul,⁶
75   and it grants you to see what you did not see before,
then when the creator of light shines in your soul, what will he
            not do,
he who said, "Let there be light," and immediately there was
            light? (Gen 1.3)
And so what do you think, if he will shine rationally⁷ in the
            heart
or in the mind like lightning or like a big sun,
80   what will he be able to produce within an enlightened soul?

⁵1 Jn 1.5; Lk 1.79.
⁶Ps 12.4; Prov 15.30.
⁷νοερῶς.

Will he not illuminate her and make himself
known in clear knowledge who he is?
Yes, truly so it happens, thus it is accomplished,
thus is the gift of the revealed Spirit,

85 and through him and in him also the Son with the Father.
One sees them, as much as it is possible to contemplate them,
and then one ineffably learns from them things concerning
    them,
and extols and writes for everyone else,
and sets forth doctrines befitting God, like all

90 the preceding holy Fathers taught.
For thus they dogmatized the divine symbol,
and having become such as we said, ‹saints who›
with God uttered and told the things of God.
For who has theologized the triune Monad,

95 or who has put heresies to flight without being known as ‹a
    theologian›,
or who was called a saint without having participated
in the Holy Spirit? No one, ever. In the same way, the rational
    light
naturally increases in the senses for those in whom it is
    present.[8]
But those who say that they partake of the light unconsciously,[9]

100 are in fact calling themselves senseless.[10]
But we call them corpses deprived of life,
even if they seem yet to live. Oh error, oh madness!
But, O Light, shine on them, shine so that by seeing
they may be truly persuaded that you are the true light, (Jn 1.9)

105 and you may render like yourself those to whom you are
    united like light! (1 Jn 3.2)

---

[8]Ὡς καὶ τὸ φῶς αἰσθήσει τὸ νοητὸν προσγίνεσθαι πέφυκεν, οἷς προσέσται. This sentence is difficult to translate because of the varied and idiomatic meanings of the verbs προσγίνεσθαι, πέφυκεν, προσέσται.

[9]ἀναισθήτως, without sense-awareness.

[10]ἀναισθήτους.

"I shine like always before the face of the blind,
but they do not want to see, rather they close their eyes,[11]
and they do not wish to look toward me, my child!
And they even turn away their eyes to somewhere else,

110   and I turn with them. I stand in front of them,
and again they send their eyes elsewhere,
and they do not look upon the light of my face at all.
Some of these cover their eyes with a veil,
and others flee away and hate me in every way.

115   So what should I do with them? I am utterly at a loss.
Perhaps if I were to save them by force against their will,
but even this would seem a calamity ‹to them›, for they do not
          wish to be saved.
For the good by choice will be good indeed,
but the unwilling good is not good,

120   and for this reason I see those who want ‹the good› and I am
          seen by them,
and I make them co-heirs of my kingdom.
But for those who do not wish the good, I allow them free will
          in the world,
and they become judges of themselves before the trial.
          (Titus 3.11)
Because while my unapproachable light was shining

125   they alone procured darkness for themselves; (Jn 3.19)
they did not wish to see the light, and they remained in
          darkness." (Jn 12.46)

---

[11]Is 6.9; Acts 28.27.

Hymn 35

That all the enlightened saints are illuminated, and they contemplate
the glory of God insofar as it is allowed for human nature to see God.

Look down from on high, my God,
and consent to appear
and to associate with a poor person!
Reveal your light by
5   opening the heavens to me,
or rather, unfold my mind
and enter now within me![1]
Speak, as before,
through my dirty tongue,
10   ‹respond to› what some people say,
that now there is no one
who has knowingly seen God,
nor has anyone before now
seen God except the apostles. (1 Jn 1.1–3)
15   "But not even the apostles themselves,"
they say, "saw clearly
your God and Father, (Jn 14.9)
but he is unknown to everyone,
and likewise unseen."
20   They declare,
citing the word
of your much loved
disciple John who
says: "No one among human beings
25   has ever seen God." (Jn 1.18)
Yes, my Christ, speak quickly,
so that to the stupid
I may not seem to speak foolishness!

[1]Acts 7.56; Lk 24.45; Lk 17.21.

"Write," he said, "what I say.
30   Write and may you not shrink back.
I am God before every
day, hour, and time, (Col 1.1/)
but also before all aeons, (Ps 54.20)
and before all creations
35   both visible and imaginary.[2]
I was above mind and reason,
and above all thought,
alone with the alone, alone.
But none of the visible things, (Col 1.16)
40   but not even the invisible things,
existed before they actually came into existence.
I alone am uncreated
with my Father and my Spirit.
I alone am without beginning
45   from my eternal Father,
but none of the angels,
nor any of the archangels,
nor any of the other heavenly orders
has ever seen my nature,
50   nor me myself, the Creator,
‹nor seen› the whole of what I am.
But only the ray of glory
and an emanation of my light
do they contemplate, and they are deified.
55   For like a mirror that
has received the rays of the sun, (1 Cor 13.12)
or like a crystalline stone
illuminated in midday,
so they all receive the rays
60   of my divinity.
But no one has yet been deemed worthy

[2]νοουμένων.

to contemplate the whole of me,
none of the angels, nor human beings,
nor the holy powers.
65 For I am outside all things
and invisible to everyone. (1 Tim 1.17)
It is not because I bear any malice at all toward
them that they do not see me,
nor because I am not beautiful
70 that I hide myself so as not to be revealed,
but ‹it is because› no one was
found worthy of my divinity.
There is no creature
equal in power to the creator;
75 for this is not fitting.
But those who see even a small radiance
learn that truly *I am*, (Ex 3.14)
and they know me as the God
who brought them into existence.
80 And in astonishment and fear
they sing my praises and they worship me.
For it is not possible for another
to be created God by nature,
equal in power to the creator,
85 and of the same nature as him,
for it is not at all possible
for something created
to become the same essence as the creator.
For how would something created
90 ever be made equal to the Uncreated?
Likewise the created things are inferior
to him who is always
both without beginning and uncreated.
For you will testify that such is the case
95 and support that there is as much difference

between a wagon or a saw
and the one who fashioned them. (Is 10.15)
And so how would a wagon
know fully the one who made it?
100 And tell me, how will a saw
know the one who moves it
if the maker does not give the knowledge to them,
if the one who made them
does not put the vision into them?
105 Is this not impossible
for all created things?"
And so no one at all among human beings,
and none of the angels
has received the authority
110 to give spirit to others,
or to procure life for them.
But the Lord of all things
alone has the authority,[3]
alone has the lordship,
115 since he is the fount of life. (Ps 35.10)
he brings forth animated life forms,
and whatever he shall wish,
and he freely gives to each
(as artisan, as master)
120 as much as he wants and desires.
To him be the glory and the power
now, always, and forever and ever. Amen. (1 Pet 4.11)

[3]Rom 10.12; Mt 28.18.

Hymn 36

Thanksgiving for the exile and afflictions which he endured in the persecution against him.

I thank you, Lord, I thank you alone,
the knower of hearts, just king, all-merciful!
I thank you all-powerful Logos without beginning,
My God who descended upon the earth and became
      incarnate,

5   you who became what you were not, a human being like me,
without change, or transience, or all sin, (Heb 4.15)
so that you who are dispassionate, by suffering unjustly under
      the lawless ones,
would procure dispassion for me, for me who was condemned,
by imitating your sufferings, my Christ! (1 Pet 2.21)

10   And so your judgment is just, and at the same time so is your
      command (Rev 16.7)
which you have commanded us to keep, All-Merciful One.
And this is the imitation of your humility,
so that just as you who are without sin have suffered,
so also we who have committed all sins may endure

15   temptations, and persecutions, and scourges, and afflictions,
      (Rom 8.35)
and finally death from lawless people.
For you were said to have a demon, and the godless supposed
      that you were
a deceiver opposed to God, and a transgressor of the Law.
      (Jn 10.20)
You were apprehended and led away alone in chains,

20   all your disciples and friends had abandoned you.
      (Mt 26.55–56)
And you stood before the judge like one condemned, O Logos,

and you received the judgment which was carried out against
　　you.
And when you spoke you endured a slap from a slave,
　　(Jn 18.22)
and when you were silent at once you were condemned to
　　death.

25　For your words were a sword to the lawless, (Mt 10.34)
and your silence, O King, the cause of your condemnation.
On which account they could not bear to see you alone as the
　　just one.
The unjust ones handed you over to a most shameful death,
whence you were beaten on the head and crowned

30　with thorns, and clothed with a purple cloak.[1]
Your face was spat upon, woe is me, and you were mocked,
"Hail King," you heard the Jews mockingly say.[2]
You carried the cross, Savior, on your shoulders,
and you were crucified and raised upon it, my God. (Jn 19.17)

35　You were bound[3] hand and foot, and given vinegar to drink,
and your side was pierced by a spear, O All-Merciful One.
　　(Jn 19.29, 34)
The earth would not bear these things, and trembled with fear,
and in haste she gave back the dead that were in her. (Mt 27.52)
The sun changed into blood on seeing you,

40　and the moon was then clothed in darkness.[4]
Then the curtain of the temple was torn
into two from top to bottom. (Mt 27.51)
And the criminals understood nothing at all of these
　　phenomena,
but even when you lay in the tomb they posted guards,
　　(Mt 27.66)

[1]Jn 19.2; Mt 27.27ff.; Jn 19.3.
[2]Mt 26.67; Jn 19.3.
[3]ἠλώθης from ἁλίσκομαι. Various translations are possible, e.g., caught, seized,
condemned. The context would suggest tied or nailed.
[4]Mt 27.45; Acts 2.20.

45   and they sealed the stone, and supposed that they had
          overcome you.
     And so you arose, Master, by your own power
     and you left the seals secured for the sinners.
     The presence of angels rolled the stone
     and struck down with fear those who guarded the place,
50   and they did not want to understand even a little bit,
     but their mind remained blind,
     they kept their heart hardened until the end. (Mt 28.2–11)
     And so what is so great for me, if I should also suffer these
          things
     which you yourself—being without sin—have suffered
55   on behalf of the world, Master, in order to save the world,
          (Jn 12.47)
     I who have committed innumerable sins from my early youth
     and have provoked your anger, Christ, in both my works and
          words? (Deut 32.21)
     Truly what is great for me, or rather beyond all glory,
     is that which makes me a participant in your unspeakable
          glory,
60   that is the sharing of your sufferings, the imitation of your
          works,
     and your humility is the agent of your divinity
     for those who go in quest of it with knowledge.
     I thank you, Master, I suffer more unjustly,
     but if justly, let it be for the expiation of my failures,
65   for the purification, O Christ, of my immeasurable trespasses,
     and may you not ever allow my troubles to increase
          (1 Cor 10.13)
     beyond my strength, Master, nor temptations, nor afflictions,
     but always give to me the way out, my God,
     and the strength to be able to endure the sufferings!
70   For, from the beginning, you are the provider of goods

for those who from their soul prostrate worthily before your
    supremacy,
you give them gifts of faith, of works, and
of good hopes, and all the presents
of your divine and worshipped Spirit, O Compassionate One,
    (Acts 2.38)
75   now and always, and at all times forever and ever. Amen.

Hymn 37

Symeon's supplication and prayer to God for his help.

Master Christ, life-saving Master,
Master God of all visible
and invisible powers, as creator
of all things in heaven, of things above
5   heaven and above all heavens,[1]
creator of things above the earth and likewise things on the
    earth,
you are the Lord of all these, both God and Master, (Jude 4)
by your hand you control creation
because in your hand you encompass all things.
10 Your hand, Master, is a great power
which, by fulfilling the will of your Father, (Lk 22.42)
fashions, and accomplishes, and creates,
and unspeakably manages things concerning us.
And so your hand, having brought me forth
15 just now, made me into a being out of non-being,
and I was born in this world (Jn 1.9)
not knowing you at all, the good Master,
you my creator, you, O my Maker.
And I was like a blind man in the world,
20 like an atheist, not knowing my God.

[1]Ex 20.11; Col 1.16.

And so you yourself had mercy and watched over me,
and having shone your light in the darkness for me, (2 Cor 4.6)
you turned me around and dragged me to yourself, O Sculptor,
and you brought me out of the lowest pit, (Ps 87.6)
25 from the darkness of the passions, from the deepest darkness
of desires and of life's pleasures. (Lk 8.14)
You showed me the way, you gave to me a guide[2]
who guided me to your commandments.
Following him without care, I continued on,
30 I rejoiced with unspoken joy, O Logos,
seeing him following your footsteps
and often conversing with you.
But I also saw you, the good Master,
together with my guide and father,
35 I had ineffable love and desire,
I was beyond faith and hope,
and "Behold," I said, "I see the things to come,
and the kingdom of heaven is at hand, (Mt 3.2)
and also the good things that eye has not seen,
40 ear has not heard, I see before my eyes." (1 Cor 2.9)
And having these, what more shall I hope for,
or in what other things will I show my faith?
For there will not be another thing greater than them.
For having been in them and revelled in them,
45 alas you took my father from the earth,
you raised my guide from my eyes, (Acts 1.9)
O Benevolent One, you also left me alone,
completely orphaned, completely forsaken,
being by all means without any help at all,
50 and, alas, you appointed me shepherd of a flock,
I who was truly like a stranger without protection,
and you yourself established this by judgments that only you
    know.

[2]I.e., Symeon Eulabes.

Because of this I now beg you,
now I pray, prostrating I entreat you:

55   May you not turn away, may you not abandon me,
may you not leave me alone, O my Master!
You know that to run this route is to trod in sorrow,
you know the robbers' madness against us,
you know the crowd of evil wild beasts,

60   you know my weakness, my Christ,
and my ignorance that, like a human being, I have.
Moreover, I do not suppose that I am completely human,
but rather much inferior to human beings.
For in every way I am the last of all

65   and I am truly the least of all human beings. (1 Cor 15.9)
My King and my God, pour upon me (Sir 18.9)
your great mercy, I beg you,
so that your mercy, Savior, may fill up
my needs and my defects (1 Cor 16.17)

70   and make me a totally saved person
lacking nothing of the necessities,
and may your mercy place me before you, Logos,
not condemned, but your blameless servant,
singing your praises forever and ever. Amen.

Hymn 38

Concerning theology and that when the mind is purified of the material of the passions it immaterially contemplates the Immaterial and Invisible.

What sort of road should I travel, what sort of path do I turn
    away from? (Is 40.3)
What sort of ladder would I ascend, what kind of gate would I
    enter, (Gen 28.1)

or how shall I open the door and of what bedchamber?
    (Mt 25.10)
In what sort and what kind of house will I find
5   him who holds all things in his hand and palm? (1 Kg 8.27)
What sort of mountain should I climb, from what part
    (Ex 24.12)
and in what kind of cave shall I there feel around, (1 Kg 19.9)
or by traversing what swamp would I the wretch be worthy
of contemplating and possessing him who is
10   everywhere, and inapprehensible, and invisible?
To what hell would I descend, and to what heaven
should I climb, and to the ends of what sea
that I may find him who is utterly unapproachable,
    (Ps 138.8–9)
altogether uncircumscribed, wholly impalpable,
15   the Immaterial in matter, the Creator in creation,
the Imperishable in the perishable, tell me, how shall I find
    him?
And how may I come outside the world, I who am in the
    world,
how should I be united to the Immaterial, I who am united to
    matter?
How would I be entwined with the Imperishable, I who am
    wholly perishable,
20   how shall I who am in death draw near to Life at all,
how shall I, a corpse, approach the Immortal One?
I who am all grass, how shall I dare to touch fire? (Is 40.6)
But at the same time, listen to the unraveling of these
    unspeakable mysteries!
Before heaven came into being, before earth was brought into
    existence,
25   there was God, the Trinity, alone, solitary, (Prov 8.24ff)
Light without beginning, Uncreated Light, Light in every way
    inexpressible,

at the same time immortal God, without end, alone,
eternal, everlasting, very much the greatest good.
Consider well that in the beginning was God alone, the Trinity
30   being absolutely without beginning, beyond all beginning,
incomparable, without measure in height, depth and breadth,
       (Eph 3.18)
and having no limit to his greatness and light!
There was no air, as now, nor was there any darkness at all,
nor light, no water, nor atmosphere, no other beings.
35   But there was Spirit alone, God, in every way luminous,
       (Gen 1.2)
he was at the same time all-powerful and Immaterial.
And he made angels, dominions, and powers,
the cherubim, and the seraphim, lordships, thrones,
and unnameable ordinances ministering worship
40   for him and standing by in fear and trembling.
And afterward he created the heavens like a canopy, (Is 40.22)
material and visible, perceptible and thick,
and in a flash he stretched it out, as only he knows.[1]
And at the same time both earth and waters, and every abyss
45   in the middle of the heavens, only by thought itself
he made them, such as are all now seen by us. (Prov 8.23)
And so creation remained, it did not have the Immaterial light
       within,
the perceptible heaven was stretched out like I said,
it did not cut through the radiance of the Immaterial light.
50   For since it is material, as was said, the sky is found outside the
       Immaterial,
not with respect to place, but by its nature and essence.
For the Immaterial is separated from material things;
he does not have his own particular place, for he is boundless.
He himself creates all things in himself by his word,
55   and he is by nature completely separated from creatures,

[1]Ps 103.2; Is 44.24.

and he bears all things in himself; he is outside all.
For just as a mind or an angel may be outside a house,
without being confined by walls and doors, nor held within,
so the Maker of these is not at all outside,
60 nor within the heavens, nor in another place.
But God is by all means everywhere separated from
all material creatures created by him.
And so material heaven was also made and, as we said,
set apart by its nature from the Immaterial Light,
65 and remained without light, like a large house. (Gen 1.14ff)
But the Master of all has ignited the sun
and the moon in order to shine perceptibly for perceptible
        creatures,
and he put in our hands a light to shine in the night,
inexplicably produced from iron and stone.
70 But he is separated from all light,
beyond light, exceedingly bright, unendurable to every
        creature.
For just like when the sun shines the stars are not revealed,
so also if the Master of the sun wants to shine,
every living thing will not bear his dawning. (Mt 24.27)
75 On which account he has yoked together mind with material
        dust, (Gen 2.7)
and placed all of us human beings among material things,
so that by steadfast faith and by keeping the commandments,
when we again purify the mind that we have confounded by
        the gloom
of our transgression, this immaterial mind subject to the
        yearning
80 of material passions, and to the tasting of pleasures,
we may contemplate the Immaterial Light immaterially in
        material things,
the light which, as I said, was God beyond beginning,
invisible to perceptible and material eyes,

unapproachable to the rational eyes of the heart.
85 For I marvel how the soul which is wholly immaterial
    and possessing the rational eye of the mind
    stoops to peep through and receive sense messages[2] through
    the eyes of the body like two windows, and she sees
    through them all visible things, and again turns back
90 and contemplates intellectual[3] and immaterial things
        immaterially,
    and how the soul is ineffably held between imperishable and
        perishable realities.
    On the one hand she is drawn by the perishable toward
        pleasures, toward passions.
    On the other hand the imperishable gives her wings to fly to
        heaven.
    She is under pressure to remain there in heaven, but she is
        nevertheless
95 dragged down and always strives vigorously to be borne up
        again;
    she wants to be one who walks in the air away from beings that
        are seen.
    For she sees all things in the world as traps,
    she wholly fears to walk or settle on earth,
    lest by all means she be held and stuck in them
100 and become the food of savage beasts. (Ezek 34.5)
    Such is the life of all the pious, and faithful,
    and holy ones, a life that is necessary for all to imitate,
    so that they may stand blamelessly with
    the saints before Christ, God, Judge of all,
105 and they shall be participants in his glory and kingdom forever.
        Amen. (1 Pet 5.1)

---

[2] αἰσθητῶς.
[3] νοητά.

Hymn 39

That the yearning and love for God surpasses all love and human long-ing.[1] And the mind of those who are purified is plunged in the light of God, and completely deified, and thence styled the mind of Christ.

Your beauty is impossible, your appearance incomparable,
your timeliness is unutterable, your glory beyond words,
your character, Christ Master, is good, and meek,
and lies above the thoughts of all the earthborn.
5   And because of this, love and yearning toward you
more than conquer all love and yearning of mortals.
       (Rom 8.37)
Insofar as you lie above visible things, Savior,
so much also is yearning for you greater,
and completely covers all human love,
10   and turns away passionate love for carnal pleasures,
and quickly repels all yearnings.
For yearning of the passions is truly darkness
and the practice of shameful sins is deep night,
but, Savior, passionate love and love for you are light.
15   For this reason when love springs up in God-loving souls,
immediately and within she produces the day of dispassion,
       my God.
She chases away the darkness of passions and pleasures.
O marvel, O paradoxical work of God most high,
and power of secretly accomplished mysteries!
20   You generously give to us both incorruptible and perishable
       realities,
and you give earthly things, God, with heavenly things,
both present and at the same time future things, Logos,
since by all means the Maker of everything has the authority

---

[1]There are four terms for love and desire that are used in *Hymn 39*. They are translated as follows: ἀγάπη = love; ἔρως = passionate love; πόθος and ἐπιθυμία are both be translated as "yearning," sometimes as "longing."

of the heavens, Master, and of the underworld. (Phil 2.10)
25 And how do we miserable people love human beings
more than you, and how wretchedly do we become their
    servants,
so that we may receive small and perishable things from them,
and we surrender to them our miserable souls
and bodies as cheap equipment of abuse?
30 And being members, Master, of the holy Master of all things,
    (1 Cor 6.15)
by all means holy members of the absolute Master,
how do we not shudder to voluntarily throw ourselves
to wicked demons for unworthy works of sin?
And so who among your legitimate servants would not weep,
35 who would not bewail the audacity of so much stubbornness?
And who would not tremble at your copious forbearance, my
    God,
who would not tremble at the retribution of divine judgment,
    (Is 34.8)
the unbearable and unquenchable fire, alas, of Gehenna,
where there is weeping, and gnashing of teeth,
40 and relentless trouble, and unspeakable suffering? (Mt 13.42)
But, O Sun, Creator of the sun and moon,
Creator of all the stars and all other light,
hide me outside these lights and in your light,
so that by seeing you alone in your light,
45 I will not see the world nor the things in the world,
but looking I shall also be as though not looking,
and hearing as though not hearing, Logos,
and just like the experience of those who
sit in the darkness of the pleasures of this life
50 —those who are covered by the darkness of the love of glory,
looking they do not see your divine glory, (Mt 13.13)
and hearing they do not understand
your commands and your ordinances at all—

thus also shall I be in your light,
55 seeing neither the world nor the things in the world.
For who, once having seen you and having had their senses
     enlightened
by your glory, by your divine light,
has not been transformed in mind, soul, and viscera,[2]
and was not deemed worthy likewise to see
60 and to hear, Savior, in another utterly extraordinary way?
For the mind is plunged into your light,
and made bright, and transformed into light
similar to your glory, and is called your mind,
and one who has been deemed worthy to become like this
65 is then also deemed worthy to possess your mind, (Rom 11.34)
and they become inseparably one with you.
How then does such a one not see like you do, and not hear
all things dispassionately? And how would one who
has become God yearn at all for anything perceptible,
70 or for any transient and perishable reality, or any glory,
when they are above all these
and beyond all visible glory?
For once one has come above all visible things
and associated with God,
75 or rather once one's self is reckoned as God,
how would they want to seek after glory
or the pleasure of things lying below?
For these are truly a disgrace for such a one:
wantonness, emptiness, and dishonor.
80 But glory, and pleasure, and wealth
are God, the Trinity, and the divine things of God,
to whom is fitting all glory, honor, power, (1 Pet 4.11)
always, and now, and unto all ages. Amen.

[2]τὰς φρένας.

Hymn 40

Admission of the grace of God's gifts, and how the father writing these things was energized by the Holy Spirit, and a lesson proclaimed by God on what one must do to obtain the salvation of those who are saved.

Again the light shines for me, again it is seen clearly,
again it opens the heavens, again it divides the night, (Mt 3.16)
again it creates all things, again the light alone is seen,
again it transports me outside all visible things,
5 and likewise it separates me from perceptible things—what a
        surprise!
Again the light is above all heavenly things (Eph 4.10)
that no one among human beings has ever seen, (1 Tim 6.16)
not opening the heavens, not splitting the night, (Acts 7.56)
nor dividing the air, nor the roof of the house,
10 it becomes wholly indivisible with me the wretch,
within my cell, within my mind,
and the middle of my heart—oh awesome mystery!
When all things remain as they are, the light comes to me,
and bears me up above all things, (Eph 4.10)
15 and in the middle of everything it transports me outside of all
        things.
And I do not even know if with my body, but for a time I
        become (2 Cor 12.2)
entirely there in truth, there is only the light,
simple, when I see it I become simple without guile.
These are the paradoxes of your wonders, my Christ,
20 these works of your lordship and benevolence
which you do for us unworthy ones.
And so because of this, fear of you grips me and I tremble,
and I worry constantly, and I am much consumed
with how I may repay you, what I may offer you

25   for such great gifts, such great compassion,
     innumerable gifts that you have accomplished for me.
     But finding nothing in me, nothing is mine in life,
     but all things are your servants, all are works of your hands,
     even more greatly I am put to shame, suffering more greatly,

30   I am more ashamed to learn, Savior, what
     I must do to serve you, so to please you,
     in order to be found uncondemned, Savior, before
     your awesome judgment seat in the day of judgment.[1]
     "Listen to what everyone who intends to be saved should do,

35   especially you who first of all call to me!
     Today, resolve! You have died. Today you have renounced,[2]
     today consider that you have left all the world behind!
     Today, having got rid of your friends, family, all vainglory,
     and at the same time having renounced concern for things
         below, (Mt 16.24)

40   bear the cross on your shoulders, and bind it vehemently,
     and carry it unto the last sufferings of the trials,
     receive joyously the sufferings and nails
     of painful afflictions like a crown of glory. (1 Pet 5.4)
     And being struck by spears of insolent violence each hour,

45   and being stoned violently by every disrespect
     you will be a martyr shedding your tears instead of your blood,
     and bearing mockeries and slaps on your face with complete
         goodwill,
     you shall be a participant in my divinity and glory.
     And if you show yourself to be the last of all,

50   both the slave and servant, in future I will (Mt 19.30)
     render you the first among all of these, just as I have promised.
     If you love your enemies and all who hate you, (Lk 6.27)
     and from your soul you pray for those who threaten you,
     and if you do good to them according to your power,

[1] 2 Cor 5.10; Mt 12.36.
[2] Cf. Heb 3.7; Ps 94.8.

55   then you have truly become like your Father above,
      and having acquired a pure heart from these virtues, (1 Tim 1.5)
      in your heart you shall see God whom no one has ever seen.
      And if it should happen that you are persecuted
      for righteousness, then leap ‹for joy› because the kingdom
60   of Heaven has become yours, and what greater joy is there than
            this? (Mt 5.10)
      These things, and more, that I have enjoined, (Jn 15.14)
      practice and teach them to others, you and all others (Mt 5.19)
      who believe in me, if you wish to be saved,
      and to abide with me forever and ever!
65   And if you reject my commands and you are vexed by them,
      and you consider it a shame and a dishonor
      to suffer and to lay down your soul for my commands,
            (Jn 15.13)
      then why do you ask to learn how you must be saved,
      and by what practices you may befriend me?
70   And why do you call me your God?
      And why do you stupidly think that you believe in me?
      For I willingly suffered these things for your sake.
      I was crucified, I suffered the death of criminals, (2 Tim 2.9)
      and the disgrace against me became the glory of the world,
75   the life and splendor and resurrection of the dead, (Phil 3.11)
      and the boast of all who believe in me, (2 Cor 12.9–10)
      and my shameful death was a garment of incorruption,
            (1 Cor 15.52)
      and true deification for all the faithful.
      For this reason those who imitate my sublime
80   sufferings are participants in my divinity,
      and shall be heirs of my kingdom; (Rom 8.17)
      they shall become co-partakers of unspeakable,
      secret goods, and they shall be with me forever.
      But as for the others, who will not weep, who will not bewail
            them,

85   who will not let fall a tear from a sympathetic heart,
      who will not mourn their great insensitivity,
      because they have sent away life, and betrayed themselves to
          death,
      cutting themselves off from God terribly?"
      Rescue me from their portion, Master of all things,
90   and deem me, the worthless and least of your servants,
      to become a participant in your immaculate sufferings,
          (2 Cor 1.7)
      so that—as you said, O God—I also will be a participant
      in your glory and the enjoyment of your goods, Logos,
          (1 Pet 5.1)
      for now as in an enigma, and an image, and a mirror,
95   but then I shall know you as much as I have been known.
          Amen. (1 Cor 13.12)

Hymn 41

Thanksgiving to God for the kindnesses done by him, and a request to learn why the perfected are submitted to temptation by the demons, and a lesson and a model from God concerning those who leave the world.

      You know my poverty, you know my orphanhood, (Rev 2.9)
      you understand my isolation, you see my weakness
      and my powerlessness, you my God who formed me,
      you do not ignore me, but you see and know all things.
5   See my humble heart, see my crushed heart, (Ps 50.19)
      see me approaching in despair, my God,
      and give your grace from on high, give your divine Spirit!
          (Lk 24.49)
      Give the Paraclete, Savior, send him as you promised,
      send him even now to the one sitting
10   in an upper room, Master, truly above (Acts 1.13)

all earthly concerns, outside the world,
and seeking you and awaiting your Spirit!
And so do not delay, Compassionate One, nor disregard,
      Merciful One,
nor forget the one who seeks you with a thirsting soul!
15 Do not deprive unworthy me of this life,
nor loathe me, God, and do not abandon me!
I throw myself before your affections, I hold out your mercy
and I offer your benevolence to you as a mediatrix.
I have not labored, I have not practiced works of righteousness,
      (Titus 3.5)
20 I have never observed one of your commandments, (Mt 5.19)
but I have passed all of my life as a profligate,[1] (Lk 15)
nevertheless you did not overlook me, but when you searched
      you found
me straying, you turned me from the road of error, you lifted
me upon your immaculate shoulders by the light of your grace,
      (Lk 15.4–5)
25 Christ, you carried me, Merciful One,
and you did not allow me to feel any toil,
but as though resting as in a carriage
you gave me to travel the rough roads with ease,
until you restored me to the fold of your sheep,
30 until you united me to and appointed me among your servants.
I proclaim your mercy, I sing your compassion,
thanking you I marvel at the wealth of your kindness.
      (Rom 2.4)
And I was called up by you, as was said, my God,
and now I am, it seems to me, wholly given to your service,
35 nailed to the light, and glued to you,
gripped by your desire, chained by your love,
I am at a loss, I am dumbfounded, and I cannot understand.
How then would affliction reach my wretched soul,

---

[1]ἀσώτως, in debauchery or without hope of salvation.

how would sorrow come upon me, how would it wholly
trouble me,
40   how deprive me of your sweetness, my God,
how would the affliction of earthly things separate me from
your grace?
Why such a one as I who have stumbled and sinned,
why after I have angered you more, my Christ,
do you abandon me, O Good One, to greater sorrow
45   beyond that when my soul was impassioned?
Tell me and teach me now the depth of your judgment,
(Rom 11.33)
tell me and do not loathe me who speaks unworthily,
you who of old feasted with sinners and prostitutes,
and dined, Master, with profligates and publicans! (Mt 9.10ff)
50   To these things the Master answered me and said:
"I brought you from the world, like a little child
in my arms I carried you, certainly you know what I say,
and I wrapped all of you and all of your members in swaddling
clothes,
and I raised you on milk over food and drink.[2]
55   For what pertains to me is inexpressible and by all means
inexplicable.
And I gave you to a pedagogue—you know whom I mean[3]—
and like a little child growing by the hour
he assisted you to the utmost, he nourished you worthily.
Already you became an adolescent, and indeed even a young
man.
60   And you are not unaware that I am always with you,
and increasing in you, and protecting you on all sides,
until you have completed well the stages of growth.
And so now are you not in your prime? Or rather truly a man,

[2]Rom 14.17; 1 Cor 3.2.
[3]I.e. Symeon Eulabes.

and by now becoming perfected as you lean toward old age?
    (1 Cor 13.11)
65   How is it that you wish to be carried in my arms like an infant?
How do you ask to be wrapped in swaddling clothes and
    carried again?
How should you be nourished with milk and be under
a pedagogue? Tell me, do you not blush to say these things?
Since you are a man, do service for others, and nourish them,
70   and practice all things for their growth!
Stand up to enemies and respond blow for blow!
You know the enemies of whom I speak, armies of demons.
When you have received a blow, strike without mercy, falling,
    get back up again,
when arrows are sent, do not forbear to throw them back again
75   at those who throw them, and at those who contrive these evils
    against you.
But those who wound you with despair,
may they be wounded by hope sent from you,
and when they punch you with anger, and they are forced on
    you by rage,
may their face be slapped by your meekness,
80   may they be thrown out far from your house!
For, as I said, are you an infant or a child,
or do you now have weakness of soul,
or is your mind too utterly weak for resistance?
You know how to flee the enemies and to conquer them again,
85   for when you fight you also have me as an accomplice and
    protector,
and when you flee you possess me as a strong and secure
    shelter. (Sir 6.14)
And, tell me, why do things in the world distress you? What
    sort of things?
Gold, or silver, or precious stones? (1 Cor 3.12)
And what stone is more brilliant or shinier than me,

90 or what kind of stone is priceless like me?
But does deprivation of lands, or lack of bread,
or forsaking wine utterly agitate you?
And what other paradise is such as I,
or what land of transients here below is like the land of the
　　meek? (Mt 5.5)
95 And what prepared bread or wine in the world
is like my grace, like the divine Spirit,
what is like the bread of life that I provide, (Jn 6.35)
and my body and blood, for the pure of heart (Jn 6.54)
and unhesitant faith, for those who eat and drink me with
100 fear and trembling, both spiritually and perceptibly,[4]
what pleasure, what joy, what glory, tell me,
on earth is greater than to see me alone,
me alone as in an enigma reflected in a mirror, (1 Cor 13.12)
to contemplate only the radiance of my glory, (Heb 1.3)
105 and through it to be instructed in these things, and more than
　　these,
and ‹to learn› precisely that I am God creator of all things,
　　(Sir 24.8)
to know and understand that the person sitting
in the deepest pit has been reconciled to me, (Ps 87.7)
and converses with me without mediation like a friend to a
　　friend, (Ex 33.11)
110 having passed beyond the rank of hired servant and the fear of
　　slavery,
serving me tirelessly, attending me with love,
associating with me by obedience to the commandments.
I do not mean those who serve me as employees,
nor again those who come to me as slaves, but I speak of
115 those who are my friends, familiars, and my sons by their
　　actions.
Write briefly what these actions are:

[4] νοερῶς αἰσθητῶς τε.

to suppose themselves to be the more worthless than anyone in
    the world,
not only among their fellow ascetics and worldly people,
but even considering themselves truly worse than the gentiles,
120 to reckon a small transgression of even one
of the least commandments to be the loss of eternal life,
      (Mt 5.19)
to regard little children as perfect men
and to prostrate before them as to the famous.
Likewise to assign honor to the blind,
125 while I watch from on high the deeds of all persons,
and to do things on my behalf—again, write these down!—,
to hold nothing at all against anyone in your heart,
even unto a bare emotion or a little suspicion,
to pray from your soul with a suffering heart,
130 and with sympathy for all those who sin against you,
likewise also for those daring to do such things against me,
with tears begging their conversion,
at the same time to bless those who curse you,
and to praise those who always abuse you with jealousy,
135 and to hold as benefactors those who threaten you, (Lk 6.28)
and those who do not submit to you nor obey you,
constantly to weep and to bewail those who
utterly deny me as their master, do not stop admonishing
    them!
For one who receives you receives me, I have said, (Mt 10.40)
140 and one who hears you certainly hears me.
But one who does not receive your words and admonitions
with trembling, and fulfill them unto death,
such a one shall not have a share in my eternal glory,
will not be ranked with the crucified one,
145 with me who obeyed the Father unto death, (Phil 2.8)
nor will they stand on my right, nor do such people
become co-heirs of those who crucified themselves. (Rom 8.17)

Hereafter do not cease admonishing, hereafter do not cease
      weeping,
hereafter do not cease seeking their salvation,
150 so that if they should obey, and if they should repent,
you will have them as brothers, you shall gain them as your
      members, (Mt 18.15)
and lead them to me sincere and obedient,
so that I also may receive them through you and glorify them,
I may offer them with you to my Father as gifts!
155 But if they will not renounce their own will,
if they will not despise their own soul, as I have said, (Mt 16.25)
if they will not become dead to their own private will,
and in this life live according to your will,
fulfilling my will through you, you will not
160 lose your reward, you will not be deprived of it,
but I will give to you a double portion in place of the single
      reward,
because even though you were not obeyed you did not refrain
      from speaking,
but you were hated even more, and the more you were turned
      away,
and loathed by them, as I myself was hated
165 then and now by them and people like them.
Through works such as these I want you to serve me,
hasten to please me through such things and
similar such things, for I rejoice in such things.
Do not prefer to be idle nor choose at all
170 another thing in the world over the benefit of your soul!
For what will it profit one who gains the world,
or one who nurtures everyone in it, or teaches,
or even saves everyone, if one's self is not saved? (Mk 8.36)
And so who, or even how could any poor wretch save others
175 and not save their own soul, but rather destroy it?

One who dissolves my command, the Master of all things,
(Mt 5.19)
and as if trampling through it, and stepping outside it,
and side-stepping my law, transgressing my ordinances,
and getting outside the courtyard and fence of the
commandments,

180 if such a one were to save the world and everyone in the world,
still they shall be a stranger to me and far from my sheep,
just as certainly as if they had dissolved the fence of the
courtyard,
and ‹permitted› the sheep to exit, not only through the gate,
but even unjustly provided an entrance for wild beasts.[5]

185 Such a one will endure an unspeakable judgment on account of
all the sheep,
and the wretch shall be cut in two for the fire,
and the dark abyss, and shall be the food of worms."[6]
For the Father said this through the Son and
the Spirit who is the mouth of the Master,

190 the angels uttered approval and unceasing voices,
the just ones fell prostrate when they heard and said:
"Your decision is not bribed, your judgment is without
suspicion,
for you have judged free from the passions,[7] O all-merciful
God.
For how is it that one who has not abandoned their own will,
and has not given

195 first place of honor and kept free of damage the will of your
representative as they should your will—the will of the
Master—just as
you yourself have observed the will of your Father, Merciful
One, (Jn 15.10)

[5]Jn 10.1ff.; Ezek 34.5.
[6]Mt 24.51; Mk 9.48.
[7]ἀπροσπαθῶς, that is "objectively," or "without self-interest."

⟨how would such a one⟩ be seen as your co-heir, and your full
    partner,
and as one who heeds God's will unto death?
200 Which means not doing one's own will in anything,
not to give in to blood relatives, nor to prefer the flesh
    (Gal 1.16)
that is kin and natural bonds, the affection that
binds those on earth to the things they have renounced,
that turns them completely around backwards?"[8]
205 The martyrs cried out: "Truly the judgment is just! (Rev 16.7)
For as one eagerly gives oneself for martyrdom,
if their family comes to them, both women and children,
saying these things with mourning: "Do you not have mercy
    on your children,
do you not feel pity, heartless one, for the widowhood of your
    wife?
210 Are you not bent sympathetically by their beggary,
do you not consider their destruction and have pity,
but will you leave them orphans, strangers, beggars,
and your wife a widow, and do you prefer to save only yourself?
Do you not rather expect to be condemned like a murderer
215 because you abandoned us all to destruction
and you seek to save only your own soul?" One ought
not to listen to their voice for even a moment,
nor give ear at all to their complaints,
neither to escape the chains and prison by gifts,
220 nor to be released from them by denial of you, Christ,
but rather one must remain in the torments as though already
    dead,
to persevere in the jails,[9] in hunger and thirst,
not remembering one's affairs or property,
not allowing, if possible, one's thought

[8]Jn 6.66; Mk 13.16.
[9]φυλακαῖς, perhaps a pun that also suggests vigils.

225   to wander outside the jail for a moment,
        but to contemplate you in it, Master of all things, and
        be wholly occupied by contemplation of the heart turned
              toward you,
        to persevere unto death by your desire alone,
        nor in the least should one look at those who turn away,
230   nor look at those who deny you and turn back again
        to their previous vomit, to their previous practices,[10]
        to their worries of wife and children on earth,
        nor by any excuse whatsoever be fettered in them,
        for one no longer exercises power over one's own soul.
235   For this reason many, when the prisons were opened by you,
        and the chains were completely loosened from the body,
              (Acts 16.26)
        your servants did not choose to get out
        and flee, but remained as if still chained.
        And so thus, Savior, those who are now in the world,
240   and who renounce the world, and at the same time renounce
              all relatives,
        friends, companions, and every concern for things
        in the world, and before all these their own will,
        they no longer have any authority over themselves,
        but even if they are not restricted by their abbots,
245   they ought to observe the rule for you the Master.
        For they have not said to human beings, but to God,
        to keep obedience and service, to abbots and to all
        the brothers with them who practice asceticism in the
              monastery.
        And so like being an island in the middle of the sea
250   they ought to dwell, and to consider the whole world
        as utterly inaccessible for settlement by themselves,
        as though a great chasm was established around (Lk 16.26)
        their whole monastery, so as those who are in the world

[10]Prov 26.11; 2 Pet 2.22.

do not pass through to the monastery nor do those on this
island
255 go over to them in the world, and look upon them with strong
affection,
nor turn a memory of them in heart or mind,
rather monks ought to be disposed like corpses to corpses,
regarding them as not perceived by their senses,[11]
and they become as lambs, truly willing victims."
260 These all-holy words of the martyrs,
these words filled with desire and full of affection for the
Master,
the cherubim heard them and in fear they sang:
"Glory to you," they said, "King, glory to you, All-Merciful,
you who revealed martyrs on earth without tyrants,
265 bearing witness[12] to you each hour by their desire alone!"
Yes, again said the Father through the Son, and the Spirit
proclaimed: "Truly those who love[13] God from their heart,
and remain faithful to his love alone,
and hourly die to their own will,
270 these are genuine friends, these are co-heirs,
and these are martyrs by their free choice alone,
without scrapings, the rack, hot coals, and cauldrons,
and without burning fire and swords cutting them!"
To this all the hyper-cosmic hosts at once
275 gave a great shout: "Your judgment is just, All-Merciful One!
(Rev 16.7)
Let it be written, let it be sealed both now and forever!" Amen.

[11]τῇ αἰσθήσει.
[12]μαρτυροῦντας, "martyr" means witness.
[13]φιλοῦντες.

Hymn 42

That those who henceforth are already united to God through partici-
pation in the Holy Spirit when they travel from this life will be with
him there forever. But it will then be the reverse for those who live
otherwise.

The beginning of life is the end for me and the end is the
    beginning for me.
The place from whence I have come, I do not know, where I
    am, I know not,
and again where I shall arrive, I the wretch do not know.
I am born earth from the earth, body from body, (Gen 2.7)
5   perishable by all means from perishable, and since I am wholly
    mortal
I waste a little time on earth living in the flesh and I then die,
passing over from this life I begin another life.
I permit my body that waits in the earth to be resurrected
and to live a life without end forever.
10 And so now look at me, God, now be moved with compassion,
    One Alone,
now have mercy upon me! Behold, my strength has left me,
    (Ps 70.9)
I have approached old age, Savior, unto the gateway of death.
The prince of the world comes wishing to inspect (Jn 14.30)
my works and practices, the shameful and the impure,
15 the executioners stand ready looking at me harshly,
and they await the command to take and pull down
my wretched soul into the perdition of hell.
And so you who are compassionate by nature, who alone are
    benevolent,
who are the all-merciful Lord, then have mercy on me,
20 and do not bear a grudge against me, nor abandon me,
do not give place against me to my treacherous enemy

who each hour overwhelms me with threats,
who howls against me, gnashing his teeth,[1]
and who says to me: "How do you have confidence, and how
    do you hope
25   to escape from my hands, just because you leave me and go to
Christ, and only just now cheat my commands?
But there is no way that you will escape, for where will you go?
You will never be able to run through me at all,
I who have brought Adam and Eve from paradise,
30   I who made Cain the murderer of his brother,
I who since the deluge made everyone fall
wretchedly by error and dreadful death,
enticing them to the end with my gross deceits,
I who led David astray into adultery and murder,
35   I who raised battle against all the saints,
and many died, how do you have confidence
and expect to get past me, you who are utterly weak?"
Hearing this, Master, my God and Creator,
my Maker and Judge, you who have authority
40   over my soul and body as the sculptor of both,
I tremble and utterly dread, I shudder all over, a wretch.
     (Lk 12.4–5)
My Christ, the deceitful one cites evidence and says to me:
"Behold you do not lie awake, behold you do not practice
    self-control,
behold you do not possess prayer, you do not make
    prostrations,
45   you do not demonstrate the labors like you did before,
and because of these alone I will separate you from Christ,
and I will take you with me into unquenchable fire." (Mt 3.12)
Therefore you know, Master, since I never entrusted
the salvation of my soul to works or practices,
50   but to you, Benevolent One, I ran to you for mercy

[1] 1 Pet 5.8; Mk 9.18.

having confidence that you would save me as a gift, All-
    Merciful One,
and you would have mercy as God, like you did on the
    prostitute, (Lk 7.36 50)
and like the prodigal son who said: "I have sinned." (Lk 15.21)
So thus having faith, I run, thus having confidence, I come,
55   thus hoping, Master, I draw near to you.
And now may he not boast over me your slave.
May he not say: "Where is your Christ, where is your helper?
Did not he himself surrender you to my hands?"
For if he would deceive me and take me at spear point,
60   it would not be attributed to my free choice,
nor to my laziness, but to your abandonment of me,
and publishing the whole affair he would say such things to me
    as:
"Behold One in whom you had confidence, behold the One to
    whom you had gone,
behold the One whom you thought was your friend,[2] whom
    you believed loved[3] you,
65   and you boasted that you were his brother and friend,
his son and heir, see how he has abandoned you,
he has surrendered you to my hands, your enemy,
and unawares he has turned away from you, suddenly he has
    hated you."
May I not hear such things, Savior, do not abandon me!
70   Do not let me become your disgrace, my God,
do not, King, do not, Lord, you who of old led me out
of darkness, and from his hands, and from his jaws,
and you set me free by your light!
For seeing you I am wounded in my heart,
75   and I cannot look at you, and I cannot bear not to look.
Your beauty is unapproachable, your appearance is inimitable,

[2]φιλεῖν.
[3]ἀγαπᾶν.

your glory is incomparable, and who has ever seen you,
or who is able to see you fully, you my God? (1 Tim 6.16)
For what sort of eye would be able to contemplate the all?
80   What sort of mind would be able to comprehend,
or to grasp, or to stretch entirely to the whole,
and to contemplate the Upholder of all things
who is outside all things, and fills the all and all things,
and again him who is ineffably outside?
85   Nevertheless I see you as a sun and I look at you like a star,
and I bear you in my bosom, just like a pearl,
and I see you as a lamp lighted in an earthen vessel.
But because you do not increase, because you do not
render me completely light, and you are not wholly revealed to
     me, what kind
90   and how great you are, I do not seem to have you fully, you my
     life,
but I grieve like someone having gone from wealth to beggary,
and from fame to dishonor, and having no hope. Therefore
when he sees this, the enemy says to me: "You are not saved.
For behold, you have fallen out, you have lost hope,
95   for you do not have boldness before God as before." (1 Jn 3.21)
I do not speak a word to the enemy, I do not so honor him, my
     God,
but I blow on him and immediately he vanishes.
So I ask, Master, thus I call upon you then
to give to me also your compassion, my Savior,
100 when my soul goes out of my body, to be able
with a single breath to put to shame all
who are against me your servant, all who intend to attack me,
and so that I can pass over unharmed, protected by the light
of your Spirit, and stand before your judgment seat,
105 having your divine grace present to me, Christ,
sheltering me and rendering me wholly without shame.
For who would dare to be seen before you

if they had not put on your grace, if they did not
possess it within and had not been illuminated by it? How
    would anyone
110   at all be able to contemplate your unendurable glory?
For how will a human being, humble human nature, be able
to look upon the glory of God and the nature of divinity?
For God is uncreated, and we are all created,
he is imperishable, we are perishable and ashes,
115   he is Spirit and beyond all spirit,
as he is the maker of spirits and their master,
we are flesh that is of dust, and earthly essence,
he is maker of all things, without beginning and
    inapprehensible,
we are worms and at the same time mud and ashes,
120   and who among us will ever be able to see him
by their own power or energy,
if he does not send his divine Spirit,
and by the Spirit provide for one's weakness of nature,
strength, might, and power, and make the person
125   capable of contemplating his divine glory?
For otherwise no one among human beings will contemplate
nor be able to see the Lord coming in glory,[4]
and thus the unjust will be separated from the just,
and all the sinners shall be covered with darkness,
130   however many do not have the light in them here below.
And those who are united to him now, then also
will be joined to God mysteriously and legitimately,
and they will be inseparable from his communion.
But if those who go away from his light are separated,
135   how then shall they be united or in what manner?
I want to learn from you, or to teach you.
God became a human being, and he was united to human
    beings,

[4] 1 Tim 6.16; Mt 24.30.

he participated in humanity and gave a share to all
who have faith in him, and who show their faith
140 by works, by participation in his divinity. (Jas 2.17)
And so he said that only those who participate
in his divinity are saved, thus he himself participated
in our nature, the Maker of all things,
as Paul testifies: that the Church of Christ
145 will become the one and divine body of the master,[5]
spotless, blameless, without any wrinkle, (Eph 5.27)
whomsoever are the faithful with Christ as head.
Therefore if it shall be thus, as also it is,
who then, being dirty, would dare to touch him,
150 or who, being unworthy, would be attached to him?
For if even now sinners are thrown out of the Church
and prevented from communicating at all,
and even more they are deprived from the view of divine
        things,
then those who are not holy, how, alas,
155 would they be united to the all-blameless body of God,
and become members of Christ when they are stained?
        (1 Cor 6.15)
This is not possible, this could never be!
Those who are separated from the body of God;
that is to say, the Church and chorus of the elect, tell me,
160 to where would they go, to what kingdom,
to what place, tell me, do they hope to encamp?
For by all means paradise, and the bosom of Abraham,
        (Lk 16.22)
and every place of repose belongs to the saved.
And the saved are certainly all the saints,
165 as all the divine Scriptures teach and bear witness.
For there are many mansions, but within it the one bridal
        chamber, (Jn 14.2)

[5]Eph 1.22–23; 4.4.

just as there is one heaven, and in it stars that
surpass one another in honor and glory, (1 Cor 15.41)
so also there is one bridal chamber and one kingdom.
170 But even paradise, and the holy city,
and every place of repose is God alone.
For as a human being does not have repose in this life
when one does not remain in God and God in the person,
    (Jn 15.4)
so also after death outside God alone,
175 alas, there is no repose, no place without suffering,
no place completely free of groaning and affliction.
And so let us hasten, brothers, let us hasten before the end
to adhere to God the Maker of all things,
to the One who came down to earth for the sake of us
    wretched ones,
180 to him who has bowed down the heavens and the angels, yet
    escaped notice, (Ps 17.10)
and pitched his tent in the womb of the holy virgin,
and who immutably and ineffably took on flesh from her,
and came forth unto the salvation of us all.
But our salvation is certainly this,
185 just as we have said many times and now we shall say again,
we do not speak from ourselves, but the divine mouth
has revealed the great light of the age to come.
The kingdom of heaven has come down upon the earth,
rather, the Absolute Monarch of beings on high and beings
    below
190 has arrived, he wanted to be made like us
so that all who partake of him as from a light
may be rendered a second light similar to the first,
and be partners in the kingdom of heaven,
and participants in his glory, and heirs
195 of eternal goods, which no one has ever seen. (1 Cor 2.9)

And these goods are, as I am persuaded, and I believe, and I
    say,
Father, Son, and Holy Spirit, Holy Trinity,
this is the source of goods, this is the life of beings,
this is the pleasure and repose, this is the robe and the glory,
200 this is the inexpressible joy and salvation of all
who participate in his unspeakable illumination,
and who have communion with him in their senses.
Listen, for on account of this he is called Savior,
because he provides salvation for all to whom he has been
    united,
205 and the salvation is release from all evils,
and the eternal discovery of all goods in this ‹salvation›:
life from death, daylight out of darkness,
absolute freedom from the slavery of the passions
and from very shameful practices, granted to all
210 who have been united to the Christ and Savior of all.
And then they possess all endless joy,
and all exultation, and all merriment,
but those who are separated from him,
and who have not sought him, nor have been united to him,
215 and who have not been rescued from slavery of the passions
    and from death,
even if they are kings, even if they are princes, even if great
    people, (Rev 6.15)
even if they suppose that they enjoy pleasure and have
    happiness,
and think that they possess good things,
still they will never attain so much merriment
220 as the servants of Christ. Those who are free of all
unnatural yearnings for pleasures and glory
have ‹joy› beyond telling, that is utterly ineffable,
that no one has ever known, nor learned, nor looked upon,

unless they have been genuinely and fervently united to Christ
  (1 Cor 6.17)
225 and mixed with him in a mysterious union,
to whom is fitting glory, and honor, praise, and every hymn
by every creature and breath forever. Amen.

Hymn 43

*That it is better to be shepherded well than to shepherd others against
their will. For there will be no profit for one who hastens to save others,
but destroys oneself through leading others.*

Speak, Christ, to your servant, speak, Light of the world,
  (Jn 8.12)
speak, Knowledge of the universe, speak, Logos, Wisdom,
All Foreknowledge, All Premonition,
teaching us useful things generously.
5   Speak and teach me the saving ways
of your will, Savior, and of your divine commands!
Speak and do not disregard me, nor hide, O my God,
your divine will from your unworthy servant!
What is better on your part, what is pleasing to you (Wis 9.10)
10   of the two, tell me, O Benevolent Savior:
that I be in worry over the affairs of the monastery
and that I be ungrudgingly concerned about bodily necessities,
and claim justice for everything with hostility and fighting,
or that I always persist in solitary quietude,
15   and preserve my mind and my heart untroubled,
and that I receive the illumination of your grace,
and the senses of my soul should always be illuminated,
and echo[1] mystically divine words, and that
I teach others meekly, and likewise be taught myself,
20   for one who speaks says what is said for himself also,

---

[1] ἐνηχεῖσθαι: to echo, to resonate, to teach by voice.

and must by all means be the first to practice them.
Of these things therefore speak to me, O my God and Sculptor,
what is better for me, what is useful,
and what pleases you and what is perfect? (Rom 12.2)
25 Yes indeed, may you not hide from me, O all-merciful Logos!
"Listen to what you ask, write what you hear!
I am God before eternity, I am Master by nature,
and king of the heavens and of the underworlds,
and all are my servants even if not wishing to be.
30 For I am creator, and judge, and master of all things,
I am now and I shall be forever and ever.
But I never coerce one who is unwilling,
and I want those who obey me to do service,
to be moved by fear, and to show love
35 by their own power and free choice.
For such as these are my slaves, such are my employees,
and I yearn for such as these to be my friends,[2]
and the others I have not yet known nor have I been known by
        them, (Jn 10.14)
because of this they say that I am harsh, they call me
        unsympathetic,
40 the children of the unjust one name me Unjust.
And so those who maltreat me and revile me,
those who reproach me, how would they obey you
or how would they accept you as a teacher, tell me?
And how would wolves consider you their shepherd?
45 Being wild beasts, how would they follow your voice? (Jn 10.5)
Go out, flee and get out of the midst of such as these,
for if you will save yourself, it will be sufficient for you!
But if you were to save the world, but perish yourself, (Lk 9.25)
what profit for you would there be in your having saved the
        world?

[2]Cf. *Hymn* 41.109–15.

50   For I do not want you to shepherd anyone of those who are not
          willing.
      See that even I observed this in the world.
      For I am both shepherd and master of those who so desire.
      But I am by nature creator and God of the others,
      but indeed I am not the king nor prince at all
55   of those who do not take up their cross and follow me.
          (Mt 16.24)
      For they are children of the one who is against me, his slaves
          and tools.
      Look at the frightful mysteries, look at their callousness.[3]
      Behold and bewail them, if possible, every hour!
      For being called from darkness to endless light, (1 Pet 2.9)
60   from death to life, from hell to heaven, (1 Jn 3.14)
      from the temporary and the perishable to eternal glory,
          (1 Pet 5.10)
      yet they get angry and furious against their teachers,
      and they weave all sorts of plots against them,
      and they prefer to die than to shun darkness
65   and the deeds of darkness, and to follow me. (Rom 13.12)
      Tell me, how will you shepherd them, how will you guide
          them,
      how will you lead, tell me, the ones who desert to fire,
      who associate with the enemy, and with him
      eagerly do things contrary to my commands?
70   How will you shepherd them like sheep, how will you lead
          them, tell me,[4]
      into the pasture of my commandments, how do you lead them
          out
      to the water of my wishes, to the mental[5] mountains
      of mystical contemplations, of my inexpressible glory,

[3]ἀναισθησίαν.
[4]Ps 22.1; Jn 10.9.
[5]νοητά.

through which those who see it despise the glory
75 here below, and forget all perceptible things,
and they consider them all as a shadow and smoke?
Tell me, how will you make an opponent your advocate,
how will you persuade the enemy who fights you to be your
friend?
For friends more easily become enemies
80 when they find a small pretext, but with difficulty
can enemies become friends even when they are shown
kindness,
even when they partake of great and sublime gifts
they have poison hidden in their heart,
and seizing the right moment they suddenly vomit it forth,
85 without pity or compassion they do not fear
to kill their benefactors. Oh ultimate madness!
These imitate Cain, they are worse than Lamech, (Gen 4)
they are of the same habits as Saul, they are imitators of the
Hebrews, (1 Kg 13)
emulators of Judas, heirs of hanging! (Mt 27.5)
90 If you seek to lead them, look to where you will arrive!
For they will not repent, like you want,
but they will force you to walk in their own path,
and to fall to destruction before them,
and to descend lower to the depths of hell
95 as you have them follow you. (Pr 14.12)
But if you do not wish to become at all like them,
and if you do not want to accommodate yourself to their
designs,
nor to participate in their wicked practices, (2 Jn 11)
you will have an uprising, a fight, and an irreconcilable battle.
100 What will happen to you under them? And what will you
meet?
And what will you gain? Listen, and I will tell you at once.
First of all you will not be at all able to be my servant,

for I absolutely do not want my servant to fight. (2 Tim 2.24)
And they will possess irrepressible hatred toward you,
105 urge murder against you both openly and secretly,
and you will give an account of their condemnation.
For your death will not benefit anyone else.
Whereas my death was the life of the world,
but you will become the cause of condemnation for them,
110 and you will go out from this life unable to speak freely.
Therefore it is better to be shepherded than to shepherd
such as these, but better still to be anxious for your own
     interests,
and to pray for them and all human beings
to repent, and for all to come to full knowledge. (1 Tim 2.4)
115 Teach and instruct ‹only› the willing among them.
And may you not compel them to do what you teach,
but speak my words and exhort them
to keep my words as the providers of eternal life! (Jn 5.24)
And these words will stand up when I come to judge, (Jn 12.48)
120 and they will judge each of them all according to their
     worthiness,
and you will remain without responsibility, not at all
     condemned,
because you did not hide from them the silver of my oracles,[6]
but however much you yourself received, you set down before
     all.
This is acceptable to me. This became the work
125 of my apostles and disciples according to my commands,
to proclaim me as God to the whole world,
and to teach my desires and ordinances,
and to leave them in writing for all human beings.
Thus also ‹may you› struggle to do and to teach, (Acts 1.1)
130 and say to those who do not want to listen to my words
what I myself said to them when they said:

[6]Mt 25.18; Ps 11.7.

"Your word is hard, and who will be able to
listen to it?" And so I responded: "If you do not want to hear
        thus,
go and may you each do what you want!"[7]
135 I left everything to their own power and
free will to choose death or life. (Deut 30.19)
For no one ever became good unintentionally,
and the unfaithful will not be faithful unless they want to,
nor will a friend of the world be a friend of God.
140 A mischievous person will not unwillingly change
their purpose and become entirely good,
for no one will become wicked by nature, but by intention.[8]
So in turn no one will become good and virtuous
from having been wicked and sinful by purpose and intention
145 unless they so desire. But if one is not willing, this will never
        be.
No one who does not want to accomplish virtue in the world,
no one who does not want it is saved. Do not seek more than
        this,
but hasten to save yourself and those who hear you
if you would but find a person on earth who has ears
150 to hear and to obey your words!" (Mt 11.15)
So shall I do, Master, as you have commanded me,
but may you give your aid and your grace to me
your unworthy servant, O my God,
so that I may always glorify you and sing your power
155 in unceasing songs forever and ever. Amen.

[7]Jn 6.60; 6.67.
[8]Cf. *Catechesis* 4; SC 96:322; deCatanzaro, *Discourses*, 72.

Hymn 44

What it is to be created according to the divine image and how a human being is reasonably considered the image of the Prototype. That one who loves enemies as benefactors is an imitator of God, and thence one becomes a participant of the Holy Spirit, and, by adoption and grace, becomes God. This is made known only to those who are moved by the Holy Spirit.

Glory, praise, hymn, and thanks
to him who brought all creation
from non-being to being
by just a word
5   and his personal will.
To the God of everything, worshipped
in Trinity of hypostases
and in one essence!
For God is one, Holy Trinity,
10   essence beyond essence,
one in three persons,[1]
and three hypostases
neither separated nor divisible,
one nature, one glory,
15   one power,
and likewise one will.
This Trinity alone is creator of all things,
She molded all of me
from clay, and giving me a soul,
20   put me on the earth. (Job 10.9)
And She gave to me light to look
and to see everything in this
perceptible world:
the sun, the moon I say,

[1]προσώποις.

25 the stars and the sky,
earth and sea, and everything
that is within them.
She also gave to me mind and reason,[2]
but pay attention to this word![3]

30 Therefore, according to the image of the Logos
reason was given to us. (Gen 1.26)
For we are given reason from the Logos,
the eternal, the uncreated,
the inapprehensible, and my God.

35 Truly the soul of every human being,
according to his image,
is a rational image of the Logos.
How? Tell me! Teach me!
Listen to the Logos himself:

40 The Logos, God from God,
is also coeternal
with the Father and the Spirit.
And so truly my soul is also
according to his image,

45 for having mind and reason
the soul bears these by her very essence,
without separation or confusion,
likewise all three are of the same essence,
three united as one,

50 but also distinguished.
And always they are united,
and yet they are reckoned as parts.
For they are united without confusion,
and distinguished indivisibly.

---

[2]Symeon employs an understanding of the human soul in terms of ψυχὴ, νοῦς, λόγος, that is soul, mind, and reason. The latter term lends itself to a variety of word play. When λόγος refers specifically to the second person of the Trinity I have simply transliterated it as Logos.

[3]A pun on λόγος, implying Symeon's words, reason, and Christ.

55   If you were to take away one of them,
     you certainly take all three with it.
     For a soul without mind or reason
     is equal to irrational beasts,
     and it is not possible for either the mind
60   or reason to subsist without the soul.
     And so truly understand
     the Prototype by the image!
     Without the Spirit there shall be
     neither Father nor his Logos,
65   but the Father is Spirit, (Jn 4.24)
     his Son too is Spirit
     even if he has put on flesh,
     and the Spirit in turn is God;
     for they are one
70   in nature and essence,
     like mind, soul, and reason.
     But the Father ineffably
     begot the Logos.
     Just as my mind from my soul,
75   or rather in my soul,
     so also the Spirit from the Father,
     or rather both remain in the Father
     and proceed ineffably.
     And again just as my mind
80   always begets reason,
     and proclaims, and sends it forth,
     and makes it known to all,
     yet the mind is not separated from it,
     but it both begets reason
85   and possesses it within.
     So consider the Father,
     that he begot the Logos,
     that he begets continuously,

but the Father is not separated at all
90   from his Son.
But he is seen in the Son, (Jn 14.9)
and the Son remains in him. (Jn 17.21–22)
This exact image
—even if it is obscure—
95   my discourse has sketched out,
an image you will never contemplate
nor will you ever understand,
unless first you purify,
unless first you wash away,
100 the filth of your image,
if you do not bring out the image that
has been buried in the passions,
and wipe it off perfectly,
and likewise strip it,
105 and make it white as snow. (Is 1.18)
And when you have done these things,
and well purified yourself,
and the image has become perfect,
you shall not see the Prototype,
110 nor will you understand
if he has not revealed it to you (1 Cor 2.10)
through the Holy Spirit.
For the Spirit teaches all things (Jn 14.26)
shining in unutterable light.
115 He shall mentally provide for you a glimpse
of all rational things,
as much as you are able to see,
as much as is accessible to a human being,
in proportion
120 to the purification of your soul,
and you will be made like God
by exact imitation of his works

of discretion, and of courage,
but also of benevolence,
125   and patient endurance of temptations, (Jas 1.12)
and by love toward enemies. (Mt 5.44)
For this is philanthropy:
that you do good to enemies,
and love them as friends,
130   as genuine benefactors,
and pray on behalf of all
who threaten you abusively, (Lk 6.28)
and to keep equally toward all,
both the good and the wicked,
135   a deep-seated love,
and each day lay down your soul
on behalf of all, (1 Jn 3.16)
for their salvation I say,
so that one may be saved,
140   or even all of them if possible.
These things, child, shall render
you an imitator of the Master,[4]
and show you to be
a true image of the creator,
145   an imitator, in every respect,
of the divine perfection. (Mt 5.48)
And then the creator—pay attention
to what I am about to tell you!—
shall send the divine Spirit.
150   I do not mean another soul for you
such as you have, but the Spirit
who comes from God, I say to you,
and he shall inspire, and dwell,
and in essence he shall pitch his tent,
155   and illuminate, and make brilliant,

[4]Eph 5.1; 1 Cor 11.1.

and refashion you entirely,
and he shall make the perishable imperishable,
and, moreover, he shall renew
the dilapidated house
160   —I mean the house of your soul!—
And by this he shall render completely immortal
your whole body as well,
and he shall render you God
according to grace,
165   like the Prototype. O marvel,
O mystery unknown
to all those who are driven by the passions,
unknown to the worldly,
unknown to the lovers of glory,
170   unknown to the arrogant,
unknown to the truly irascible,
unknown also to those who bear a grudge,
unknown to those who love the flesh,
unknown to the money lovers,
175   and unknown to the envious,
unknown to all the abusers,
unknown to the hypocrites,
unknown also to the gluttons,
unknown to the compulsive eaters,
180   and the drunkards and fornicators,
unknown to the blabbermouths,
unknown to those who use foul language,
unknown to the lazy,
unknown to those who neglect
185   hourly repentance,
unknown to those who do not mourn
continuously each day,
unknown to the unruly,
unknown to those who contradict,

190 unknown to those who follow their own devices,
    unknown to those who suppose they
    are something, but are nothing,
    unknown to those who boast, (Gal 6.3)
    but also unknown to those who enjoy
195 the greatness of their body,
    whether its strength, or beauty,
    or any other gift
    whatsoever, I tell you,
    unknown to those who have not gained
200 a pure heart, (Mt 5.8)
    unknown to those who do not beg
    to receive in the fervor of their heart
    the divine Spirit,
    unknown to those who do not believe
205 that even now the divine Spirit
    is given to those who seek him.
    For unbelief hinders
    and chases away the divine Spirit.
    Anyone who does not believe does not ask,
210 without begging they do not receive, (Mt 7.8)
    having not received they are a corpse.
    Who will not weep over a corpse,
    because even though it is a corpse, it seems to live? (Rev 3.1)
    The dead are not as yet able
215 either to see or to bewail
    other corpses at all. The living mourn
    when they see them.
    For they see a strange wonder,
    the corpses not only living,
220 but also walking about,
    they are blind yet suppose that they see,
    and also those who are truly deaf
    imagining they hear.

For they live, and see,
225 and hear like an ox;
they perceive like unintelligent beasts,
in unfeeling sense perception,
in a dead life.
For is it to live without living?
230 Is it to see, without seeing?
Or to hear without hearing? (Mt 13.13)
Tell me how?! I will say briefly:
however many live according to the flesh, (Rom 8.12ff)
however many look at things here present,
235 and hearken to divine words
with fleshly ears alone,
all these are, according to the spirit,
deaf, blind, and dead cadavers.
For they were not begotten from God at all (Jn 1.13)
240 so that they also may live.
But they have not received the Spirit,[5]
they have not cast up their eyes,
they have not looked upon the divine light,
and failing this,
245 they have remained utterly stupid.
Tell me, how would such as these
be called Christians?
Listen to what the divine Paul
has wisely revealed to you,
250 or rather what Christ has said:
the first human being was created
from earth, truly dust,
but the second human being
descended from the heavens. (1 Cor 15.47)
255 Pay attention to what is said.
It follows that in as much as the first is dust,

[5]Jn 20.22; Acts 8.15–16.

so all those who are begotten
from him are also dust. (1 Cor 15.48)
But in as much as Christ
260 is a heavenly Master,
so also all who have believed in him
are also heavenly,
and begotten from above, (Jn 3.3)
and likewise baptized
265 in the all-holy Spirit. (Acts 1.5)
Such a Spirit who begets is
truly God, and from him
such types who are begotten
from God are really adopted gods
270 and all of them children of the Most High,[6]
as the divine mouth says.
Have you heard the words of God?
Have you heard how he separates
the faithful from the others?
275 How he has given to his servants
a sign and a proof
so that they are not led astray by the words
of foreign teachers?
He says the first human is from the earth
280 because he was created of dust,
but the second human being,
the Master of all things,
descended from the heavens. (1 Cor 15.47)
The first procured death
285 for all human beings, (Rom 5.17)
and mortality by a transgression.
But the second gave
to the world, and even now
provides for all the faithful,

[6]Jn 1.13; Ps 81.6.

290 light, life, and incorruption. (2 Tim 1.10)
Have you heard what he says to you,
he who is initiated into the mysteries of the heavens?
Have you heard Christ speaking
through him, and teaching
295 what kind of people
are those who have believed in him,
and who show their faith
by their works? (Jas 2.18)
Therefore doubt no longer.
300 If you are a Christian,
inasmuch as Christ is
heavenly, so also
you should be heavenly.
But if you are not so heavenly,
305 how will you be called a Christian?
For if he says that insofar as
the Master is heavenly
so also those who believe in him
310 are by all means heavenly, (1 Cor 15.48)
then however many think worldly things,
however many live according to the flesh, (Rom 8.12)
they are not of God the Logos
who descended from above, (Jn 3.13)
315 but they certainly belong to the man of dust
who was formed out of earth.
Think thus, understand thus,
thus believe and seek
to become such
320 heavenly types, as he has said,
he who has visited from heaven
and given life to the world! (Jn 6.33)
He is also the bread
descending from heaven;

325 those who eat him
shall never see death. (Jn 6.50)
For being heavenly,
they shall certainly be forever
stripped of corruption,
330 and having put on incorruption, (1 Cor 15.53)
they throw off death,
and cleave to life.
For they become immortal,
incorruptible, and because of this,
335 they are called heavenly.
For who has ever
been reckoned as such
—I mean from among the sons of Adam—
before the Master of all the heavenly beings,
340 of all the terrestrial beings,
descended from heaven? (Phil 2.10)
He received our flesh
and gave the divine Spirit,
as we have often said,
345 and this Spirit, as God,
provides all things for us.
All of what things? Things of which I have often spoken,
but I shall now tell of them again:
He becomes like a divine,
350 most radiant bath,
he embraces everyone
who is worthy, those whom he discovers within.
But how shall I say it, how shall I
worthily express what happens?
355 Give to me a word,[7]
my God who gave to me a soul.
The divine Spirit, being God,

[7]Symeon again plays on the word λόγος, meaning both speech and reason.

whomsoever he may find within himself,
he reforms them completely.

360 He renews them,
and paradoxically makes them something new.
How, and in what manner,
does the Spirit not in the least
partake of their filth?

365 Just as the fire does not partake
of the blackness of iron,
yet it gives to iron
a share of all its properties,
so also the divine Spirit,

370 being incorruptible, gives incorruptibility,
and being immortal,
he gives immortality,
and being never-setting light,
he turns everyone into light

375 in which he shall pitch his tent,
and being life to everyone,
he provides life for them,
And as he is the same nature as Christ,
likewise the same essence,

380 and being the same glory,
and being united ‹with Christ›,
he renders them absolutely
like Christ himself.
For the Master is not jealous

385 that mortals should be seen
equal to himself by divine grace.
And he does not deem his servants
unworthy to be like him,
but he is delighted and rejoices

390 seeing us transformed from human beings
into such divine beings

according to grace, just like he
is and was by nature.
For being a benefactor,
395 he wishes us to be ‹divine›
inasmuch as he is himself.
For if we were not so much
like him in exactness,
how shall we be
400 united to him, as he said,
and how do we remain in him,
if we are not like that,
and how would he remain in us
when we are unlike him? (Jn 15.4)
405 Therefore you who wisely know this,
hasten to receive the Spirit
who is divine and from God,[8]
so that you may become as divine
as this word has shown,
410 so that you may be both heavenly and divine,
as much as the Master said,
so that you may also become heirs
of the kingdom of heaven
for all ages. (Jas 2.5)
415 But if you have not been divine,
or if you do not become
heavenly here below like I said,
how do you suppose you will
dwell with him in heaven?
420 And how also will you
enter into the kingdom with
the heavenly ones, and reign,
and live with the King
and Master of all?

[8] Acts 19.2; 1 Cor 2.12.

425 Therefore run with haste all of you,
   so that we may be deemed worthy
   to be in the
   kingdom of heaven,
   and to reign with Christ (2 Tim 2.12)
430 the Master of all things,
   to whom is fitting all glory
   with the Father and the Spirit
   forever and ever. Amen.

Hymn 45

Concerning a most exact theology, and that one who does not see the light of God's glory is worse than blind.

   O my God who is prone to pity, my Maker,
   shine your unapproachable light for me some more
        (1 Tim 6.16)
   in order to fill my heart with joy!
   Yes, may you not grow angry, yes, do not abandon me,
5   but beam upon my soul with your light.
   For you are your own light, my God.
   For, though you are called by many and different
   names, still you are One.
   But this One is unknown to every nature,
10   and invisible, and inexpressible.
   He who shows himself is called all names.
   And so this One is one nature in three hypostases,
   one divinity, one kingdom,
   one power, for the Trinity is one,
15   for my God is one Trinity, not three,
   but the One is three with respect to hypostases,
   being of the same nature as each other by nature,
   entirely of the same power, of the same essence,

indeed united beyond the mind without confusion,
20 but in turn separated indivisibly,
the Three into one, and the One into three.
For he who has made all things is One,
Jesus Christ with the Father without beginning,
and with the Holy Spirit who also has no beginning.
25 And so the Trinity is one indivisibly in every way,
but the Three in the One, and the One in the Three,
or rather to me the Three are one and the One is three.
Understand now, fall prostrate in worship, and have faith
        forever!
For this One has been revealed, shining and illuminating,
30 shared, communicated, he is all good.
Because of this he is not called one by us but many:
light, and peace, and joy, life, food, and drink,
clothing, robe, tent, and divine home,
sunrise, resurrection, repose, and bath,
35 fire, water, river, source of life, and stream,
bread, and wine, the new richness of the faithful,
the lavish banquet, the pleasure that we mystically enjoy,
the sun that truly never sets, and the ever-shining star,
lamp shining within the house of the soul.
40 This is the One purifying and creating the many,
this One produced all things with a word,
and by his Spirit of power holds all these together. (Ps 32.6)
This One produced heaven and earth out of non-being,
he gave them existence, he organized them mysteriously,
45 this One made the sun, moon, and the stars
by his will, strange and new wonder.
This One produced quadrupeds, reptiles, and wild beasts,
and birds of every kind, and all creatures of the sea,
by his command, like all things seen.
50 And last he made me like a king,
and gave all these to me for service

like slaves, and they slavishly fulfill my need.
And so, I say, everything has guarded and even now keeps
the ordinance of this One God of the universe,
55   and I alone, the wretched one, am shown to be ungrateful,
hard-hearted, and deaf to God who formed me,
and who provided all these good things abundantly,
having transgressed God's command I became foolish,
and was rendered worse than all beasts, both wild and
      domestic,
60   worse than reptiles, and birds, the wretch,
and I turned aside from the straight and divine road,
and wretchedly fell from the glory given to me,
and I took off the shining and divine robe,
and having come into darkness I now lie in the darkness,
65   and I do not know that I am deprived of light,
and I say: behold, the sun illuminated the day,
and I see it. Again night having come, the sun sets,
and I light candles and lamps for myself and I see.
And of all human beings, does anyone have anything more
      than I?
70   For certainly human beings see in the world,
and no one ever sees more than this.
And so, saying these things, I lie and I mock myself,
and boasting about myself, Savior, I deceive myself,
not wanting to know myself because I am blind,
75   and not wanting to grow weary, I do not wish to regain my
      sight,
and being condemned, I do not want to know my blindness.
      (Jn 9.41)
And I say: who has seen God, the light of the world? (Jn 1.18)
And saying this, Master, I am utterly insensitive,
not perceiving that I reckon and I speak wickedly.
80   For one who does not see your light and says that they see fully,
      (Jn 9.41)

or rather they say that it is impossible
to look upon the light of your divine glory, Master,
they deny all the writings of the prophets, the apostles,
and your words, Jesus, and your divine plan.

85   For if you shone from on high, if you appeared in darkness, (Lk
  1.78–79)
and you came, Compassionate One, into the world with
  human beings,
wishing to live like us benevolently, (Bar 3.37)
and you sincerely say that you are the light of the world,
  (Jn 8.12)
but we do not see you, are we not utterly blind

90   and more wretched than the blind, my Christ?
Yes, certainly, yes, we are truly like both the dead and the blind,
not seeing you the vivifying light.
The blind do not see the perceptible sun,
but they also live, Master, and they are moved somehow.

95   For the sun does not give life, but only vision.
But you are all good things, you always give
them to your servants who see your light,
as you are life, and you provide life with all other
good things which, I say, are you yourself.

100   And one who has you truly has all things in you.
May I not be deprived of you, Master, may I not be deprived of
  you, Creator,
may I not be deprived of you, Compassionate One, I the
  humble stranger.
For your good pleasure I have become a stranger here and a
  sojourner, (Eph 2.19)
not by free choice, a stranger not by my own wish,

105   but by your grace I know myself to be a stranger
to visible things, mentally[1] illuminated by your light,
and knowing that you lead and resettle

---

[1] νοερῶς.

the human race to an immaterial and invisible world,
and you divide and distribute things worthy of the settlement
    to each person,
110 as each has kept, Savior, your commandments.
So on this account I beg you to appoint me to you,
even if I have committed many sins beyond that of all human
    beings,
and I am worthy of punishment and torture,
but I beseech you like the publican, (Lk 18.13)
115 and like the prostitute, Master, even if I do not cry like her,
    (Lk 7.37)
if I do not wipe your feet with my hair in the same way,
if I do not likewise groan and wail, Christ,
but you pour forth mercy and you are full to bursting with
    compassion,
you pour out very good things, through which you have mercy
    on me!
120 Yes, you whose hands were impaled, yes, you whose feet were
    impaled
on the cross, and whose side was pierced with a spear. All-
    Merciful, (Jn 19.34)
have mercy and rescue me from the eternal fire,
deign me worthy to serve you well here below,
and then to stand before you without condemnation,
125 and to be received within your bridal chamber, Savior,
where I will rejoice with you the Good Master,
with unspeakable grace unto all ages. Amen.

Hymn 46

Full confession united to a prayer, and concerning union of the Holy Spirit, and dispassion.

I have removed to a distance, Benevolent One, I dwelt in the
      desert, (Ps 54.7)
and I was hidden from you, the sweet Master. (Gen 3.8)
I came under the night of life's worry,
and there I sustained many stings and wounds,
5   having gone up I bear many blows in my soul,
and I cry out amid the suffering and trouble of my heart:
have mercy, have pity on me the transgressor!
O soul-loving doctor who alone loves mercy, (Wis 11.27)
who heals the weak and wounded as a gift,
10   cure my bruises and wounds!
Drip the oil of your grace, my God, (Lk 10.34)
and anoint my injuries, wipe out my infections,
form scar tissues and bind up my severed
members, and remove all the scars, Savior,
15   and heal the whole of me completely as before
when I did not have defilement, when I did not have any
      bruise, (Is 1.6)
nor infected injury, nor stain, O my God,
but calm and joy, peace and meekness,
and holy humility, and patience,
20   the illumination from long-suffering and excellent works,
long-suffering and utterly unconquerable power.
Hence much comfort[1] from tears each day, (Mt 5.4)
hence the exultation in my heart
gushed forth like a spring, flowed everlastingly,
25   and was a stream of dripping honey, and a drink of merriment,
continuously turning in the mouth of my mind.

---

[1]παράκλησις also means prayer.

Hence all health, hence purity,
hence cleansing of my passions and vain thoughts,
hence dispassion was with me like lightning,
30 and always associated with me. Understand me spiritually,
I who say these things, be not wretchedly defiled!
The dispassion produced in me is the unutterable pleasure of
     communion,
and boundless desire for the wedding feast, for union full of
     God,
partaking of which I also became dispassionate,
35 I was burned up with pleasure, blazing with desire for it,
and I shared in the light, yes, and I became light, (Eph 5.8)
higher than all passion, outside all wickedness.
For passion does not touch the light of dispassion,
just as the shadow or darkness of night cannot touch the sun.
40 And so having become such, and being such a kind,
I was relaxed, Master, as I took confidence in myself.
I was dragged down by worry about perceptible matters,
I fell down, wretched, to the concern of life's problems,
and I became cold like black iron,
45 and lying around for a long time I took on rust.
Because of this I shout to you asking to be purified anew,
Benevolent One, and to be lifted up to the first
beauty, and to enjoy fully your light
now and always unto all ages. Amen.

Hymn 47

Concerning rational paradise. Far-shining contemplation, and concerning the tree of life in it.

You are blessed, Lord, you alone are blessed,
you are blessed, Compassionate One, blessed above all,

you who gave the light of your commands in my heart,
  (Prov 6.23)
and implanted your tree of life in me, (Gen 2.9)
5   and revealed me as another paradise among the visible things,
rational among perceptible, and rational in sense perception.[1]
For you have united your other divine Spirit to my soul,
the Spirit whom you encamped in my guts. (Ps 50.12)
For this Spirit alone is certainly the tree of life.
10   He was planted in the very earth, that is the human soul,
and took root in the heart, he rendered the heart
at once a shining paradise, adorned by all
beautiful plants, and trees, and different fruits,
embellished with flowers and sweet-smelling lilies.
15   And these plants are humility, and joy, and peace, (Gal 5.22)
meekness, and sympathy, remorse, rainstorms of tears,
and a strange delight in them, the radiance of your grace
shining upon all who are in this paradise.
You are a bowl pouring forth your stream of life for me,
20   and you give abundantly the words of divine knowledge into to
       my power. (1 Cor 12.8)
But when you do not wish, but when you cancel them,
  (Ps 50.13)
I am mindless, insensitive like a stone.
The trumpet without spirit[2] will never sound,
so also without you I am like one without a soul.
25   Without a soul a body cannot operate.
Thus a soul cannot be moved without your Spirit,
nor, Savior, keep your commandments,
nor can she see you, nor be present to you,
nor wisely sing your glory, O God of mine.
30   So this is why I cry to you, and on this account I groan.
You who are with the Father and with us,

[1] ἐν αἰσθητοῖς μέν νοητόν, νοητὸν δ' ἐν αἰσθήσει.
[2] πνεύματος: a blowing, breath.

not, as some reckon, by energy alone,
not, as many suppose, by your will alone,
not by your power alone, but also by your essence,

35 if one must venture to speak of or consider essence
with regard to you, Immortal, Alone Super-essential!
For if you are truly and completely unexplainable,
invisible, unapproachable, and unknowable,
untouchable, impalpable, wholly inapprehensible, Savior,

40 how may we call you by name, or dare we to speak
of you and your essence, of what nature and kind it is?
For certainly you are not among things, O my God,
but all of your works are produced from non-being.
But you alone are uncreated, alone without beginning, Savior,

45 Holy and Exalted Trinity, the God of all things,
who also provided for us the light of your immaculate glory.
Now also provide that the light be inseparable, Savior,
give for me always to reflect you through it, Logos,
and to understand well your impossible beauty,

50 which is unknowable to absolutely everyone,
it frightens my mind, and drives out my wits,[3]
and ignites a fire of your love in my heart!
When this fire becomes a flame of divine desire,
it shows to me more clearly your glory, my God.

55 Prostrating myself to worship this glory, I ask You, Son of God,
      give
both now and in the future for me to have it perpetually,
and through this glory to look upon you, God, eternally!
But do not give to me, Master, empty glory in the world,
not wealth that perishes, nor talents of gold,

60 nor lofty throne, nor sovereignty of these perishing things!
Yoke me to the humble ones, to the poor and meek, (Mt 5.3–5)
so that I also shall become both humble and meek, (Mt 11.29)
and if I do not pursue my service to be useful

[3]ἐξιστᾷ μου τὰς φρένας.

to your good pleasure and your worship,
65 may you be pleased to eject me from my service,
    and, Master, that I may bewail only my sins,
    and worry about only your just judgment,
    and how I shall explain the many times I provoked your anger!
    Yes, O Sympathetic Shepherd, Good, and Meek, (Jn 10.11)
70 who wants all who have faith in you to be saved, (1 Tim 2.4)
    have mercy, give ear to this my prayer:
    May you not be angered, may you not turn your face from me,
        (Ps 26.9)
    but teach me to fulfil your will! (Ps 142.10)
    For I do not seek that my will be done,
75 but yours, so that I shall also serve you, Merciful One!
        (Lk 22.42)
    I adjure you, have mercy, you who are merciful by nature,
        (Mk 5.7)
    do what is useful for my miserable soul,
    because you alone are benevolent God,
    uncreated, endless, truly all-powerful
80 life of all, and light of all who love you,
    and, Benevolent One, who are loved very much by you!
    Set me among them, Master, and render me
    a participant and co-heir of your divine glory.[4]
    For glory is fitting to you, the Father with the Son also without
        beginning,
85 and with the divine Spirit forever and ever. Amen.

[4] 1 Pet 5.1; Rom 8.17.

Hymn 48

That for every person who is maltreated and suffers badly on account of God's commandment, the dishonor for the sake of God's commandment is glory and honor.

Give to me the sensation,[1] Christ, that you once gave,
cover me with it, Savior, hide all of me within it,
and may you not allow the sensation of the world to approach
    me,
nor to penetrate within me, nor to wound me at all,
5 your humble slave, on whom you alone had mercy!
For worldly sensation suddenly fell upon the
one virtuous worry,[2] and at once caused
wicked yearnings in my miserable soul.
For it shows the glory, it calls to mind wealth,
10 and incites me to approach kings of the earth,
and says that this is great success.
And so from these thoughts, just like a billows is inflated
by a wind and a fire is ignited into flame,
so also this puffed-up soul is made vain,
15 and with a desire for glory vehemently contends for wealth,
and the relaxation of those who are dragged below,
she seeks to be glorified with those who are glorified,
conspicuous and seen everywhere with dignitaries,
and to possess wealth with those who possess wealth,
20 this very soul whom you yourself glorified with your
        inexpressible light,
whom you adorned with your unspeakable glory,
whom you revealed as your divine splendor.
The sensation takes its mind prisoner by force and
subtly points out kings, brings to mind glory,

[1] αἴσθησιν.
[2] The "virtuous worry" is that of one's final judgment, cf. *Hymn* 22.80ff.; 47.63–68.

25 and indicates the wealth of the present life,
  and makes the mind excited by its consideration alone.
  Oh the darkness, oh the hardness, oh the vain considerations,
  filthy intention, and stupid[3] opinion,
  because I abandon the vision of mysterious and imperishable
    things,
30 and I consider the things on earth and take them to heart!
  Shall a king not come to an end? Does glory not pass on?
  Shall wealth not be scattered like dust in the wind? (Wis 5.14)
  Shall bodies in the tombs not be utterly corrupted,
  and shall not others have power over their riches on earth?
35 And after them, then others, and after them, still others?
  And tell me, soul, to whom did the wealth belong?
  And who in the world is able to gain some small thing
  so that in death as in life they may take it with them? (Ps 48.18)
  Certainly you shall not ever be able to indicate anyone,
40 except the merciful ones who possess nothing,
  but rather, they give everything into the hands of beggars.
  For these are the ones who keep safely what they gave away,
  when they gave it into the hands of the Master.
  But all others who have their wealth stored away
45 are like beggars and are worse than all the poor, (Lk 19.20)
  for they are thrown naked like corpses into tombs,
  wretches ‹deprived› of present goods and strangers to future
    blessings.
  And so, my soul, what good do you see in them that you enjoy?
  And what of these do you judge worthy to be coveted?
50 Certainly you do not have anything to say, certainly you do not
    answer.
  Woe to those who have wealth treasured up,
  woe to those who want to take glory from human beings,
    (Jn 5.41–44)
  woe to those who impose themselves upon the wealthy,

[3] ἀναισθήτου.

and do not yearn for the glory of God,
55   and his wealth, and only to be with him.
For the world is empty, and all the things in the world
shall be most vain, everything is vanity of vanities. (Eccl 1.2)
And so shall they all pass away, and God alone shall be
eternal, and imperishable, remaining for ever, (1 Tim 1.17)
60   and with him shall be those who now seek him,
those who love him alone before all others.
And woe to those who now love the world, (1 Jn 2.15)
because in it they shall be condemned forever! (1 Cor 11.32)
Woe, my soul, to those who want the glory of humans,
          (Jn 12.43)
65   because they shall then be deprived of God's glory! (Rom 3.23)
Woe, my soul, to those who have collected wealth,
because there they shall yearn to obtain a drop of water!
          (Lk 16.24)
Woe, my soul, to those who put their hope in a human being,
          (Jer 17.5)
because humans shall die and with them their hopes,
70   and then they shall be found without hope!
Woe, my soul, to those who have their rest here,
because there they shall have eternal affliction!
Tell me, my soul, why do you grieve? What do you seek in life?
Tell me, and I shall teach you the use of each one.
75   Learn and be taught the good in each!
Tell me, do you wish to be glorified, and do you want to be
          praised?
Then hear what is honor and what is dishonor.
Honor is to honor everyone, but God before all,
and to obtain his commands like wealth,
80   and on account of them to suffer abuse, for their sake to be
          reviled,
and because of them to endure insults of every kind.
For when, my soul, on some occasion, you are attacked

in order to honor God, so that you may glorify him,
and on account of this you are maltreated and set at naught,
85   then you have obtained honor and ever-standing glory,
because the glory of God will by all means have come upon
     you. (Is 60.1)
Then all the angels shall praise you
because you have honored God whom they praise in song.
You wish, my soul, to acquire clothing and wealth?
90   Listen now, I shall show to you eternal wealth:
weep, repent, despise all things,
become poor in spirit, become also poor at heart, (Mt 5.3)
become impoverished of property, become a stranger to the
     world,
become an enemy of your own contrary desires,
95   and submit only to the will of your master,
and vigorously follow in his footsteps! (1 Pet 2.21)
And then the master proceeds more slowly
as he wishes to be overtaken by miserable you. (Phil 3.12)
And having beheld him, shout and cry loudly,
100 and he shall return with a gracious eye,
and he shall see and grant for you to behold him a little bit,
and again he will abandon you, concealed from your eyes.
Then you shall wail, wretched soul, then you shall cry
     diligently,
then you shall beg for death, not bearing the suffering,
105 not enduring the separation from the sweet Lord.
But he, the good Lord, seeing you in great difficulty,
and stubbornly continuing with weeping and sorrow,
again of a sudden he shall appear, and again he shall illuminate
     you,
again he shall give a glimpse of inexhaustible wealth to you,
110 the imperishable glory of his paternal face, (2 Cor 3.7)
and he shall make you happy like before, and fill you with joy,
and thus he shall leave you filled with joy.

And little by little the joy shall abandon you because of words,
and thoughts of the world, and sorrow shall come upon you.

115 And so again, as before, you shall be wailing violently,
screaming with wailing, and seeking him,
the Provider of merriment, the Giver of joy,
the wealth established and truly being for all time.
So while he tests your free will, watch out

120 lest you grow weary, O my soul, may you not turn back,
> (Lk 17.31)

> may you not say: "How long shall he thus be inapprehensible
> to me?"

> May you not say: "Why is he revealed and immediately he is
> hidden again?

> And, without mercy, how long will he give this suffering to
> me?"

> May you not say: "And how am I able to toil until the end?"

125 And, O my soul, may you not shrink from seeking out the
> Master,

> but like a soul giving herself to death once and for all,
> may you not grope about for relaxation, may you not seek out
> glory,

> nor pleasure of the body, nor the affection of relatives,
> nor look around to the right nor to the left,

130 but as you begin, or rather running more vigorously,
hasten always to overtake and to seize the Master! (Phil 3.13)
Even if he disappears ten thousand times, as many times is he
> revealed to you

and so the inapprehensible shall be within your grasp,
many thousands of times, or rather, so long as you breathe at
> all,

135 more zealously seek him and run to him!
For he shall not forsake you, nor shall he forget you,
and little by little he will most certainly be revealed even more,
and, my soul, the Master will be with you more frequently,

and when you have been perfectly purified by the illumination
     of the light,
140 the whole of him shall come, he himself shall dwell in you,
and he shall be with you, he who created the world,
          (Acts 17.24)
and you will have the true wealth that the world does not have,
but only heaven and those who are inscribed there. (Heb 12.23)
If it shall be thus for you, tell me, what more do you want?
145 Tell me, ungrateful soul, tell me, arrogant soul,
tell me, my lowly soul, what is better among the things
in the heavens or on earth that you would rather seek?
The Maker of heaven, and the Master of earth,
and of all in heaven and all in the world,
150 Creator, Judge, and himself sole King
who is abiding in you, wholly showing himself to you,
all of him illuminating you with a light, and he gives a glimpse
     of the beauty
of his face, and he provides for you to see him
in high relief, and renders a share of his very own glory.
          (1 Pet 5.1)
155 Tell me, what else is better than this?
"By all means, nothing," you say to me. And again I say:
after having been deemed worthy of such great glory, O soul,
why do you still gape at the world, and why are you enchanted
     by things here below,
and why do you cling to perishable things when you have
     received imperishable,
160 why are you devoted to present things when you have found
     the things to come?
Hasten to obtain these things, my soul,
attach the whole of yourself to them, my soul,
so that also after death you will be found among them,
          (Phil 3.9)
the eternal goods that you have obtained here below,

165   and with them you may stand by the Maker and Master
      enjoying yourself with him forever and ever. Amen.

Hymn 49

*It happens that by care for and reform of the neighbor the teacher may
be pulled down into the weakness of the neighbor's passion.*

    Have mercy on me, Lord, have mercy on me, One Alone,
    the Savior who protected me from my youth,
    you who in your own personal goodness had sympathy
    in all the many times I knowingly stumbled,
5   you who rescued me from the terrible and vain world,
    and from relatives, and friends, and unnatural pleasures,
    and you have deemed me worthy to settle here as on the
        mountain. (Mt 17.1)
    And you have shown to me your wonderful glory, my God,
        (Ex 33.18)
    and you have filled me with your divine Spirit, my Christ,
10   and you have poured spiritual Illumination into the whole of
        me!
    Give to me your servant, my God, your
    irrevocable grace perfectly unto the end!
    May you not cancel it, Master; may you not turn away, Creator;
        (Ps 50.13)
    nor may you disregard me whom you once set before your
        face,
15   and you have set me among your servants, and sealed
    me with the seal of your grace, and declared me your own!
    May you not again disown me, may you not again hide
    the light of your face, lest darkness also cover me,
    and the abyss engulf me, and heaven oppress me (Ps 68.15)
20   whom you have brought up above heaven, my Savior,
    even with the angels, rather with you the Creator of all,

you have deemed me worthy to be with you, and to be glorified
    with you,
and to see the incomparable glory of your face,
and to enjoy the unapproachable light to the full, (1 Tim 6.16)
25   and to rejoice, and to enjoy unspeakable merriment
in the communion, Master, of your inexpressible radiance.
And delighting in that mysterious light,
I was leaping for joy, I rejoiced with you the Maker and
    Sculptor,
understanding the impossible beauty of your face.
30   But after I brought my mind down to earth again,
having been illuminated in you, I did not see the world,
nor, Master, the affairs that are in the world,
but I was above the passions and worries,
and I was whirled about by these matters, and I confronted
    evil.
35   At first I no longer took part in human vices,
but as I passed time among them, I put before me the affairs of
    others,
and, Master, I was drawn in among contentious men,
I shared a hope of reforming their vices
and, alas, I foolishly shared in the darkness of the passions,
40   and having been overpowered by savage beasts, I am in danger
because I wanted to draw others out from their maltreatment,
I first became prey to the wild beasts. (Ezek 34.5)
But I anticipated your mercy, for your sake, Benevolent One,
I hastened to rescue someone who fell among the wild beasts!
45   For according to your commandment, Merciful One, I laid
    down
my all-miserable soul for the sake of my brothers. (1 Jn 3.16)
And so if I have been wounded, you are able to heal me, Savior,
if I was overpowered by enemies, a wretch taken prisoner at
    spear point,
still you are powerful, and strong in every way,

50   you are able to redeem me by your will alone.
    And if I was caught by the jaws and paws of beasts,
    still when you appear they shall die at once and I shall live.
    Yes, you are abundant in pity, extraordinary in mercy, (Ex 34.6)
    have mercy, have pity on me the fallen one!
55   I descended into the well to rescue my neighbor
    and I myself fell down with him, just Judge, Savior.
    May you not allow me to lie in this pit to the end!
    Yes, I know you have arranged, my All-Merciful God,
    that it is certainly necessary to rescue one's brother from death,
60   and from the sting of sin, but not to be destroyed
    with him through sin—which I the wretch have suffered,
    and having been negligent, I fell because I had confidence in
        myself,
    but ‹it is necessary› to rescue the neighbor and likewise myself,
    and if not, then to remain above ‹the pit›, and bewail the fallen
        neighbor,
65   and flee, with full power, from falling with him.
    But now, raise me up, bring me up from the chasm,
    and stand me upon the rock, Christ, of your commandments,[1]
    and show to me again the light that the world cannot contain,
    the light that brings the one who contemplates it,
70   my Savior, outside the world, and outside visible light, and
        outside
    perceptible air, and out of all perceptible things of heaven,
    and whether without the body, or fully with it,
    one does not know, God, at that hour. (2 Cor 12.3)
    But it seems to me that one was then like an immaterial star
75   illuminated with the beauty of the rational[2] sun,
    not able to look upon one's own light with the senses,
    but seeing only that non-setting star,
    understanding the impossible beauty of God's glory,

---

[1]Ex 33.21; Mt 7.24.
[2]νοητοῦ.

and being so very astonished, one has no way to learn fully,
80   nor to comprehend the manner of contemplation,
how or where the one who is inexplicably everywhere
can be seen; as he wishes, he is circumscribed within the saints.
All of us who are initiates in such matters know this:
namely that when outside the world, then we are
85   and we remain in the truth for as long as we see the light,
and then we find ourselves again in the body and in the world.
But remembering the joy and that light,
and the sweet pleasure, we wail and mourn,
like a little baby seeing its mother,
90   and when it remembers the sweetness of the milk, it cries
until it is picked up and suckled unto satiety.
And we demand this for ourselves now, for this we importune
        you,
we prostrate ourselves to receive this and not to be taken away,
        Savior,
so that even now we may be sustained, All-Merciful One, by
        this
95   bread which mentally[3] descends from heaven, (Jn 6.31)
giving a share to those who participate in life,
and having departed, making the journey to you,
we may have the viaticum,[4] both helper and rescuer,
and with it and through it we may draw near you, Savior,
100 and at the awesome judgment it may cover
our sins, Master, lest they be disclosed
or revealed to all the angels and humans,
but it may become a brilliantly arrayed garment for us,
and glory, and a crown forever and ever. Amen.

[3] νοητῶς.
[4] συνοδοιπόρον; literally, traveling companion.

Hymn 50

Concerning contemplation of God, and of divine matters, and of the paradoxical energy of the Holy Spirit. And concerning the special characteristics of the holy and consubstantial Trinity. And that one who has not anticipated entering the kingdom of heaven will not be helped, even if he were outside the punishments of hell.

What is this that is accomplished in me by you,
O God, Cause and Guardian of all things?
For what shall I say and what shall I think?
Indeed a great marvel is seen by me,
5   but it is unknown and invisible to all.
—Tell me, what is this?—I shall speak faithfully.
I am seized by darkness and shadow, perceptible things and the
       senses,
by material creation, and by both blood and flesh.
I am beaten black and blue, Savior, a miserable wretch.
10   But, unhappily and wretchedly, under these conditions
astonishment embraces me when I want to speak.
I see rationally:[1] where, what, or how I do not know.
For the *how* is in every way inexpressible,
and the *where*, it seems to me, is both known and unknown,
15   for on the one hand, it is known because it is seen by me
and at least it is shown from a distance, but on the other hand
the *where* is unknown since it also takes me away with it
in a place that is absolutely nowhere at all,
and it gives to me forgetfulness of perceptible realities,
20   and all material and visible things,
and leads me naked out of my body.
So what is this that does these things for me, (Eph 1.11)
things that I say I see? I cannot say.
Listen nevertheless and you will understand this thing.

---

[1]νοερῶς.

25 It is utterly beyond everyone's grasp,
   but for the worthy it is graspable, and shared,
   communicated, incomprehensibly united,
   made one with the pure without confusion,
   and mixed by an unmixed mingling,
30 whole to the whole who live blamelessly.
   This gives light in me like a lamp,
   rather it is first seen in the heavens,
   and infinitely above the heavens,
   obscurely, altogether invisibly it is seen.
35 But when I will diligently seek
   and constantly demand that it give light,
   or that it be seen there more clearly,
   and it separates me from things below and unites
   me mysteriously to its splendor,
40 or all at once it shows itself within me,
   a spherical light, calm and divine,
   formless, shapeless with a formless form,
   seen and saying these things to me:
   "Why do you circumscribe me within heaven?
45 And why do you seek me there and assume that I dwell there?
   Why do you suppose that I am on earth?
   And why do you proclaim that I am with all ‹creatures›?
   And why do you decree that I am everywhere?
   The *everywhere* attributes magnitude to me,
50 but I am absolutely without magnitude;
   know that my nature is beyond magnitude!
   And the *on earth* reflects circumscription,
   but I am once and for all in every way uncircumscribed.
   And when you say that I am with all ‹creatures›,
55 you make evident your ignorance to everyone.
   For you hear that I am with the saints,
   the whole of me by essence, in sense perception,
   and in contemplation, and also by participation

with my Father and the divine Spirit,
60 and plainly I repose in the saints. (Is 57.15)
So if you say we are with each saint individually,
you will make us many and divided among many.
If you say I am One, how would the One be also in each saint?
Or rather, how would the One be both above and below,
65 and how shall he be joined with everyone?
How shall he who fills the universe dwell in just one?
    (Eph 4.10)
How shall he who is in one also fill the universe?"
Hear the mysteries of the ineffable God:
ineffable, paradoxical, and in every way strange mysteries.
70 On the one hand God truly exists, he certainly *is*
—on this all religious people agree—
but then he is nothing of which we know at all,
for even the angels know not of what he is.
And by this I say that God is nothing,
75 nothing among ‹created› things since ‹he is› creator of all
    things,
but he is beyond the universe. For who would ever say
what God is, so as to say: "He is
this or perhaps that"? I do not know at all
what kind, how great, what sort, or how big.
80 Therefore I do not know God, the nature of
his form, appearance, magnitude, his beauty.
How shall I explain his energies?
How he is seen when he is invisible to everyone,
and how he is with every created nature,
85 how he dwells in all the saints,
how he fills the universe yet in no way is he filled, (Eph 4.10)
how he is above the universe and also everywhere,
for no one shall be able to say these things fully.
But, O you whom none among human beings has fully seen, (1
    Tim 6.16)

90 O Absolute Monarch, who alone are supremely
         compassionate,
    I thank you from all my heart, (Jn 11.41)
    because you did not look away when I lay below (Is 42.7)
    in darkness, but you touched me with your divine hand.[2]
         (Mt 8.3)
    When I saw her, at once I got up rejoicing.
95 For she shone brighter than the sun.
    I, the wretch, strove to seize your hand,
    and immediately she vanished from my eyes, (Acts 1.9)
    and again I was entirely in darkness.
    I fell to the floor mourning and weeping,
100 rolling about and groaning vehemently,
    yearning to see again your divine hand.
    You reached out, she was seen more clearly by me,
    and embracing her I kissed her.
    Oh kindness and abundant compassion,
105 the creator has given his hand to be kissed,
    the hand that sustains the universe with her strength,
    oh gift, oh inexpressible present!
    And again the Sculptor withdrew her,
    in every way testing my good zeal,
110 whether I yearn for her and her Giver,
    whether I despise all and honor her before all else,
    and remain in her love. (Jn 15.9)
    Immediately I abandoned the world and things of the world,
    at the same time I closed all my senses,
115 my eyes, ears, nose, mouth, and lips.
    I died to all my relatives and friends;
    yes as I truly died to my will
    and sought only the hand of God.
    And God's hand herself seeing me acting thus,

---

[2]χείρ, "hand," is grammatically feminine so the feminine pronoun (she, her) will
be used in the remainder of this hymn.

120 secretly touched my hand, she seized me
     and led me who was in the middle of darkness. (Ps 138.10)
     And so I was perceiving by my senses and I followed rejoicing.
     I ran vehemently in the night and day.
     I walked vigorously with eagerness,
125 but while walking again I became immobile,
     and it was then that I advanced toward the things ahead.
     Oh mysteries! Oh prizes! Oh the awards!
     Running thus in the middle of the race course, (1 Cor 9.24)
     the hand secretly overtook me
130 when my holy father[3] served as my intercessor,
     and the hand touched my miserable head,
     and gave to me the garland of victory,
     or rather the hand herself became my garland,
     and seeing this I had unutterable merriment,
135 unutterable joy, unutterable delight.
     For why not? Having conquered the whole world, (1 Jn 5.4–5)
     and having put to shame the prince of the world, (Jn 12.31)
     I received a divine crown from the hand of God,
     or rather I received the hand of the Master of the universe.
140 O marvel! The hand herself instead of a garland,
     the hand was seen by me shining immaterially,
     incessantly, and without setting
     she reached out to me like a breast
     for me to suckle imperishable milk,
145 as for a son of God she supplied milk abundantly,
     oh sweetness, oh ineffable pleasure!
     And she became the cup of divine drink,
     and an immortal stream for me,
     from which I partook and I was filled full of heavenly
150 nourishment with which only angels (Wis 16.20)
     nourish themselves and keep themselves immortal,

[3]I.e., Symeon Eulabes.

by participation they are second lights of the First.[4]
So also we all become
participants of divine and secret nature, (2 Pet 1.4)
155 children of the Father, and brothers of Christ[5]
when we are baptized by the All-Holy Spirit.[6]
But certainly we have not all recognized the grace,
nor the illumination, nor the participation,
because we have not all been thus begotten. Scarcely
160 one in thousands or even tens of thousands
recognized this begetting in mystical contemplation.
But all the others who do not know who
begot them are stillborn children.
For just as corpses when baptized with water
165 or even with fire do not feel at all,
so also they are dead by their faithlessness,
and they lack the commandments because of their laziness.
They do not know that they are just like those who have
    suffered
a frightful sign, an erroneous faith.
170 They suppose themselves to be children of God,
yet they do not discover their own Father.
And so if you say that you know this by faith,
and you suppose that you are a son of God by faith,
then let also the Incarnation of God be "by faith,"
175 and may you not say he became human in deed,
or that he was made in a perceptible manner.
But if he truly became the Son of Man,
certainly he makes you in deed a son of God.
If he did not become a body in imagination,
180 then certainly we are not hypothetically[7] spirit,

[4]Cf. Symeon, *Hymn* 42.192.
[5]1 Cor 9.5; Mt 5.45.
[6]Mt 3.11; Acts 1.5.
[7]ἐν ἐπινοίᾳ.

but just as the Logos was truly flesh, (Jn 1.14)
so also we are mysteriously transformed,
and in truth he makes us children of God.
The Logos, remaining immutable by his divinity,
185 became human by taking on flesh,
and maintaining the human being immutable in flesh and soul,
he made the whole of me God.
He assumed my condemned flesh,
and dressed me in full divinity,
190 for having been baptized I put on Christ, (Gal 3.27)
not perceptibly, but by all means mentally.[8]
And how is one not God by grace, and adoption,
and perception, and knowledge, and contemplation
‹when one› puts on the Son of God?
195 If the Logos God became human
without knowing it, then I also in ignorance became
God as is fitting and reasonable to suppose.
But if in knowledge, and practice, and contemplation
God is called fully human,
200 then I have become fully God by communion with God,
in perception and knowledge,[9] not in essence, but in
        participation
as it is necessary to think according to orthodoxy.
For just as God was immutably begotten
as a human in a body seen by all,
205 so also he begot me ineffably and spiritually
and though remaining human he makes me God.
And just as when he was seen in the flesh
he was not known as God by the crowds,
so also—O wonder!—we were seen by everyone
210 as what we were, human in every way,

---

[8] νοητῶς.
[9] αἰσθήσει καὶ γνώσει.

but what[10] we have become by divine grace
was not seen by the masses.
But only to those who have purified
the eye of their soul, are we revealed as in a surveying scope.

215 But to the impure neither God nor we
are at all seen as we are,
such as we certainly believe we are.
For they are faithless if they rely
only on faith without works. (Jas 2.17–18)

220 But even if they are not faithless, still they are like corpses in
     every way,
just as the divine Paul demonstrates.[11]
May you not be faithless, but speak to me and answer wisely!
Which of these two shall you prefer:
dead faith deprived of works,

225 or faithlessness in the works of faith? (Jas 2.18)
Certainly you will say to me: "What is the gift of works
without straight and perfect faith?"
And again I will argue against you: but what is
the use of faith without works?

230 Therefore if you want to know the things about which
we have been speaking, and to become God according to grace,
not by word, not by opinion, not hypothetically,
nor by faith alone deprived of deed,
but by experience, actual fact, both mental[12]

235 contemplation, and most mystical knowledge,
then do whatever the Savior commands you,
and the things he underwent for your sake,
and then you see the very bright light appear
in the completely whitened atmosphere of your soul,

240 you see immaterially but plainly the immaterial essence

[10]That is, God.
[11]Symeon confuses James for Paul; see *Hymn* 15.35.
[12]actual fact . . . mentally = πράγματι . . . νοερᾷ.

penetrating completely whole through the whole air,
but the whole body in its entirety is apart from this essence
which is of itself a bodiless soul,
and your body shall shine like your soul,
245 while your soul in turn, like the grace which has shone forth,
will be flashing like lightning, just like God.
But if you will shrink back from imitating the humility
of the creator, his sufferings and assaults,
and if you will not consent to endure these things
250 either mentally, or better physically,[13]
then you have been abandoned—Oh the stupidity!—
in the gloom and netherworld of your flesh (2 Pet 2.4)
that is mortality. For what else is this
if not death in an immortal vessel?
255 And indeed being confined forever,
and deprived of all good things in the light
and of the light itself! For I do not mean
being given over to fire and gnashing of teeth, (Lk 13.28)
to weeping and to the worm, (Mk 9.48)
260 but to dwell in the body as in a clay jar
after the resurrection just as before,
and never to look outside of the body,
nor to receive any light at all within it,
but thus to lie there deprived
265 of all pleasures here and hereafter,
as I said before. And so tell me, you who hear,
you who say: "I do not want to be
within his pure kingdom
nor to enjoy those good things,
270 but I wish only to be outside punishment
and to not receive the experience of fire at all."
Like I said, what benefit is that for you?
Answer me, most wise one, and say!

[13]νοερῶς . . . αἰσθητῶς.

Do you think there is another torture
275   that is worse or would become worse?
Go away, for when you are alone in tortures,
then you will say that you are being punished.
For would you also say that then you shall receive
a spiritual body? How then will the soul be
280   enclosed in that body as in a clay jar? (1 Cor 15.44)
Listen, learn how this shall be!
Just as seed is sown according to its kind
—I tell you seed of wheat and barley, and others—
and according to its kind in turn it grows up,
285   so also the bodies of those who die
fall to the ground as whatever type they happen to be.
      (1 Cor 15.42–44)
Therefore the souls that have been separated from their bodies
in the resurrection of the dead that is to come,
each of them finds, according to her worthiness,
290   a dwelling full of light or of darkness.
On the one hand the pure souls having had a share of light,
and having ignited their own lamps, (Mt 25.7)
shall certainly be in endless light.
But on the other hand, the souls that are full of darkness
295   and have the eyes of their heart blinded,
how will they see the divine splendor?
"No way," you would say. And so tell me,
who will hear them begging after death,
and who will open the eyes, alas,
300   of those who did not want to see willingly,
or to light the lamp of their own soul?
And so a darkness without light shall receive them.
And their bodies, like we said, equally
are ruined and decayed, even those of the saints,
305   but they are raised up just as they were sown,
pure wheat, sanctified wheat,

holy vessels of the Holy Spirit, (Num 18.3)
as absolutely pure as they were before,
anew they are raised up glorified,
310 shining, flashing like divine light.
The souls of the saints dwelling in these ‹glorified bodies›
will shine beyond the sun (Mt 13.43)
and they shall become like the Master
whose divine laws they kept.
315 The bodies of sinners in their turn will also be raised up
as they were when sown in the ground:
muddy, stinking, full of rottenness,
impure vessels, weeds of wickedness, (Mt 13.25)
absolutely unenlightened since they practiced the works of
        darkness (Rom 13.12)
320 and handled the instruments of every sort of evil
belonging to the evil sower.
And these bodies are resurrected immortal
and spiritual, but more like darkness.
And so the wretched souls are united to these bodies;
325 they also are unenlightened and impure.
They shall become similar to the devil, (Jn 8.44)
since they imitated his works,
and they kept his rules,
and with him they shall be assigned to unquenchable fire,
        (Mt 3.12)
330 to darkness, and be sent to hell. (2 Pet 2.4)
Or rather they shall be led down to hell in proportion
to the weight and merit
of the sins that each carries,
and there they shall remain forever and ever.
335 But the saint, as we said, again,
each provided with the wings of virtues
shall ascend to the meeting of the Master, (1 Thess 4.17)
each according to their worthiness,

according to how they have prepared themselves beforehand
340 shall they be near to or far from the creator,
united to him for endless ages
leaping for joy and delighting in everlasting pleasure. Amen.

Hymn 51

That when the Holy Spirit shines in us, all things of the passions are
banished like darkness is banished by light. But when he reduces his
rays we are again struck by passions and wicked thoughts.

Your light shining round vivifies me, my Christ,
for seeing you gives life and resurrection.
I have no way to speak of your light's energies,
yet I have learned this in deed, and I know, my God,
5   that even in sickness, Master, even in affliction and grief,
even in fetters, and even in hunger, and even when I am held
          in jail,
and even when I am oppressed by worse pains, my Christ,
your shining light expels them all like darkness,
and your divine Spirit suddenly puts me
10   in relaxation, and light, and enjoyment of the light.
I knew the afflictions as smoke, the thoughts as darkness,
the temptations as arrows, the anxieties as gloom,
and the scheming passions as wild beasts, Logos,
from which you have set me free, from which you rescued me
          long ago,
15   and little by little you shone your divine light in me,
and now when I am in the middle of these afflictions, Christ
          my God,
you guard me unharmed, sheltering me with your light.
But when I often stumble, sinning by the hour,
but when I am arrogant, when I anger You,
20   I beg your compassionate education, my Christ,

which I strongly perceive happening in me,
Master, by the retreat from me[1] of the unapproachable, all-
    shining,
and divine light of God that was sheltering me.
For just as when the sun sets, night and darkness begin,
25 and they send out the beasts to feed, (Ps 103.19–21)
so also, O my God, when your light no longer covers me,
at once the darkness of life and a sea of thoughts
cover me all round, and the beasts of the passions devour me,
and I am wounded by the arrows of all my thoughts.
30 But when again you have compassion, when you have pity,
when you hearken to my mournful complaints,
and hearken to my groans, and you accept my tears,
and you want to look upon my humility, (Lk 1.48)
when I have committed unpardonable sins, my Christ,
35 you are seen from afar like a rising star, (Num 24.17)
you enlarge yourself little by little; you yourself do not undergo
    this change,
but you open the mind of your servant to see.[2]
Little by little you are seen more, like the sun,
for when the darkness flees and disappears,
40 I reckon that you come, you who are present everywhere.
And when, as before, you envelope the whole of me, Savior,
because you shelter me completely, you surround all of me,
I am liberated from evils, and I am ransomed from the
    darkness,
and from temptations, and from passions, and from all
    thoughts,
45 for I am filled with kindness, I am filled with cheerfulness,
and I am filled full of joy, unutterable delight,
seeing the awesome mysteries, seeing the strange wonders,
seeing what the eye has not gazed upon, nor the eye

---

[1]Read the variant text ἀπ᾽ ἐμοῦ rather than τοῦ θείου (SC 196:186).
[2]Lk 24.45; Mt 17.2.

of any human would be able to see, nor also ear to hear
50 what has not at all ascended the heart of mortals. (1 Cor 2.9)
And I am exceedingly astonished, I am beside myself among
        these things,
and I am wholly estranged from all things on the earth,
singing your praises with unceasing phrases, my God,
perceiving full well the strange transformation in myself,
55 and the manner of defense of the All-Powerful's hand,
        (Wis 11.17)
how by the shining and the appearance of your light alone
you have chased away all sorrow. You have snatched me away
        from the world,
and mysteriously united with me, and at once
set me up in heaven, in which there is no sorrow, (Rev 21.4)
60 no groaning, no crying, no snake biting the heel,[3]
and you revealed the opposite path that is untiring, without
        suffering, (Mt 7.14)
narrow, and impassable to human beings,
or, to say more truthfully, it is untrodden by all.
For who ever had the strength, or who among human beings
65 would ever be able to get to heaven in their body,
or even without their body, flying with some sort of wings?
        (2 Cor 12.3)
Elijah was lifted up in a chariot of fire, and before him
Enoch, but not into heaven, rather into another place,[4]
and not by his own power, but nevertheless he was removed.
        (Heb 11.5)
70 But what are such things compared to what happens in us?
How shall there be a comparison of shadow and truth?
Or, tell me, a comparison of a ministering and servile spirit
        (Heb 1.14)
to the masterful, and all-working, and divine Spirit

[3]Gen 3.15; 49.17.
[4]2 Kgs 2.1ff.; Gen 5.24.

who strengthens and empowers every created essence?
75 For the others are a thing made, but the Maker is unique
since he is inseparable from the Father and likewise the Son.
The Three are God for the Trinity is one God.
She[5] gave existence to everything, She created all things,
She created in the world the Logos and Son of the Father
80 according to the flesh unto our salvation,
being inseparable from the Father and the Spirit.
He truly is made flesh by the arrival of the Spirit,
and he becomes what he was not, a human being like me
except for sin and every lawlessness, (Heb 4.15)
85 he was at the same time both God and human, being seen by
    all,
having the divine Spirit who is united with his nature,
with whom he has given life to the dead, opened the eyes of the
    blind,
cleansed lepers, and driven out demons. (Mt 10.8)
He suffered the cross and likewise death,
90 he was resurrected in the Spirit, and taken up in glory,
    (1 Tim 3.16)
and he has renovated[6] the path to heaven for all (Heb 10.20)
who have faith in him, a faith without doubt,
and he has poured out copiously the All-Holy Spirit (Titus 3.6)
on all who show their faith by their works. (Jas 2.18)
95 Even now he pours out the Spirit abundantly on such people.
And he deifies by the Spirit those to whom he has been
    ungrudgingly united.
He changes them from human beings without changing,
and renders them children of God, siblings of the Savior,
co-heirs of Christ, and heirs of God, (Rom 8.16–17)
100 gods joined to God in the Holy Spirit,
prisoners indeed by flesh alone, but free in spirit,

---

[5] αὕτη; the word for Trinity is grammatically feminine.
[6] ἐγκαινίζω also means to consecrate.

easily rising together with Christ into heaven,
and obtaining full citizenship there (Phil 3.20)
in the contemplation of good things which eyes have not seen.
    (1 Cor 2.9)
105 And so what is the chariot of fire that snatched away Elijah,
    (2 Kg 2.11)
and what is the taking up of Enoch compared to these graces?
    (Gen 5.24)
I would think that as of old the sea was divided by the staff ‹of
    Moses›, (Ex 14.16)
and manna descended from heaven, these are certainly[7]
only types and symbols of the truth: (1 Cor 10.6)
110 the sea of baptism, the manna of the Savior.
So even these are symbols and a type
of the things that possess incomparable superiority and glory,
as much as the Uncreated by nature surpasses the created.
For the manna, which is called bread, is the food of angels;
    (Wis 16.20)
115 the human beings then ate it in the desert, (Jn 6.49)
they vanished, they were obliterated, and they all died
whosoever ate it, for they did not partake of life.[8]
But the flesh of my Master, having been deified,
is full of life and renders all who nibble it
120 participants in life, and makes them immortal. (Jn 6.54)
His flesh does not transport them through the depths of the sea,
nor set them free from Egypt, and guide them to another land
that produces perishable fruit again for the human beings.
Nor does the Redeemer of the world
125 order us to march for forty years (Ex 16.35)
in order that we may take possession of the land of promise,
    (Heb 11.9)
but all at once when we are baptized in doubtless faith,

[7]Ex 16.33; Jn 6.32.
[8]Read here the variant lines 51.116–17 (SC 196:194).

and we have partaken of his blood and flesh, (Jn 6.53)
from death to life, and to light from darkness,[9]
130 from earth to heaven, immediately he bears us up.
Previously he stripped me of the ruin of death,
and freed the whole of me in sense perception and knowledge,
—but most spine-chilling of all—he rendered me a new
heaven, (Is 65.17)
and the creator of all things dwelt within me.
135 None of the ancient saints was deemed worthy of this grace.
At first he spoke through the Holy Spirit, (2 Pet 1.21)
and by his energy he did wonders,
but he was never essentially united to anyone
before Christ my God became human.
140 For having taken a body, he gave his divine Spirit,
and through him he unites himself to all believers,
and their union becomes inseparable.
Woe is me! I groan bitterly for the error of humans.
How do we not have faith in Christ, how do we not follow
him,
145 how do we not yearn for life, how do we not long for
his inviolate wealth, imperishable wealth,
the undecaying glory of passing our lives with him?
How do we believe ourselves to be saved when devoted to
perishable things,
we who do not love[10] Christ more than visible things,
150 we who do not seek to be with him after death?
But we are more insensitive than wood and stones.
But, O my Christ, rescue me from their absurdity,
and teach me to love[11] you, the life of all the faithful!
For glory and praise are fitting to you with
155 the Father and your divine Spirit, honor and worship

[9] 1 Jn 3.14; 1 Pet 2.9.
[10] φιλοῦντες.
[11] φιλεῖν.

now and always as to a king forever and ever,
and to the Maker of all things, God and Master. Amen.

Hymn 52

Concerning theology, and that it is not permitted for one who has not been transformed by participation in the Holy Spirit and has not knowingly become God by adoption to teach the divine things to human beings.

Who shall comfort the suffering of my heart?
But when I said "suffering" I disclosed my yearning for the
    Savior.
But the yearning is the energy of the Spirit,
or rather it is essentially his presence
5   substantially[1] seen as light within me.
But the light is incomparable, it is wholly unutterable.
Who shall separate me from perceptible things from which I
    was once released
and from which I was hidden when I was outside the world?
Who shall give to me calm and stillness of all things
10 so that I may have my fill of the light's beauty and vision?
The incomprehensible in it ignites my yearning
and insofar as it is comprehensible, it is a substantial yearning.[2]
For love is not a name, but divine essence, (1 Jn 4.16)
participatable and ungraspable, but by all means godly.
15 What is communicated must be achieved, but not more than
    this.
Therefore on account of this I told you that the yearning is
    achievable

---

[1]ἐνυποστάτως.

[2]ἐνυπόστατος πόθος. The point is that the yearning *is* the real presence of God. Whether ἐνυπόστατος means "Substantial/essential," or "personal," or both, is not clear, but not necessarily significant (cf. *Graces* 2.271; SC 113:352; deCatanzaro, *Discourses*, 376).

and substantial in so much as it is communicated and grasped.
For all that is grasped and communicated is by all means
substantially communicated essence, and likewise grasped.
20 For that which has no essence is called nothing and is nothing;
but the divine, uncreated, and super-essential nature
is called super-essential because this nature exceeds the essence
of all created things. Nevertheless it is essential,
and it is substantial, above all essence,
25 and next to a created hypostasis it is in every way perceived as
incomparable, for it is entirely boundless by nature.
But how would you say that the uncircumscribed is an
        hypostasis?
That which has no substance is nothing, and how would it be
        communicated to me?
But if you do not believe it, I refer you to Paul giving witness
30 and confirming for you that both things are credible.
For when Paul says that he has Christ speaking within
and that he himself speaks by the All-Holy Spirit, (2 Cor 13.3)
he says that the divine Spirit is participatable and
        circumscribable;
in him the divine Spirit is present boundlessly and
        inapprehensibly.
35 But when Paul mentions "dwelling in unapproachable light,"
and testifies that he has never been seen by a human being,
        (1 Tim 6.16)
then he shows the Uncircumscribable and Inapprehensible.
For how has Paul partaken of, or at all touched
that which no human has ever seen?
40 Certainly, if you are not quarrelsome, you will say: "No way."
But when again Paul says to you: "The God who long ago
ordered the light to shine out of darkness, who has shone
        within me," (2 Cor 4.6)
what other god does he offer for you to know, tell me,
if not that God who dwells in unendurable light

45   and whom no human has ever in any way seen? (1 Tim 6.16)
For he is super-essential, uncreated before
he took on flesh and appeared to me as created;
in some strange way he himself took hold of me and deified all
     of me.
Tell me, do you thus believe and in no way doubt?
50   So if God has become human, as you believe,
he deified me, the human who was made a partner,
having become God by adoption; I see the God himself
by nature,[3] whom no human has ever been able
to see, nor is ever able to contemplate fully. (1 Tim 6.16)
55   And so those who have received God by the works of faith,
and who are styled gods when they were begotten by the Spirit,
     (Jn 3.5)
they see him himself, their own father,
who always dwells in unapproachable light. (1 Tim 6.16)
They possess him as an inhabitant dwelling within them (2 Cor
     6.16)
60   and they dwell in him who is absolutely inaccessible.
This is the true faith, this is the work of God,
this is the seal of Christians, this is the divine participation,
     (2 Cor 1.22)
this is the communion and divine pledge,
this is the life, this is the kingdom,
65   this is the garment, this is the robe of the Lord (Mt 22.11)
that the baptized put on in faith, (Gal 3.27)
not in ignorance, I tell you, nor without perception,
but through faith with perception and knowledge.[4]
So that you may not say: "I believe that I have put on Christ!"[5]
     (Gal 3.27)

[3] τὸν φύσει θεὸν βλέπω ἐκεῖνον.

[4] αἰσθήσει καὶ γνώσει, the latter, in this context, might be translated "consciousness."

[5] The point being that it should be a matter of experience, not just belief or supposition.

70　I do not say: believe this! But have the work of faith,
　　and confirmation of faith, and the seal of faith,
　　and the unambiguous perfection of faith
　　that comes from putting on Christ in perception and
　　　　knowledge,
　　the Christ who illuminates, who flashes with the glory of
　　　　divinity,
75　and who transforms all of you in a most clear light,
　　you remain unchanged yet double since you are both
　　God by adoption and fully human by nature!
　　And having become totally like this, like I told you,
　　then come and stand with us now, O my brother,
80　on the mountain of divine knowledge, and of divine
　　　　contemplation,[6] (Ex 34.2)
　　and together we shall hear the paternal voice. Alas! (2 Pet 1.18)
　　How much we forsake the divine dignity,
　　how much we abstain from eternal life!
　　As far as heaven keeps away from earth's subterranean regions,
　　　　(Is 55.9)
85　and from those who are held there unhappily from of old,
　　so much the more do we all truly abstain
　　from the dignity of God and from divine contemplation
　　even though we may say paradoxically that we dwell with him,
　　and that we have him who dwells in unapproachable light
　　　　(1 Tim 6.16)
90　remaining and inhabiting entirely within ourselves. (Eph 3.17)
　　And while we sit in the subterranean regions we want
　　to philosophize about the things above earth, and even the
　　　　things in heaven,
　　and above the heavens, as though we saw clearly,
　　and to explain to everyone, and to be called knowledgeable,
95　consummate theologians, and mystics of the secrets;
　　this is certainly proof of our insensitivity.

[6]"knowledge . . . contemplation" = γνώσεως . . . θεωρία.

For one who was unhappily begotten in the subterranean
    regions,
and inhabiting the darkness of the present world,
and not seeing the light of the age to come
100 —a light that shone on earth and shines everlastingly—
and who says that they think and see the things in heaven,
that they see all things there and teach them to others,
is not such a person insensitive and even worse than that?
For such a one is like a blind person quarrelling with those
    who see, saying:
105 "The coin is bronze," or "This is the seal of another,
and the writing on it signifies such and such."
Truly this marvel is paradoxical to those who hear,
who also see that the coin is gold from a perfectly good source,
and is the true seal of the King,
110 showing his genuine image,
and the writing indicating his name,
so also we suffer without thinking what it is to suffer.
Nor do we feel shame before any person or the saints,
or the angels who look upon our concerns from above.
115 But the word of the Lord is fulfilled concerning us,
when he says: "seeing, they do not see." And again: (Mt 13.13)
"Hearing, they plug the ears of their soul all the more," (Ps 57.5)
and they in no way hear the words of the Spirit.
For they hear bodily with their ears of flesh,
120 but the spiritual ears of their heart they keep covered,
and they cannot hear God at all.
For in no way are they able to lift from themselves
the shroud of pride and insensitivity, (2 Cor 3.15)
for they put it over themselves by their own choice,
125 they want to cover their eyes and ears,
and because of this they imagine that they both see and hear.
But if someone were to say to them: "Listen to me, children,
and lift the shroud from your heart!"

They would grow angry at these words because
130   the speaker did not call them "fathers," but said "children,"
and they add more hatred to the speaker from these words,
and they are not able to be conscious of their passion[7] present
      in them,
or rather the passions that darken their mind and heart,[8]
and separate them from God, those who have already been
      selected[9] beforehand,
135   the slaves of self-conceit and of arrogance,
having given ear to their will and having been taken prisoner,
they always fulfill their personal will.
These people shun the laws of God and are a law unto
      themselves,
and they serve not God but themselves. Oh the audacity!
140   In place of the glory of God they seek their own, (Jn 5.44)
and they seek to establish their glory by all works and means.
And so the glory of Christ is his cross and his sufferings
that he submitted to for our sake in order to glorify us.
But they do not want to suffer these things like he suffered,
145   and they refuse to become participants in God's glory
by their refusing to suffer like he suffered.
And they want even more, alas, the honor from human beings,
      (Jn 12.43)
and they willingly prefer separation from God.
But, O my Christ, deliver those who are obedient to you
150   from defiled conceit and arrogance,
and make them partners of your sufferings and glory,
and deign us worthy to be inseparable from you,
now and unto the future ages forever! Amen.

[7]πάθος could also be rendered "suffering" in this context; Symeon perhaps intends both meanings. Πάθος in Symeon's works is always a negative term, except when referring to the sufferings of Christ (see line 142).

[8]Φρένας: guts, wits.

[9]Προληφθέντας is a bit obscure in this context, it could also be rendered "preferred," "anticipated," or "seized."

Hymn 53

A lesson in the form of a discussion between God and the author. And how this divine father who is enlightened by the Holy Spirit converses with God, and by him was initiated into divine and human mysteries.

Behold, Christ, my affliction,
behold my faintheartedness,
behold my powerlessness,
behold also my beggary.
5   Behold my feebleness,
and have pity on me, O Logos!
And shine on me now as of old,
and illuminate my soul,
enlighten my eyes (Ps 12.4)
10 to see you, light of the world, (Jn 8.12)
the joy, the merriment,
the eternal life, (1 Jn 5.20)
the pleasure of the angels,
and kingdom of heaven,
15 you are also a paradise,
the crown of the just ones,
both judge and king. (2 Tim 4.8)
Why do you hide your face?
Why do you separate yourself from me, my God,
20 you who never wish to be separated
from those who have affection[1] for you? (Prov 8.17)
Why do you flee from me, why do you burn me,
why do you cut me and beat me to a pulp?
You know that I love you (Jn 21.15)
25 and I seek you from my soul. (Deut 4.29)
Reveal yourself like you said

---

[1] φιλούντων.

and show yourself to me![2]
For I know that you are truthful;[3]
I recognize that you are sincere,
30 and you are fond of[4] those who are fond of you, (Pr 8.17)
and you converse with them as with friends,
not in shadow, nor reflection,
not like one mind to another mind,
but as the Logos who is from the beginning, (Jn 1.1)
35 and inherent[5] life, (Jn 1.4)
you who are begotten from the Father,
and made one with him,
and an ineffable companion.
In this way those whom you yourself beget (Jn 3.5)
40 by your Holy Spirit,
and whom you reveal as your children,
and indeed your siblings,
and children of God, of your Father,
with these you converse, and
45 when you see them you are also seen
by them in turn.
Therefore show your compassion, (Ps 84.8)
show your benevolence, (Titus 3.4)
and also your mercy, Savior,
50 that you have poured out profusely (Titus 3.6)
upon all flesh that has
truly maintained faith in you,
and open for me the doors
of your bridal chamber, my God, (Mt 25.10–11)
55 yes, may you not close the gate
of your light on me, O my Christ!

[2]Mt 11.27; Jn 14.21.
[3]Mt 22.16; Jn 5.20.
[4]φιλεῖς.
[5]ἐνυπόστατος.

"Why do you expect to constrain me
with words, O son of humans?
And why do you senselessly say
60 that I hide my face from you?
And why do you suspect that I shut
the doors and gates?
And why do you also suppose that
I ever separate myself from you?
65 And why did you say that I
burn, and ignite, and beat you to a pulp?
Your words are not straight,
nor is your understanding straight.
But rather listen to the words
70 that I am going to say to you:
I was light even before I created
all the things seen by you.
I was everywhere and I was also
creating the whole creation.
75 I am everywhere and in everything.
Listen to words of wisdom,
understand the depths of mysteries! (1 Cor 2.4)
Yet I was not a thing at all,
nor in any way with all things,
80 nor was I within all things,
and while not being united to anything,
still I was with all things.
Therefore being none of all things,
I was in all things without being there,
85 but in the middle of the visible things,
‹amidst› the animate and inanimate,
creatures with sense perception and those without,
‹amidst› things separated from me
and not knowing me at all,
90 I formed the dust into a body, (Gen 2.7)

and I inspired a soul,
not out of my essence,
but out of my strength.
Understand what I teach you!
95 And so I have said: by my power
I blew a soul into you, (Gen 2.7)
a soul both logical and rational,⁶
which, as though entering a house,
was united ‹to your body›
100 and took it as an instrument,
the one ‹being› appeared out of the two.
I tell you a rational living being,
a human who is double from two
natures inexpressibly;
105 from a visible body that is
without senses and irrational,
and from an invisible soul
according to my image (Gen 1.26–27)
both logical and rational
110 —strange marvel—amidst all things,
between creatures, I say.
Between what creatures?
The material and the immaterial.
For the material creatures are what you see,
115 but the immaterial are angels.
And so between these, I tell you,
the double living creature, the human being,
who is immaterial in perceptible creation,
but perceptible in immaterial creation.
120 And so I made him as perceptible
lord and master
of the visible creation,
setting all visible things

⁶λογικὴν καὶ νοεράν.

as servants under him alone (Ps 8.6)
125 so that he would see my works
     and glorify me the Creator.
     And since he was rational
     and contemplating rationally,
     I granted that he see me,
130 and by this I established him
     in the dignity of angels.
     Look, understand what I say to you:
     a human being, being double,
     saw my creatures with
135 perceptible eyes,
     but he saw the face of me
     the creator with rational eyes;
     he contemplated my glory
     and conversed with me by the hour.
140 But when he transgressed
     my command, when he ate from
     the tree, he became blind
     and entered into the darkness
     of death, like I said;
145 that is, "he hid himself,"
     for he then foolishly
     supposed that he could hide.[7]
     For where did he have to hide from me,
     in what sort of place, tell me?
150 But now you reckon even worse,
     more foolishly than Adam,
     you suppose that I hide myself, not wanting
     to be seen by you at all. (Job 34.29)
     For if I wish not to be seen,
155 then why did I appear in the flesh? (1 Tim 3.16)
     And why did I come down at all?

[7]Gen 3.11,17; 3.10.

And why was I seen by everyone?
Do not be ignorant of my deeds,
nor of my divine plan.
160 Adam was first blinded
and when he was cross-examined
and taught by me he
did not wish to repent, but was found
without any humility,
165 but instead he said: "The woman
whom you gave to me has sinned" (Gen 3.12)
as if he meant to show that I
was the cause of his sin.
Likewise the woman in turn
170 blamed the snake, (Gen 3.13)
and no one confessed
to have sinned at all.[8]
On account of this he was thrown out
of the pleasure of paradise, (Gen 3.23)
175 and he remained in perceptible creation
alone with the irrational beasts,
he became irrational and material
out of logical[9] creatures,
separated from the immaterial creatures.[10]
180 Strange marvel the soul
that has been blinded,
she became like a body without eyes,
and did not contemplate God.
Indeed, if the body is blinded
185 it is moved by the soul.
But if the soul is blinded,
what sort of movement will she find?

[8]Cf. *Catechesis* 5.160–75; SC 96:388–90; deCatanzaro, *Discourses*, 94–97.
[9]ἐκ λογικῶν.
[10]Angels, see 53.115.

And how will she be able to live at all?
No way, rather she will die
190 the death forever that,
as I said, the first-formed
parents died by their folly,
and they descended into hell,
and they were brought down into destruction. Having mercy
        upon them
195 I descended from above. (Jn 3.31)
Being invisible in every way,
I took on the thickness of flesh,
and assumed a soul;
being God unchangeably,
200 I the Logos became flesh. (Jn 1.14)
And from the flesh I received a beginning;
I was seen by all as human.
And so for what reason
did I undertake to do this?
205 Because, like I said,
I created Adam
to look upon me.
But since he was blinded,
along with everyone after him,
210 and his descendants,
I have not submitted to be
‹only› in divine glory,
and to look away from those who were blinded
by the treachery of the snake
215 whom I created with my hand.
But I became like human
beings in every way, (Heb 2.17)
perceptible to the perceptible beings,
and I wanted to be made one with them.
220 Look how much desire

to be seen by humans I have,
even to become human
and to want to be seen.
And so how do you say that I hide myself
225 from you and that I am not seen?
Truly I shine, but you do not look.
Pay attention to the mystery:
Adam saw the glory
of my divinity and lived,
230 but having transgressed he was blinded
and immediately turned into a corpse
when he did not repent
and say: "I have sinned against you."[11]
Because of this he was justly
235 condemned to return again
into earth from which he was taken. (Gen 3.19)
And afterward this was by all means
given as a judgment,
and reckoned by everyone
240 as an inescapable punishment.
But it is not a punishment,
rather death is a kindness.
For I have not allowed the perishable
to be united with the imperishable.
245 For to have been bound together forever,
and for the evil to exist
immortally in both body and soul
would be worse than the soul being released.
For if the soul, having fallen out
250 of the life here on earth
also had to bear
the decaying body
united with her,

[11]Ps 50.6; Lk 15.18.

how would it not be worse than death,
255   I tell you, worse than the separation of the soul?
And so there are two deaths,[12]
that of the body and that of the soul.
One who dies by the soul, tell me,
and thence carries around
260   a perishable body united to her,
and little by little the body grows old,
and dissolves, and perishes,
if the soul will not be released
and separated from the body,
265   but were eternally
tied to this body,
how would this life not
be worse than all other
tortures in hell?
270   Look at those who are stricken
with the sacred disease,[13]
how their flesh
is wasted and consumed,
and they are without hands, and feet,
275   and eyes, and lips,
and noses, and ears,
how they are utterly immobile,
and how both deaf and dumb
they call to God
280   with unutterable voices
to release them from their flesh!
Again I say, if a soul
were destined to live
that way forever, would not

[12]Rev 2.11; 20.14.
[13]"Sacred disease" is a common term for epilepsy, and sometimes, as in this case, for leprosy (SC 196:231n1).

285   it be worse to live than to die?
      So the punishment
      becomes a kindness,
      or rather not a punishment,
      but a divine plan.
290   For the death of human beings
      is death of troubles,
      death of worries is a release,
      death is freedom from
      diseases and all manner of suffering,
295   death of sins,
      and amputation of injustice,
      and death is deliverance
      from all of life's evils,
      and for those who live virtuously
300   death is the agent of everlasting joy,
      and of eternal pleasure,
      and light without evening.
      Nevertheless instead of being separated
      from the body, I tell you,
305   look at the kind benefits,
      see the divine plan,
      learn of my gifts!
      I have manifested myself
      and my Father to the world,[14]
310   and I have poured out copiously
      my Holy Spirit
      truly on all flesh,[15]
      and I have revealed my name
      to all human beings, (Jn 17.6)
315   and by my works I revealed
      that I am creator and maker,

[14]Jn 17.6; 7.4.
[15]Titus 3.6; Joel 3.1.

I have shown and I now show
all things that are necessary to do."[16] Amen.

Hymn 54

That God suitably gives to each human being in accordance with a fitting gift through the Holy Spirit, to work with, not as one wishes, but as was predetermined by him, so as not to be useless in the middle of his Church.

What would a product ever know without its maker?
For the product would certainly have demanded of it, justly
  and fittingly,
the know-how which it had received, that is its action and its
  function.
For even a mattock, a scythe, a dagger, and a saw,
5 an axe, a staff, a spear, and both sword and bow,
an arrow, and all the remaining tools in life,
each possesses its own function, but it
does not take its function from itself, but certainly from us.
For the artisan of each tool, for whatever desired purpose,
10 equips the tool to operate according to its art.
Because it is not possible to reap corn with a mattock,
nor to do carpentry with a scythe, nor to build with a dagger,
nor to dig with a saw, nor to sew with an axe,
nor to cut wood with a staff, nor is it custom to saw with a
  spear,
15 nor to sling stones with a sword, nor to cut with a bow,
but it is necessary to use each tool in a way suitable for its
  purpose.
But if you were to use them for purposes other than for what
  they were made
then your life and all your works destroy themselves.

---

[16]The abrupt ending suggests that this *Hymn* is incomplete.

Therefore understand me that so also God has made us
20   each faithfully to operate in the works of this life,
putting some to teach, and some to study,
others to rule the masses, and some to yield to them.
     (1 Cor 12.8–10)
And to some he gave wisdom, and to others knowledge and
     reason,
and to others to prophesy, to others to speak in tongues,
25   and to the rest to work miracles and deeds of power,
others he has rendered leaders. And these are spiritual gifts,
but let us tell also the charisms of the creator,
what he has given to human beings, to each according to their
     worthiness.
One he made manly of body, and to another ‹he gave a› more
     youthful beauty,
30   and to another the sweetest voice of all.
He has given simply to each human person
a gift and an advantage according to what is worthy,
as God, the creator of all things, alone knows
to operate fittingly, ineffably in this life.
35   On this account each person is suited not to whatever
art one wants, but to whatever art one was created for,
and to this art one is disposed suitably and affectionately.
And you would see the sailor ingeniously sailing across
the open sea and enjoying it more
40   than a man sitting upon a racing horse,
and ‹you may see› a farmer cutting furrows of earth with a
     plow;
he reckons the pair of oxen working with him to be
much better than a king's four-horse chariot
from whence the farmer rejoices in their uses and revels in
     hope.
45   And again the soldier regards himself best above all:
farmers, and sailors, and artisans,

and he is conceited in glory when he runs
to the slaughter and death, to destroy out of time.
Therefore this soldier will never bear to drive an oar,
50   nor to grab a hoe, nor to become a carpenter,
nor a sailor, nor a farmer, nor will he choose to be
a husbandman. But like I said, each person shall
operate according to what operation one has received from
     God,
otherwise a human in this life will not be able
55   at all to accomplish anything or to desire at all.
For behold—again I say to you what I said before
just as it is never possible that any of the
tools mentioned moves itself to its work,
or anything operates without a human hand
60   taking something and making something else with it,
so also a human being without the divine hand
cannot know or do anything good.
For behold, the Artisan, the Logos, made me,
and he has placed in the world whatever kind he wanted.
65   Therefore how, tell me, how shall I be able to think, or to make,
or to operate anything without divine strength?
He who granted to me a mind, whatever kind he wanted,
and he gives to think what things he knows to be useful,
and he provides for me power to operate what he wants.
70   And so if I would do them, he certainly will give more,
          (Mt 25.21)
and benevolently provide for me to think more perfect things.
But if I were to despise even the small things
entrusted to me, I would truly and justly suffer
deprivation by God who has given ‹to me›,
75   and I shall become an unprofitable and useless tool
because I did not wish to accomplish the commands of my
          creator,
but instead I surrendered myself to timidity and to laziness.

And because of this I have been cast out of the hands of the
    Master
by disobedience and insubordination toward him;
80   I have been thrown out of paradise, (Gen 3.24)
becoming far from God and the hands of the saints.
The all-wicked serpent found me lying abandoned
and wholly given to laziness from virtues.
Deceitfully he ill-treated me by all dishonorable deeds,
85   and taking pleasure in these I appeared rejoicing,
instead of this I should have mourned and wailed and cried
because I voluntarily set aside what I was created
to do, I the miserable, and by self-will
I surrendered to the things against my nature,
90   having fallen all-wretchedly by the impure hands of the enemy
by whom I was overpowered and wholly moved,
and I was not able to withstand him, O wretch,
for how could I resist when I am a corpse?
I became an organ of every wickedness,
95   a tested tool of every transgression and sinful work,
the miserable one deceitfully cheated.
For he grabbed me by the hand and powerfully dragged me,
he defiled me with the carrying of dung and all sorts of mire,
and he threw me into bitter stench,
100 and made me rejoice in this work, oh the insensitivity!
To rapines, and to jealousies, to unjust deaths,
to abuses, to angers, to every form of evil,
to make a long story short, he found me doing these,
or rather, he himself used me against my will.
105 From when I renounced myself willingly
from the hand of God, and from his saints,
and the terrible, soul-destroying prince snatched me away,
when I willed this he held me by his hand,
I could no longer avoid doing his deeds,
110 but I was performing all his desires.

For the sword knows not to speak against the one who holds it,
but the one holding it uses the sword however they want.
And so God made me and looked upon me from above,
>   (Ps 32.13)
and seeing me oppressed by the hand of the tyrant
115 he had pity on me, he snatched me away from his hand,
and again led me into divine paradise,
into his vineyard; he gave me into the hands
of the holy farmers to operate the divine works, (Mt 20.1)
to accomplish the virtues, to keep the commandments,
>   (Gen 2.15)
120 and not to be moved without the hand of the saints,
lest again the worker of evil find me
living away from the holy hand and he snatch me away,
and he prepare me again to do his deeds.
And so the good and sympathetic farmers
125 took my whole will into their hands
and immediately they entrusted me to work
by repentance and humility, and to mourn without ceasing.
"For," they said to me, "those who keep these three
and who persevere by their good work are
130 immediately, as one knows not, led to glory,
to purification, and to dispassion, and to divine contemplation,
and nevermore are they overcome by the hands of the hostile
>   one,
but from God they receive remission of all their sins
and failures, and at the same time they truly also
135 become children of the Most High, and gods according to
>   grace, (Ps 8.1–6)
and useful tools, working every novel ‹deed›,
or rather they become divine farmers guiding others
to good practices, to works of salvation."
Everyone listen! Having believed and done these things,
140 and given my whole self into the hands of God's farmers

and servants according to his commandment,
I found to my astonishment that in me everything
turned out accordingly. And I scream to everyone,
shouting out with a loud voice, and exhorting, and saying:
145 —for I cannot bear to cover these graces with a heap of
       silence—
run, however many of you feel that you are
outside the hands of God and of his saints!
Hasten and be glued to them inseparably
by faith, and by fervent love, and by total free choice,
150 throw away all arrogance, and selfish desire,
and give your souls to their hands,
like inanimate tools doing, or moving, or operating
nothing at all without them!
Let their purpose become yours,
155 and likewise their holy will, which
like the will of God, let it be fulfilled by you and thus
when you have traveled the stumble-free and shortened road,
then you shall become friends of God Most High,
and in a few days you shall be seen as heirs
160 of the kingdom of heaven and of inexpressible goods! (Jas 2.5)
For as soon as you walk on the straight road
you will become numbered with all the saints,
and it will eventually make you all happy.
For me who has sinned above all mortals,
165 for me who has also traveled this rugged road,
the road that is narrow, and short, and without danger,
that leads to the breadth of eternal life, (Mt 7.14)
because I have shown this road to you, may you all pray for me,
you who most eagerly want to walk on it,
170 and to follow fervently after the feet of Christ,
so that both I and you may be found on the road
marching blamelessly unto the end of life.
But pray also for whoever yearns to see Christ

in order that together with joy, leaving our bodies, (Rom 1.11)

175   we may withdraw to the rest up there, to the breadth of
      paradise,

and we may be rendered heirs of life, (Titus 3.7)

and inseparable from God and all the saints,

we shall be in Christ the only begotten Son, and in God the
      Logos,

with the divine Spirit of the Holy Trinity,

180   now, and always, and unto all ages forever. Amen.

Hymn 55

That the Holy Spirit stands by those who keep their holy Baptism pure.
But the Spirit departs from those who defile their baptismal purity.

You know me, O Christ, as a worker of every
transgression, but certainly also as a vessel of every sort of evil.
By all means, I know also that I am full of shame,
and the pain of reproach and affliction embraces me,

5   and intolerable suffering grips my heart.
But the light of your face shining mystically for me (Ps 4.7)
has driven away my thoughts, banished my suffering,
and substituted joy in my humble soul.
And so I want to be afflicted, Christ, yet affliction does not
      stick to me,

10   and I am afflicted so that because of this affliction
I may neither lose nor be deprived of the joy that is to come.
But, Master, may you never deprive me of this joy,
not now, nor in the age to come, my King!
For joy is the contemplation of your face,

15   for you alone, my God, are every good,
but you also prepare every good for those who see you,
you fill those whom you look upon with communion and
      participation,

not only in the age to come—woe to those who say that!—
but even now and in the body those who are worthy of you;
20   that is to say, you see them purifying ‹themselves› through
       repentance,
and you provide for them to see you clearly,
not just in a dream or consideration of the mind,
not by a mere memory like some would think,
but by truth of divine reality and a spine-chilling work,
25   certainly unto fulfillment of the divine plan.
For in this case you make a union of extremes;
you are God, being the salvation of all sinners. (1 Tim 1.15)
For those who have received your Baptism as infants
and have lived the life of Baptism unworthily
30   shall have a condemnation worse than the unbaptized,
like you have said, they have insulted your holy robe.
      (Heb 10.29)
And, Savior, knowing this to be certain and true,
you have given repentance as a second purification,
and you have set the grace of the Holy Spirit as the goal of
      repentance,
35   the grace we first received in Baptism.
For you have said that grace is not only by water,
but even more by the Spirit, in the invocation of the Trinity.
      (Mt 3.11)
Therefore since we have been baptized as children who were
      unaware,[1]
as unperfected persons we received the grace imperfectly;
40   we received ‹only› the release from the first transgression.
And for the sake of this alone, it seems to me, you have
prescribed this divine Baptism to be accomplished, O Master,
those who are baptized in the vineyard enter into this Baptism,
      (Mt 20.1)
and they are ransomed from darkness and hell,

---

[1] ἀναισθητοῦντες.

45 and they have been completely set free from death and
corruption.
I understand the vineyard to be paradise.
We have been summoned back to the place from which we had
been expelled.
And just as Adam was at the time before his sin,
so also everyone became, all who have been baptized with
knowledge,
50 but not those who do not receive imperceptibly rational
perception,[2]
which the Spirit makes by his energy when he comes.
Likewise all of us have received the commandments
like Adam to keep and to accomplish them as one, spiritual,[3]
and divine law both in Spirit, and in body,
55 this law bodily perfected in practice.
For the human being is double and begs a double law.
For if one were to neglect one law, then one falls out of the
other.
For the soul alone cannot work good deeds,
and the body working without divine knowledge
60 reckons like a toiling ox or a beast of burden.
And so those who have been summoned have entered into
your vineyard,
or into paradise, through your Baptism, and at the same time
are wholly blameless or even sanctified.
They have become like the first Adam.
65 But then, having neglected so great a salvation, (Heb 2.3)
and your so very great, unutterable foresight, Christ,
they have done and continue to do worse deeds than Adam,
at the same time they have also despised your benevolence;
they have not reckoned the bath of Baptism in
70 the Holy Spirit as the work of your awesome plan. (Titus 3.5)

[2]αἴσθησιν νοερὰν ἀναισθήτως.
[3]Mt 28.20; Gen 2.15.

Then could it be that, as the masses of human beings suppose,
they would be received into paradise and allowed both
to sin and to be saints again, those who have defiled
and wickedly stained your garment, my Savior?[4]

75   And would you who are pure and holy at all
consent to dwell within their filthy heart?
"Away," says God, "this would not happen to me, child!
For you know that you are baptized, but you are also defiled
and have sinned as a child, since you have been foolishly led
    astray,

80   and you know how much you wept, and how much you were
    crushed,
and how you have rejected all the world, and with pain
you were made ashamed by the intercessions of your father
    Symeon Eulabes,
from the beginning, by your mind alone, in your rational
    perception,[5]
and I deemed you worthy of my voice, and afterwards of my
    splendor,

85   and after that I was benevolently revealed to you as a ray.
Next I became a little cloud in the form of fire (1 Kg 18.44)
coming to rest over your head, and I
provided for you the lone contemplation of my appearance,
and tears of astonishment with much compunction

90   burning the thickness of your flesh, the gloom of your head,
with the result that the smell ‹of the flesh and gloom› arises like
    when
flesh burns in a fire, the smell comes from it as you know.[6]
And after these things, evils and difficulty;
you have completely forgotten how much you then endured.

[4]Rev 3.4; Jude 23.

[5]νοερᾷ αἰσθήσει.

[6]ὡς καὶ καέντος ἐν πυρὶ ὀσμὴν γενέσθαι τούτων.

κρέατος ἐξ αὐτῆς γενομένην, ὡς οἶδας. This sentence is difficult because of the
word order and the prepositional phrase ἐξ αὐτῆς. See SC 196:261n2.

95   But therefore I know, the God who knows all things,
      the faith, the humility toward your father,
      the total renunciation of your own will
      that is and is reckoned a testimony to me.
      For one who does not have their own will certainly dies,
100 but one who is found in my will also lives.
      Therefore when you were in this state each day with pain and
          toil,
      compelling me with tears, I who am good by nature,
      I began to appear to you more, as you know,
      little by little purifying your soul with repentance,
105 and consuming the stored up material of the passions,
      not thorns of flesh nor material thorns, but immaterial thorns,
      like a cloud, like thick gloom, fog, and darkness,
      clearly you have grown lean by fasting and by the labors
      of keeping vigil, of prayer, of every ill plight,
110 and the ‹toil› of being continually washed by fervent tears
      in prayer, in nourishment, and even more in your drink,
      and with difficulty I made you a suitable vessel,
      not only suitable, but purified so
      to remain unburned in the middle of fire. Pay attention!
115 And so having made you like this, the light that you then saw
      flying around in you and surrounding you entirely,
      entered into you, a light unapproachable by nature,
      and strangely the light transformed you in a beautiful
          transformation.
      And so, if you do not serve me with all your works,
120 but instead if you admit even a little thought into your heart,
      or disgust toward anyone, either reasonable or unreasonably,
      and even if inclined to temptation in word or wicked thought,
      if you do not repent fervently with tears,
      and banish these temptations from yourself with repentance,
125 as well as every worthless consideration of your heart,

it is only natural that the light does not remain. For ‹the light›
    is divine Spirit,
he is with me and the Father as of the same essence with me,
but ‹the light› secretly and suddenly flies away like the setting
    sun,
and having been hidden as in the blink of an eye, ‹the light› is
    not seen.

130 Therefore how shall ‹the light› exist in a soul not totally
    purified,
in a soul that has never come to the conscious feeling of
    repentance?
Or how would a soul also bear the nature of intolerable fire
when full of the thorns of passions and sin,
how would a soul contain the essence that is utterly
    uncontainable?

135 Being darkness, how would she be mixed with unapproachable
light and not disappear by his presence?
This, child, is not in any way the least bit possible!
For I myself am separated from all creatures.
And when I became a creature, I the creator of everything,

140 in the flesh I was just like human beings,
assuming soul and mind like them.
For by this I did not make all human beings gods
at that time, but I myself became a human being.
But by faith and by the keeping of my commandments,
    (1 Cor 7.19)

145 but also by Baptism, in the divine participation
of my spine-chilling mysteries I give life to all. (Jn 17.2)
But in saying "life" I indicate my divine Spirit.
Yet let them know this, as Paul said,
those who have my Spirit in their hearts (Gal 4.6)

150 have the Spirit shining and crying to my Father
and to me, he says through them: "O Abba, my Father!"

For they have become like children of God, and with bold
     frankness
they gain knowledge, and they see me, and call me Father.
And the Spirit says to each of those who now possess him
155 truly within themselves: "O children, do not be afraid![7]
Behold, I, as you see, am within you,
and I am with you, and once and for all I free you
from corruption and death, and I demonstrate whose children
     and friends
I have made you. Behold! Rejoice in the Lord!" (Phil 3.1)
160 And so this is a true sign for all human beings,
that they have become children and heirs of God, (Gal 4.7)
that having received they possess my divine Spirit,
and henceforth they are truly styled Christians
in truth and fact, not in name alone." (1 Jn 3.18)
165 These things are sure and longed-for promises, my Christ,
those whom you wisely foreknew and granted to be
conformed to your image in the divine Spirit, (Rom 8.29)
and these are in every way possible for them since
they were called to ineffable joy by you forever. (Mk 9.23)
170 But to all the others, these graces seem impossible,
and those who contradict have no faith at all,
and they deceive themselves, or the deranged even imagine
     (Gal 6.3)
that they are consoled in a vain hope,
talking big and in exalted terms like refined persons,
175 and they allegorize things to their liking,
completely despising your fearful commandments.
For they do not want to seek you; for they do not suppose that
     they have you.
And if they will admit that they do not have you, my God,
then they proclaim that You are in every way inapprehensible
     to everyone,

[7]Mt 28.5; 14.27; Lk 24.38–39.

180 and if no one among human beings is able to see you
      (1 Tim 6.16)
  then there is not anyone who surpasses them in knowledge.
  For they teach either that you are attainable and approachable
      for all humans,
  or that you are utterly inapprehensible and unapproachable.
  But they fail in both cases, they do not understand
185 things divine and human; they are darkened.
  Direct the light of knowledge for them, give the hand of divine
      fear,
  grant that they stand up from the pit of wicked suspicion,
  and come to the awareness that they are lying in a pit,
  and sitting in darkness, not seeing the divine light! (Lk 1.79)
190 The light to which they bear witness and that they confess,
  but they do not believe that there are now people who see you.
  But if your light will not shine for them, and they do not see in
      knowledge,
  how will they clearly believe that you are revealed to those who
      are worthy,
  and that you speak with, and abide with them now and forever
195 as friends, as your faithful servants, like you said? (Jn 15.15)
  But you are God of the faithful, but not also God of the
      faithless,
  for that reason you do not look upon them at all.
  For those who utterly reject you and say that your
  eternal light does not shine on the souls of the worthy,
200 how shall you show the face of your light, my Savior?
  No way, unless they possess much faith, like you said,
      (Mt 15.28)
  and they keep your divine law zealously
  unto death, surrendering themselves for your sake
  to true practice of your wise commands.
205 And so this is the salvation of all who are saved,
  and there is not another road, as you said, O my God. (Mt 7.14)

Give mercy, give mercy to those who beg you, Savior,
now and always forever and ever! Amen.

Hymn 56

Prayer to God concerning events that happened to Symeon: a prayer
that is both suppliant and at the same time thankful.

Lord, give to me union,[1] Lord, give to me knowledge,
Lord, teach me also to do your commandments! (Ps 142.10)
Even if I, as a human being, have sinned beyond any person,
    you know it,
but you, in your personal compassion, my God,
5   had mercy on me the beggar, the orphan in the world,
and you have done, Master, what you alone know.
From my father and brothers, relatives and friends, (Mk 10.29)
from the land of my family, out of my ancestral home,
    (Gen 12.1)
like out of dark Egypt, like out of the innermost regions of hell
    (Wis 17.13)
10 —for so you gave to me, your worthless servant,
to understand and to speak about these with understanding[2]—
you separated me, Compassionate One, and received me,
and grabbed me by your awesome hand, and then you led me
to the person whom you let become my father on earth,
15 and you threw me at his feet and into his arms.[3]
And he led me to your Father, my Christ,
and to you through the Spirit, O Trinity, my God,
weeping and prostrate like a profligate, O Logos, (Lk 15)
as you yourself know because you have taught me,
20 and you have not disdained to call me your son.

[1] σύνεσις can also mean sagacity or understanding.
[2] ἐν συνέσει.
[3] I.e., Symeon Eulabes.

Oh unworthy mouth and filthy lips!
Oh needy tongue at a loss for words to sing your praises,
to give thanks, and to tell your good deeds
that you have done for me the orphan and stranger.
25 I am a stranger on earth, for those of the world are strangers to
     you. (Heb 11.13)
But eyes do not see, and no tongue is able to tell, nor
can the world contain your graces nor those of your servants.[4]
And so on account of this, Master, the world hates us, (Jn 15.19)
it chases us away, reviles, and bears malice, rages, kills, and
30 accomplishes everything against us, surrounding us with these
     things.
But we your humble servants, as you have consented,
are strong in weakness, wealthy in poverty,[5]
we rejoice in every affliction since we are outside the world.
     (2 Cor 7.4)
We, O Master, are with you, but the world has the body.
35 Besides, the blind world is deceived, it possesses only clay
that shall not profit the world. For as you promised, the world
shall give up even this clay to become spiritual at the last
     trumpet. (1 Cor 15.52)
And the world shall then gain only its own evils along with
those who are of one mind with it, and with the blind lovers of
     the world.

Hymn 57

That one who yearns for God hates the world.

I am overpowered by a shadow and yet I see truth,
which is nothing other than a firm hope. (2 Cor 1.7)
What sort of hope? That which eyes have not seen. (1 Cor 2.9)

---

[4] 1 Cor 2.9; Jn 21.25.
[5] 1 Cor 1.25; 2 Cor 8.9.

What is it? Life which everyone longs for.
5   But what is life if not God the creator of all things? (Jn 14.6)
Yearn for him and hate the world! (1 Jn 2.15)
The world is death, for what does it have that is not transient?

Hymn 58

*Public lesson with reproach to everyone: kings, bishops, priests, monks,
laity. Proclaimed as though spoken by the mouth of God.*

O Christ, provide wise words for me,
words of knowledge and divine sagacity! (1 Cor 12.8)
For you know the weakness of my word,[1]
and that it has no share of outside education.
5   You know that I have you alone
as my life, and word, and knowledge, and wisdom,
savior God, and patron in life,
and life's breath of my humble soul.
I am a stranger and humble in words.
10   You are my hope, you are my support,[2]
you my shelter, you my refuge,[3]
you my boast, my wealth, my glory.[4]
You, Logos, according to your compassion, wanted
to receive me from the world, me the stranger,
15   the unworthy, the one more worthless than
every human being, worse than every irrational beast.
And because of this I take confidence in your mercy,
and I beg of you, and I babble, and I prostrate myself.
Give frank speech, give strength, give to me power
20   to say to all those who are dedicated to you,
and to those serving you, King of everything,

[1] 1 Cor 2.3–4; 2 Cor 10.10.
[2] Ps 21.9; 88.19.
[3] Ps 120.5; 90.2.
[4] Deut 10.21; Prov 22.4.

to proclaim to mystics, to both princes and worshippers,
to those who suppose that they see you, and worship you,
and serve you sincerely as Master.

25 All human beings, kings and rulers,
priests, bishops, monks and non-monks,
may you not disdain to hear my voice
and the words of me a worthless person,
but open the ears of your heart to me,

30 and listen, and understand what the God
of all things says, he who is also before all ages, (Mk 7.14)
who is unapproachable, who alone is all-powerful,
in whose hand is the breath of all beings! (Dan 5.23)
"Kings! You do well to fight the heathen nations,

35 if you yourselves do not do the works of the heathen nations,
and their customs, and their designs, and opinions,
and through your many works and words
you do not despise me your king.
It would be much better for you to keep my words (Lk 11.28)

40 and to do all my commands rightly,
and to pursue a good and quiet life
in the poverty that is deemed happy. (Mt 5.3)
For what is the benefit in vindicating the world
from death and seasonal slavery

45 if on the other hand you yourselves become slaves
of passions and demons by your works each day,
and you become heirs of unquenchable fire? (Mk 9.43)
For whatever other works anyone
does for my sake, and for sympathy,

50 and for charity toward one's neighbor, all such deeds are
noble but the first of all works of charity is to have pity on
    oneself,[5]
and to keep my words with all earnestness,
and to manifest sincere repentance

[5]Cf. *Catechesis* 9.117–70.

for what sins were perhaps done before,
55   and thereafter one would no longer turn back to those sins,
         (Mt 24.18)
      but would remain true to the words of me the Master,
      to my commands and laws of truth,
      and one would thus do all things steadfastly
      unto death, and not ignore a bare word,
60   nor one dot of the Scriptures. (Mt 5.18)
      For that is an offering to me,
      it is incense to me, and worthy, and a gift,
      but without these you are worse than the heathen nations.
      Presidents of the bishops, understand!
65   You who are the official seal of my image, (1 Cor 9.2)
      you who have been appointed to talk with me worthily,
      you who are set above all the just ones
      since you are in the name of my disciples,
      and you bear my divine character,
70   and you who have received such authority
      over the smallest public assembly,
      such as I the Logos received from my Father, (Jn 17.2)
      and I am God by nature, I was made flesh,
      and I became double by energies,
75   by wills, likewise by my natures,
      I who am undivided, without mixing,
      God human, and again human God—
      for as a human I have deigned to be held (Mt 26.45, 50)
      by your hands, but being God I am
80   inapprehensible to absolutely all clay
      hands, and invisible to those who do not see,
      and unapproachable, I who was murdered on behalf of all,
      I am double in one hypostasis—
      on account of this authority you bishops
85   are arrogant toward all the people of least account
      as though both humble and sitting beneath you,

you bishops who are far from worthiness.
‹I do not mean› those whose life concurs with their words,
and whose life is the seal of their God-inspired
90 teaching and divine doctrine,
but rather those whose life contradicts their words,
and to whom my divine and spine-chilling mysteries are
        unknown,
and who suppose that they hold bread that is actually fire,
and they despise me as plain bread,
95 and suppose that they see and eat a morsel,
without seeing my invisible glory.
The majority of the bishops, except for a few,
both the lofty ones and those brought low
to a wicked humiliation at the opposite extreme, (Mt 23.12)
100 those pursuing for themselves the glory of human beings,
        (Jn 12.43)
and looking away from me the creator of all things
as a beggar and a tossed away day laborer,
unworthily they touch my body, (1 Cor 11.27)
and they seek to dominate the masses,
105 without invitation they enter within my innermost sanctuaries,
and they walk within the unapproachable
bridal chamber without the garment
of my grace which they never received, (Mt 22.11)
and they see what they have no right to see.
110 And I the Benevolent One am very patient,
bearing shameless audacity.
And they enter, they speak to me as to a friend, to me
to whom they have not remained faithful, like slaves do out of
        fear,
and they present themselves like members of my household,
115 they do not recognize my grace,
and they profess to act as mediators for others.
They are themselves accountable for many failures.

They beautifully adorn the exterior body, (Mt 23.26–27)
they are seen shining and pure in appearance,
120   but their souls are worse than mud and mire,
or rather they have souls worse than every deadly poison;
they are wretched in their vice.
For just as of old Judas who betrayed me
received the bread from me unworthily and
125   ate it like a portion of common bread,[6]
and because of this Satan entered
into him immediately and made him into a shameless
betrayer of me his teacher.
Satan received him as a subservient slave
130   and fulfiller of his wishes,
so also do these bishops experience without knowing it,
whosoever boldly, and willfully, and unworthily
touches my divine mysteries,
those who in their thrones dominate others,
135   who act superior to the clergy, to the priesthood,
those who have a conscience that was already damaged,
and afterward completely condemned,
and they walk in my divine courtyard,
and shamelessly they stand in the inner sanctum
140   speaking boldly in my presence; (Job 22.26)
in no way do they see my divine glory, (Jn 11.40)
which if they did, they would not do this, (1 Cor 2.8)
nor would they presume so stubbornly to enter
the gates of my divine temple."
145   Therefore everyone who desires shall know that
all these writings are true and certain
from the works themselves which we priests do,
and one shall find no falsehood at all,
and one shall be persuaded, and will confess
150   that God himself said these things through me.

[6]Jn 13.26–27; 1 Cor 11.27.

For among those who do these things there is no one
who hastens to cover with guileful words,
to cover over their own shameful deeds (Jude 13)
that the Lord God of all things shall reveal
155 in the presence of angels and humans, (Lk 12.9)
he who reveals the hidden things of darkness.[7]
What sort of person among us priests now
has first purified his lawlessness
so that he then carries out his priesthood boldly?
160 Who would say this with frank confidence,
that he despised the glory below, and for
the sake of the glory above alone he ministers the mysteries?
And who has loved Christ alone
and disregarded all gold and property?
165 Who has been satisfied with only what is necessary,
and has not robbed his neighbor of anything?
Who does not possess his conscience
condemned by insolence through which
he is led to become a priest or to ordain
170 a priest, buying or selling the grace?
Who when promoting a religious has not preferred
an unworthy friend over a worthy candidate?
And who does not strive to make men
who are family friends bishops
175 in order to receive into one's power all the other's
property? For this is common among the temperate ones,
they also assume that it is not a sin
to take up the goods of another church.
Who, because of the request of the powerful
180 in the world, of friends, of the wealthy, and of princes,
has not elected ‹a bishop› without regard to his worthiness?
Certainly there is no one today who has
a heart pure of all these abuses,

[7]Sir 1.30; Mt 10.26; 1 Cor 4.5.

nor one who is stung by his conscience
185 because he has certainly done one of the things
that I mentioned, but we all sin freely,
without attending to the cutting out of evil,
without employing the practice of virtue.
And because of this we do not repent;
190 we have been plunged into the depths of evils,
and we are heartlessly devoted to these vices.
For we are fasting from divine glory;
we are not able to look away from the glory here below,
but passionate love of glory—I mean the glory of humans—
(Jn 12.43)
195 does not allow the soul to be humbled at all,
nor to willingly find fault with herself.
And so how, tell me, being in such condition,
will one who pursues the glory of human beings,
and who begs for perishing wealth,
200 who longs to have a pile of gold,
who is insatiate for robbery,
and bears a grudge against those who do not give often,
how shall such a one dare to say that they have God dwelling
within?
Or that they love[8] Christ, or that they have the Spirit of Christ?
(Rom 8.9)
205 But the one who has not received Christ,
and his Father, and the Holy Spirit,
conscious of the One God dwelling and
walking about in their heart, (2 Cor 6.16)
how would such a one demonstrate sincere service,
210 from whom else would they study humility,
or how shall they be taught the divine will? (Ps 142.10)
Who will intercede, or reconcile them to God, (2 Cor 5.20)
and present them as a worshipper with no cause for shame

[8] φιλεῖν.

      to God who alone is pure, (2 Tim 2.15)
215 whom the Cherubim dare not gaze at,
      who is unapproachable to all the angels?
      Who shall guarantee that he would hold him sinlessly
      and minister without condemnation
      the awesome worship of the blameless victim?
220 What angel, what human is able
      to say this or has strength to do this?
      For I myself say, and I testify to all
      —let no one be deceived, nor be misled by words!—
      whoever will not first let go the world,
225 and hate the things of the world from their soul, (1 Jn 2.15)
      and will not sincerely love Christ alone,
      and will not lose their soul herself for his sake, (Mt 16.25)
      not worrying about anything concerning human life,
      but one who is as though dying by the hour,
230 and will weep much for him, and will have remorse,
      shall have yearning for him alone,
      and through many afflictions and toils, (Acts 14.22)
      would be deemed worthy to receive the divine Spirit
      whom Christ has also given to the divine apostles, (Jn 20.22)
235 so that through him he may expel every passion,
      and easily set right every virtue,
      and procure bounteous fountains of tears:
      whence purification, and the soul's contemplation,
      whence knowledge of the divine will,
240 whence illumination of divine illumination,
      and contemplation of unapproachable light, (1 Tim 6.16)
      out of which comes dispassion. Holiness
      is given to all who have been deemed worthy
      to see and to have God in their heart,
245 and be kept by him, and to keep
      inviolate his divine commands.
      ‹Such a one› would not dare to accept or even begin

the priesthood or patronage of souls!
For just as Christ is offered and offers
250 himself to God his own Father, (Heb 9.14)
so also he himself offers us
and thus in turn he himself receives us.
Since the undertaking of such matters
shall be a matter for judgment and condemnation,
255 it is worse than murder, worse than adultery,
and worse than all other sins.
Therefore all these sins are now committed against mortals,
for by all means we sin against each other.
But one who impudently deals in divine things
260 and sells the grace of the Spirit
certainly sins against God himself. (2 Cor 2.17)
For one who has been elevated to the person[9]
of the Logos must live like him,
and thus to say as he did: "Follow me!
265 The foxes have dens by all means,
and the birds all have nests,
but I myself do not have anywhere to lay my head,
     (Mt 8.20–22)
I who have been deemed worthy to be a worshipper of Christ."
For he has nothing at all of his own,
270 and he must not possess anything of the world,
except only the needs of the body,
but everything else belongs to the poor
and to the strangers, and to their church.
But if on the other hand he will dare to use this income
275 with his authority on his own expenses inappropriately,
and to give what belongs to strangers to his relatives,
and to build houses, and to purchase fields,
and to have a crowd of foreign slaves precede him,
alas, what will be his condemnation?!

[9]πρόσωπον.

280 Certainly this one is compared to a man
    who out of thoughtlessness wickedly consumed
    the whole dowry of his own wife.
    So when he has been apprehended and does not have
    the dowry to give when the property is demanded of him,
285 along with the separation from his wife,
    he is also sent to jail to be confined.
    And thus shall we the priests and worshippers be,
    we who misuse the income of our churches
    for ourselves, and for our relatives, and our friends,
290 And we do not care at all for the poor,
    rather, we build houses, baths, monasteries, and towers.
    By giving dowries we make marriages,
    and despising our own churches
    as alien, we neglect them,
295 and we are separated from them for long periods,
    and we delay in an alien region,
    and leave our wives alone like widows,
    making no provision for them,
    but even those of us who remain steadfast and dwell with them
300 do so not because we are held by yearning for them,
    but only in order to live off their income
    plentifully, and in order to live wantonly. (Am 6.4)
    But who among us priests is worried
    about a virtuous soul espoused to Christ?
305 Show to me just one and I will be satisfied with him!
    But, alas for us in the seventh millennium,[10]
    priest, monks, bishops, and worshippers,
    because we trample underfoot the laws of God
    and the Savior as if worth nothing!
310 And if somewhere someone may appear small among humans,

---

[10] According to Byzantine computation, from the beginning of creation, Symeon lived from 6457 to 6530 (see SC 196:301n1).

but to God this individual is great because known to him,
    (Lk 9.48)
but because such a one does not come down to our passions,
at once they are expelled as one of the criminals,
and is chased away from our midst by us,
315 and is put out of the synagogue (Jn 16.2)
like our Christ was long ago by the
high priests of his day and by the terrible Jews,
as he said and always says this
with the clear voice of his mighty works.
320 But there is God who will exalt this lowly one, (Lk 1.52)
and as he receives this one in this life,
so also in the life to come he will glorify them (Rom 8.17)
with all the saints for whom they yearned.
But what does the Logos also say to us?
325 "You monks who seem in earnest!
Mold yourselves within by piety, (2 Tim 3.5)
and by all means shall your exterior be pure to me, (Mt 23.26)
indeed this shall be to your benefit,
and for the benefit of those who see your virtuous works.
    (Mt 5.16)
330 But the interior is longed for by me the creator of all things,
and by my rational and divine hierarchies.
But if you adorn the exterior image of a person
by deportment of its habits alone,
and you seem friendly to those who see you
335 through the exterior exercise of labors,
but if you do not at all take account of my dear image,
for its purification and orderliness
by earnestness, and tears, and labors,
through which you appear to me and everyone else
340 as humans who are clearly rational and divine,
then certainly you seem to me like tombs oozing with decay,
    (Mt 23.27)

just like the Pharisees, as I anticipated
when speaking in criticism of their foolishness.
Brilliant from the outside, decaying, full inside,
345 filled full with the dead bones of the worthless
considerations of a rotten heart, of words,
of passions, of designs, and treacherous anxieties.
For who among you seeks these things;
I mean fasting, austerity, labors,
350 squalid hair, nailings of iron,
hairshirt, fully callused knees,
sleeping on the ground, grass for the mattress of a marriage
    bed,
and all other ill sufferings of life?
These are virtuous if the aspects of your
355 rational and hidden works are well accomplished
in knowledge, and wisdom, and reason.
But if you, without this inner work, perhaps think
or even consider that you are something great,
even without this inner work
360 then you indeed resemble lepers who dress in splendid
    clothing
to deceive those who see them.
But having said farewell to all the exteriors,
hasten zealously to belong to the interior work
alone, in the sweat and toils
365 of divine virtues and sacred struggles,
in order that you may be seen by me as virgins in thought,
illuminated in your whole intellect,
and so that you may be united to me the Logos in the word
of my wisdom and superior knowledge!
370 The whole crowd of my sacred people
come earnestly to me your Master!
Come, be released from the shackles of the world,
hate all the error of the senses,

        flee quickly the causes of evils,

375 the desire of sight and of flesh, (1 Jn 2.16)
        and the false pretension of the viscera and of life,
        and all other empty consideration!
        Know what things belong to the world of injustice,[11]
        that they lead the one who uses them to ruin

380 ‹when they use them in› an emotional and attached state in this
            life,
        and unfortunately they make you my enemy!
        Receive yearning for my divine realities
        in your heart, for my eternal goods,
        which by my Incarnation I have prepared for you as for a
            friend, (1 Cor 2.9)

385 so that you may always be my banquet companion
        inexpressibly at the table of my kingdom,
        my table in heaven with all the saints! (Lk 22.30)
        For know yourself, that you are mortal and perishable,
        that there is little life remaining in this life,

390 and that nothing of the things in the world follow you,
        none of the splendors, nor enjoyments and pleasures
        do you take away from here to the encampment up there,
        except the results of either the virtuous or the wicked
        works accomplished by you in this life!

395 And recognizing that everything is perishable and mortal,
        leaving behind the things below, come up, I call you
        to me the God and Savior of everyone
        so that forever and ever you may really live,
        and you may revel in my blessings,

400 which I have prepared for those who love me (1 Cor 2.9)
        both now and always, amen unto the ages!"

---

[11]Jas 3.6 describes the tongue as a "world of injustice."

Abbreviations

CSS	Cistercian Studies Series
CWS	Classics of Western Spirituality
DOP	*Dumbarton Oaks Papers*
FC	Fathers of the Church
OCA	Orientalia Christiana Analecta
OCP	*Orientalia christiana periodica*
PG	Patrologia graeca
RBén	*Revue bénedictine*
SC	Sources chrétiennes
StudMon	*Studia monastica*
Philokalia	*The Philokalia: The Complete Text*. G. E. H. Palmer, Philip Sherrard, and Kallistos Ware, trs. 4 vols. London: Faber, 1979–1995.

Bibliography

The Works of Symeon: Editions and Translations

Hymns of Divine Love by St. Symeon the New Theologian. George A. Maloney, tr. Denville, NJ: Dimension Books, 1976.

Syméon le Nouveau Théologien, Catéchèses 1–5. Basile Krivochéine, ed., Joseph Paramelle, tr. SC 96. Paris: Cerf, 1963.

Syméon le Nouveau Théologien, Catéchèses 6–22. Basile Krivochéine, ed., Joseph Paramelle, tr. SC 104. Paris: Cerf, 1964.

Syméon le Nouveau Théologien, Catéchèses 23–34: Actions de graces 1–2. Basile Krivochéine, ed., Joseph Paramelle, tr. SC 113. Paris: Cerf, 1965.

Syméon le Nouveau Théologien, Chapitres théologiques, gnostiques et pratiques. Jean Darrouzès and Louis Neyrand, eds. SC 51 bis. Paris: Cerf, 1996.

Syméon le Nouveau Théologien, Hymnes 1 15. Johannes Koder, ed. Joseph Paramelle, tr. SC 156. Paris: Cerf, 1969.

Syméon le Nouveau Théologien, Hymnes 16–40. Johannes Koder, ed. Louis Neyrand, tr. SC 174. Paris: Cerf, 1971.

Syméon le Nouveau Théologien, Hymnes 41–58. Johannes Koder, ed. Joseph Paramelle and Louis Neyrand, trs. SC 196. Paris: Cerf, 1973.

Syméon le Nouveau Théologien, Traités théologiques et éthiques I: Théologiques 1–3, Éthiques 1–3. Jean Darrouzès, ed. SC 122. Paris: Cerf, 1966.

Syméon le Nouveau Théologien, Traités théologiques et éthiques II: Éthiques 4–15. Jean Darrouzès, ed. SC 129. Paris: Cerf, 1967.

Symeon the New Theologian, The Discourses. C. J. deCatanzaro, tr. CWS. New York: Paulist Press, 1980.

Symeon the New Theologian, On the Mystical Life: The Ethical Discourses. Alexander Golitzin, tr. 3 vols. Crestwood, NY: St Vladimir's Seminary Press, 1995–1997.

Symeon the New Theologian, The Practical and Theological Chapters and the Three Theological Discourses. Paul J. McGuckin, tr. CSS 41. Kalamazoo: Cistercian Publications, 1982.

Other Patristic Sources: Editions and Translations

St Basil, *In Isaiam homiliae*. PG 30:118–668.

St Basil, *Homilia*. PG 31:163–618, 1429–1514.

Diadoque de Photicé, Oeuvres spirituelles. Edouard des Places, ed. SC 5 bis. Paris: Cerf, 1955.

Grégoire de Nazianze, Discours 1–3. Jean Bernardi, ed. SC 247. Paris: Cerf, 1978.

Grégoire de Nazianze, Discours 27–31. Paul Gallay, ed. SC 250. Paris: Cerf, 1978.

St Gregory of Nazianzus: On God and Christ: The Five Theological Orations and Two Letters to Cledonius. Frederick Williams and Lionel Wickham, trs. Crestwood, N.Y.: St Vladimir's Seminary Press, 2002.

Saint Gregory Nazianzus: Three Poems Concerning His Own Affairs, Concerning Himself and the Bishops, Concerning His Own Life. Denis Molaise Meehan, tr. FC 75. Washington, DC: Catholic University of America Press, 1987.

The Ascetical Homilies of Saint Isaac the Syrian. Boston: Holy Transfiguration Monastery, 1984.

Jean Chrysostome, Sur le Sacerdoce. Anne-Marie Malingrey, ed. SC 272. Paris: Cerf, 1980.

St John Chrysostom On the Priesthood. Graham Neville, tr. Crestwood, N.Y.: St Vladimir's Seminary Press, 1977.

St John Chrysostom, *Homiliae in Genesim*. PG 53–54.

Die 50 Geistlichen Homilien des Makarios. Hermann Dorries, Erich Klostermann and Matthias Kroeger, eds. Berlin: Walter de Gruyter, 1965.

Nicetas Stethatos. *Un grand mystique byzantin: Vie de Syméon le Nouveau Théologien*. Irénée Hausherr, ed. Gabriel Horn, tr. OCA 12. Rome: Pontifical Institute of Oriental Studies, 1928.

Pseudo-Macarius: The Fifty Spiritual Homilies. George A. Maloney, tr. CWS. New York: Paulist Press, 1992.

Marc le Moine, Traités I. Georges-Matthieu de Durand, ed. SC 445. Paris: Cerf, 1999.

Marc le Moine, Traités II. Georges-Matthieu de Durand, ed. SC 455. Paris: Cerf, 2000.

Origen, *In Jeremiam homiliae*. PG 13:253–606.

Sancti Romani Melodi Cantica genuina. Paul Maas and Constantine A. Trypanis, eds. Oxford: Clarendon Press, 1963.

Secondary Studies

Alfeyev, Ilarion. *St Symeon the New Theologian and Orthodox Tradition*.
Oxford Early Christian Studies. Oxford: Oxford University Press, 1995.

Alfeyev, Ilarion. "St Symeon the New Theologian, St Symeon the Pious, and
the Studite Tradition." *StudMon* 36 (1994): 183–222.

Charanis, Peter. "The Monk in Byzantine Society." *DOP* 25 (1971): 63–84

Davis, Caroline Franks. *The Evidential Force of Religious Experience*. Oxford:
Clarendon Press, 1989.

Gardner, Alice. *Theodore of Studium: His Life and Times*. London: Arnold,
1905.

Griggs, Daniel K. *Religious Experience in Symeon the New Theologian's
Hymns*. Ph.D. diss. University of Leeds, U.K., 1999.

Hussey, Joan M. *Church and Learning in the Byzantine Empire: 867–1185*.
New York: Russell, 1963.

Jeffreys, Elizabeth M. "Kontakion." *The Oxford Dictionary of Byzantium*,
2 1148. Alexander P. Kazhdan et al., eds. 3 vols. Oxford: Oxford University Press, 1991.

Jenkins, Romilly J. H. *Byzantium: The Imperial Centuries, AD 610–1071*.
London: Weidenfeld, 1966.

Krausmüller, Dirk. "Monastic Communities of Studios and St Mamas in
the Second Half of the Tenth Century." *The Theotokos Evergetis and
Eleventh-Century Monasticism*. Margaret Mullett and Anthony Kirby,
eds. Belfast Byzantine Texts and Translations 6.1. Belfast: Byzantine
Enterprises, 1994: 67–85.

Krivochéine, Basil. "The Writings of St Symeon the New Theologian." *OCP*
20 (1954): 298–328.

McGuckin, John A. "A Neglected Masterpiece of the Christian Mystical
Tradition: The *Hymns of Divine Eros* by the Byzantine Poet Symeon the
New Theologian (949–1022)." *Spiritus* 5 (2005): 182–202.

McGuckin, John A. "Symeon the New Theologian (d. 1022) and Byzantine
Monasticism." *Mount Athos and Byzantine Monasticism*. Anthony
Bryer, ed. London: Variorum, 1996: 17–35.

Maloney, George A. *Mystic of Fire and Light: St. Symeon the New Theologian.* Denville: Dimension Books, 1975.

Meyendorff, John. *Byzantine Theology: Historical Trends and Doctrinal Themes.* New York: Fordham University Press, 1983.

Meyer, Robert. "Lectio Divina in Palladius." *Kyriakon: Festschrift Johannes Quasten.* Patrick Granfield and Josef A. Jungmann, eds. 2 vols. Münster: Aschendorff, 1970: 2:580–584.

Morris, Rosemary. "The Political Saint of the Eleventh Century." *The Byzantine Saint.* Sergei Hackel, ed. London: Fellowship of St Alban and St Sergius, 1981: 43–50.

Morris, Rosemary. "Spiritual Fathers and Temporal Patrons: Logic and Contradiction in Byzantine Monasticism in the Tenth Century." *RBén* 103 (1993): 273–288.

Schork, R.J. *Sacred Song from the Byzantine Pulpit: Romanus the Melodist.* Gainesville: University of Florida Press, 1995.

Spidlík, Tomás. *Spirituality of the Christian East: A Systematic Handbook.* CSS 79. Kalamazoo: Cistercian Publications, 1986.

Talbot, Alice-Mary. "Mamas, Monastery of Saint." *The Oxford Dictionary of Byzantium,* 2:1278. Alexander P. Kazhdan et al., eds. 3 vols. Oxford: Oxford University Press, 1991.

Trypanis, Constantine A. *Greek Poetry: From Homer to Seferis.* London: Faber & Faber, 1981.

Trypanis, Constantine A. *Medieval and Modern Greek Poetry: An Anthology.* Oxford: Clarendon Press, 1951.

Turner, H. J. M. *St Symeon the New Theologian and Spiritual Fatherhood.* Leiden/New York: E. J. Brill, 1990.

Glossary

The following terms either have a technical sense that is difficult to convey in English, or else have a breadth of meaning that is difficult to translate consistently by a single word.

ἀγαπάω (verb): to love.
ἀγάπη (noun): translated consistently as 'love'. See also ἔρως, πόθος, and φιλέω.

αἴσθησις (noun): perception by the senses, sensation, perception, senses, feelings, sense awareness.
αἰσθητός (adjective): perceptible by the senses, sensual.
αἰσθητῶς (adverb): perceptibly, physically.

ἀναισθησία (noun): want of feeling or perception, insensitivity, callousness; theologically, opposite of ἀπάθεια.
ἀναισθητέω (verb): to lack perception, to be insensitive, to be unaware.
ἀναισθήτος (adjective): unfeeling, senseless, without feeling, insensitive, stupid.
ἀναισθήτως (adverb): imperceptibly, unconsciously, without feeling.

ἀπάθεια (noun): dispassion.
ἀπαθής (adjective): dispassionate.
ἀπαθῶς (adverb): dispassionately.

γνῶσις (noun): knowledge, consciousness.

διάνοια (noun): intellect. Generally synonymous with νοῦς (mind), but used less often.

ἐνυπόστατος (adjective): having independent existence, self-existent,
    having hypostasis, substantial, inherent, self-contained, being a
    person. See also ὑπόστασις.

ἐπίνοια (noun): translated 'hypothesis' and 'hypothetically' in *Hymn* 21,
    'theories' in *Hymn* 30.144. The sense is 'notion, theory, contrived
    thought, invention, purpose, design'. In *Hymn* 21, it is contrasted with
    πρᾶγμα.

ἐράω (verb): to love or desire passionately.
ἔρως (noun): passionate love. See ἀγάπη.

θεωρία (noun): usually translated 'contemplation'. A less technical sense is
    'looking at, beholding, observing, view'.

λογικός (adjective): usually translated as 'logical' to distinguish it from
    derivatives of νοῦς. The sense is 'rational, reasonable, pertaining to
    λόγος'.

λόγος (noun): word, reason, rational faculty of the soul. Transliterated
    'Logos' when it refers to Christ.

νοερός (adjective): rational, intellectual, spiritual, mental, of the mind.
νοερῶς (adverb): rationally, mentally, spiritually, intellectually.
νοέω (verb): to perceive, to think. The passive participle is translated
    'intellectual, imaginary'.
νοητός (adjective): rational, mental, noetic, intelligible.
νοῦς (noun): mind as distinguished from heart and spirit, though these
    three terms are partially synonymous. See also διάνοια.

οὐσία (noun): translated consistently as 'essence'. The sense includes
    'being, reality, substance'. See also ὑπόστασις and φύσις.

ποθέω (verb): to yearn.
πόθος (noun): yearning. The sense is desire for something lost, usually
    longing for God. Also a divine attribute like ἀγάπη (see *Hymn* 52.3–6).

πράγμα (noun): In *Hymn* 21 translated as 'actuality, actual fact, actually', in contrast to ἐπίνοια. The usual sense is 'deed, act, fact, matter, circumstance'.

πρόσωπον (noun): person, especially a person of the Trinity. The less technical meaning is 'face' or 'appearance'; see also ὑπόστασις.

ὑπόστασις (noun): technical Trinitarian term, transliterated 'hypostasis' rather than translated. The earlier and more basic meaning is akin to substance, essence, or real nature (see οὐσία). The later Fathers gave it a technical sense more akin to 'person;' see πρόσωπον, and note at *Hymn* 31.9.
τρισυπόστατος (adjective): in three persons, of three persons.

φιλέω (verb): to love, to be a friend, to be fond of, to have affection, to kiss. See also ἀγάπη.

φρήν (noun): senses, feeling, viscera, wits. Also has the sense of 'breast, heart'.

φύσις (noun): nature, as in 'inborn quality'.

χαρακτήρ (noun): person, character.

We hope this book has been enjoyable and edifying for your spiritual journey toward our Lord and Savior Jesus Christ.

One hundred percent of the net proceeds of all SVS Press sales directly support the mission of St Vladimir's Orthodox Theological Seminary to train priests, lay leaders, and scholars to be active apologists of the Orthodox Christian Faith. However, the proceeds only partially cover the operational costs of St Vladimir's Seminary. To meet our annual budget, we rely on the generosity of donors who are passionate about providing theological education and spiritual formation to the next generation of ordained and lay servant leaders in the Orthodox Church.

 Donations are tax-deductible and can be made at www.svots.edu/donate. We greatly appreciate your generosity.

To engage more with St Vladimir's Orthodox Theological Seminary, please visit:

www.svots.edu
online.svots.edu
www.svspress.com
www.instituteofsacredarts.com

POPULAR PATRISTICS SERIES

ST VLADIMIR'S SEMINARY PRESS
1-800-204-2665 • www.svspress.com